To Peter,

Fondest Regards

Johnny

June 2008

Michel Thomas® method

The Learning Revolution

Jonathan Solity

HODDER
EDUCATION
PART OF HACHETTE LIVRE UK

Orders: please contact Bookpoint Ltd, 130 Milton Park, Abingdon, Oxon OX14 4SB. Telephone: +44 (0) 1235 827720. Fax: +44 (0) 1235 400454. Lines are open 9.00 to 5.00, Monday to Saturday, with a 24-hour message answering service. You can also order through our website www.hoddereducation.co.uk.

British Library Cataloguing in Publication Data
A catalogue record for this title is available from the British Library.

ISBN-13: 978 0340 928 33 2

First published   2008
Impression number 10 9 8 7 6 5 4 3 2 1
Year   2012 2011 2010 2009 2008

Hachette Livre UK's policy is to use papers that are natural, renewable and recyclable products and made from wood grown in sustainable forests. The logging and manufacturing processes are expected to conform to the environmental regulations of the country of origin.

Typeset by Transet Ltd, Coventry.
Printed in Great Britain for Hodder Education, an Hachette Livre UK Company, 338 Euston Road, London NW1 3BH, by CPI Antony Rowe, Chippenham, Wiltshire

DEDICATION

For
Anna and Jack
Lilian and Sidney

In memory of Michel Thomas (1914–2005)

Contents

ACKNOWLEDGEMENTS

I have been inspired by the work of a small number of psychologists who have devoted their lives to improving the educational opportunities of the most disadvantaged children in society. Their work and influence is referenced at various points throughout this book.

I have also been fortunate to collaborate with various colleagues over the years who have had a significant impact on my thinking and understanding of how psychology can enhance the teaching and learning process and raise the achievements of all students. They are my co-authors on previous books, Shirley Bull and Martin Powell; collaborators on a range of research projects, Gordon Brown, Nick Chater and Laura Shapiro; the psychologists and teachers with whom I have worked, Chis Reeve, Dave Tweddle, Kevin Wheldall, Sue Kerfoot, Brahm Norwich, Linda Siegel, Stuart Livingstone and Sue Mann, and my current colleague at KRM: Psychological and Educational Research Consultants (KRM-PER.com), Helen Wall. I would also like to thank Anna Conley and Victoria Hislop for their insightful and incisive feedback on an early draft of this book, and Emily Conley for her time, patience and expertise in discussing the teaching of foreign languages. Finally, I would like to acknowledge the enormous influence of Ted Raybould on my career, educational philosophy and psychological practice. We shared a vision many years ago of how psychology might shape children's learning experiences to prevent the occurrence of learning difficulties. I remain as optimistic and enthusiastic as ever that we may be able to take further steps towards realising our goals through our current collaborations.

Notwithstanding all the help, support and advice I have received in writing this book, the responsibility for its contents and any errors and omissions remain entirely my own.

PART I

Setting the scene

Part 1 sets the scene for *The Learning Revolution*. The introduction discusses how this book came to be written and my interest in the work of Michel Thomas. My own background as a teacher, psychologist and academic researcher led me to share Michel Thomas's philosophy about the nature of teaching and learning. Chapter 1 looks at the life of Michel Thomas and explores his family background, his involvement in the war and life in the USA developing his language courses. Links are made between Michel Thomas's family background, war-time experiences and choice of career to illustrate that his courses are not just about teaching languages but are invested with Michel Thomas's broader aspirations for the education system and the kind of society in which we live.

INTRODUCTION

The Learning Revolution is a book about how Michel Thomas set about teaching foreign languages. It describes his methods and identifies their theoretical origins within a little known area of psychology, *instructional psychology*. Instructional psychology is an analysis of the way that the environment impacts on what students learn. This addresses what is taught, teaching methods and the assessment of students' learning and is described in detail in Chapter 7.

Michel Thomas first came to the attention of the British public through a BBC documentary in March 1997, 'The Language Master', in the series 'The Knowledge', and the accompanying profiles that appeared in the national press. However, his prowess as a teacher had long been recognised and endorsed by many Hollywood stars and public figures in the USA and the UK, and past students read like the guest list on a celebrity talk show. They include Woody Allen, Doris Day, Emma Thompson, Natalie Wood, and Eddie Izzard, who have all spoken glowingly of Michel's teaching and helped to bring an awareness of his methods to a wider audience.

'The Language Master' followed Michel Thomas teaching a number of students from Islington Sixth Form College in North London, all of whom had given up learning a foreign language in the belief that this was something that was beyond their capabilities. Many had failed to pass a GCSE, with one student being totally demoralised having been advised to give up learning a language due to a lack of talent. This was just the kind of group that Michel relished teaching: students who had been written off due to a 'complete lack of ability'. If these students subsequently learned after studying with Michel there could be only one conclusion as far as he was concerned, that their learning was a consequence of the way he taught. The highly sceptical head of French in the college where the students studied monitored their progress during the documentary and conceded that she had been astounded at how much they had learned. She reported, 'It was very impressive, very impressive. I think as the students themselves said, they learned in one week what normally takes five years.'

I was attracted to Michel Thomas's method of teaching for a number of reasons: he had a clear philosophy; he assumed all students could learn whatever he set out to teach and he believed that this could be achieved through his distinctive analysis of what and how to teach. Michel Thomas's approach is underpinned by ideas that question many conventional wisdoms about how we learn and the extent to which effective teaching can meet the varying needs of students from diverse backgrounds with a range of abilities.

Michel Thomas's methods are rarely, if ever, covered on teacher training courses. I would have welcomed knowing about them during my brief teaching career in a large first school (for children aged between five and nine) on the outskirts of Bradford in the north of England. Just before I took up my first post I was a given a class list and the name of one particular child was highlighted. Linda was a non-reader and I was told not to expect too much from her as her brother had just been transferred to a special school for children with learning disabilities, her family had a history of literacy difficulties and Linda herself had been assessed by the school's educational psychologist who said that she was of low intelligence.

Although my one-year teaching course was in many ways excellent, I must admit I did not have a clue how to teach reading, but through a process of trial and error, which included daily five-minute teaching sessions at lunchtime, Linda made excellent progress. I may not have taught any of the other children in my class but by the end of the year Linda could read and write fluently. While that was clearly pleasing it was also worrying. How could I have achieved so much with a child for whom expectations were so limited, given her low intelligence and family history of literacy difficulties? What I realised was that the information I had been given about Linda was not at all helpful in working out how to teach her and that the only legitimate expectation was that students would learn if I managed to get the teaching right.

The lessons learned from teaching Linda served me well as an educational psychologist in Walsall and lecturer in educational psychology at the University of Warwick. During my time in Walsall I came across many Lindas who were expected to learn very little. However, I was fortunate to work in a ground-breaking and enlightened psychological service where measuring children's intelligence, which was common practice amongst educational psychologists at the time, was considered unnecessary and irrelevant when set alongside the knowledge gained through systematically researching the most effective ways of teaching. Many children perceived to have literacy difficulties made rapid gains despite coming from financially disadvantaged backgrounds and receiving little direct support from home. All the obvious indicators suggested that many of these children should fail but instead, after receiving appropriate teaching from their mainstream class teachers, they excelled and improved to such an extent that they were ultimately able to read and write to a standard commensurate with their peers.

Over the last 20 years at the University of Warwick I have led numerous large-scale projects that have investigated the most effective ways of teaching reading, writing, spelling and maths to children aged between 5 and 13. The research has focused on pupils in schools in some of the most financially and socially disadvantaged areas in the county and explored the extent to which attainments could be increased and failure prevented. The various studies that have been conducted have consistently confirmed that the key to what we learn is the *way* we are taught rather than the schools we attend, our abilities or family circumstances.

Given this background, it is not surprising that I was immediately drawn to the work of Michel Thomas. I shared his fundamental beliefs about how best to help students learn and, as I became more familiar with his methods, it became increasingly apparent that they were founded on very sound psychological principles. Michel's approach worked not because he was charismatic or was working with motivated students but because of his understanding of languages, his knowledge of what was useful to learners and his ability to present information in small, logically sequenced steps that minimised ambiguity and made explicit the one key skill that he wished to teach.

The views of Michel Thomas are remarkably similar to those of B. F. Skinner, one of the most important figures in 20th century psychology and whose theories are introduced in Chapter 7. He said:

> If you want to be a good teacher you have got to have the student teach you what to do. The student is always right. If the student isn't learning it isn't the student's fault it is the teacher's fault. If the student isn't learning the teacher has not created an environment in which students learn. You must let the student specify the conditions under which the student will then actually learn.[1]

The views of Michel Thomas, like those of Skinner, represent a dramatically different way of thinking about teaching and learning from the more traditional explanations discussed in Part 2 of this book.

Michel Thomas's methods were not well received by the established educational community but he was not alone in trying to bring a different philosophy and culture to bear on students' learning. This book locates Michel Thomas's methodology within a broader context and relates his efforts to instigate educational change to others who have shared the same philosophies and objectives. Significantly they have all encountered similar obstacles but have remained undeterred in their aspirations. The book not only describes the psychological theory and research that underpins Michel Thomas's methodology but covers a broad range of issues that relate to educational theory, research and practice that it is felt are essential if Michel Thomas's overall aim of a learning revolution is to be fully appreciated and realised. This was done for two reasons. The first reason was to illustrate how little educational research has revealed about how schools and teachers impact on what children learn. It appears that where children live and their family circumstances are better predictors of success than the quality of their schools and teachers. The second reason is to demonstrate how Michel Thomas's methodology provides the framework for a radically different way of thinking about raising achievements that focuses exclusively on what is taught and how, areas that are within every teachers immediate sphere of influence.

Readers of this book will have a variety of backgrounds and familiarity with the education system. I imagine that many will have had little desire to engage in any formal learning since the day they left school whereas others, perhaps through being parents or teachers, will have had more recent contact and a greater awareness of current debates and issues. Some readers might want to know about the broader implications of Michel Thomas's approach and how it relates to educational research on school improvement and teacher effectiveness, whereas others will only want to focus on those parts of the book that describe the theory and instructional principles underpinning Michel Thomas's methodology. It is therefore impossible to write a single book that will meet the needs of everyone. As a result it may well be that this is not the kind of book that every reader will read from cover to cover. Instead some may prefer to dip into the sections that focus directly on Michel Thomas, his beliefs and his methods and not engage in the broader educational issues.

I cannot claim that this book is presenting an unbiased analysis of Michel Thomas's work. I personally doubt whether that can ever be done about any topic. Inevitably a degree of bias will have influenced my own reading and interpretation of the literature and how I have marshalled the arguments to make the case for Michel's work. Similarly, Michel always spoke with great authority about his way of teaching and it might be thought that this served to pre-empt proper debate about his methodology. It might also create the impression that what is being presented in this book is the right and only way to teach foreign languages. Certainly Michel was convinced that his way of teaching was preferable to any of the alternatives.

However, it is perhaps best to view Michel Thomas's approach as representing a different way of looking at the teaching and learning process. Although Michel clearly thought he was right in the way he approached teaching, he would not have wanted others to blindly accept his word for this without first examining all the available evidence and arguments. Michel Thomas did not want to replace the traditional dogma with an alternative that was pursued uncritically. It is certainly more challenging and less comfortable for teachers to embrace Michel Thomas's philosophy, given that it places the responsibility for what students learn with the teacher. Similarly, students who have, or are thinking about following the language courses do not have to abandon views about their own learning or that of their children in order to enjoy and benefit from Michel's way of teaching. It is not so much about whether Michel was right or wrong as accepting that he offered an alternative starting point for understanding the relationship between teaching and learning.

This book has two purposes. The first is to describe Michel Thomas's teaching methods and to explain their origins, rationale and theoretical underpinnings. The second is to explain how Michel's vision for an education system based on his philosophy, assumptions and methods could be realised. The book has been divided into four parts.

Part 1 sets the scene and this introductory chapter presents the origins of the book and its purpose. Chapter 1 summarises the key events in the life of Michel Thomas, explaining why he started to teach foreign languages after the Second World War in the USA and his ultimate ambition.

Part 2 asks what we already know about effective teaching. Chapter 2 looks at the ways in which we can find out which schools are effective and reviews the different ways researchers have investigated the topic. Chapter 3 examines the evidence about how schools make a difference. It focuses on students from low income families as these were the pupils Michel Thomas was most concerned to teach and to whom he wished to demonstrate the impact of his methods. Chapter 4 reviews the evidence on how teachers make a difference and Chapter 5 looks at the conventional wisdoms on how students learn. Part 2 covers a broad range of educational issues which are necessary background to appreciate fully the potential impact of Michel Thomas's approach for achieving widespread and sustained change in the way that students are taught in schools.

Part 3 looks at the theory and practice of teaching foreign languages through Michel Thomas's approach. Chapter 6 provides a psychological starting point for teaching and introduces Pareto's Law which offers a rationale for determining what to teach. Chapter 7 introduces instructional psychology, which underpins Michel's methodology. Chapter 8 discusses the core psychological principles, derived from instructional psychology which inform what and how to teach. Chapter 9 considers how best to decide what to teach and Chapter 10 introduces the principles for teaching new concepts. Chapter 11 looks at the teaching methodology used by Michel Thomas and Chapter 12 focuses on how he engaged students in learning and assessed their progress.

Part 4 explores the wider implications of Michel Thomas's approach to teaching foreign languages. Chapter 13 considers recent trends, principles and tensions in teaching foreign languages. Chapter 14 focuses on how foreign languages are typically taught and assessed and Chapter 15 considers what foreign language teaching might look like if it drew on Michel Thomas's philosophy, principles and methodology. Part 4 concludes with Chapter 16 which outlines the framework for working towards a 'learning revolution' which Michel Thomas fervently hoped would be the ultimate outcome of his life's work.

CHAPTER I

MICHEL THOMAS:
A BRIEF HISTORY

OVERVIEW

This chapter covers three areas. It summarises the life of Michel Thomas, explains why he started to teach foreign languages and looks at the impact of family background, both from a personal perspective in terms of the impact Michel's family life had on his career, and also from a general viewpoint: how family background affects our willingness to accept ideas and educational philosophies and practices because they are different from those with which we are familiar and have experienced success.

In the autumn of 1999 *The Guardian* published a profile of Michel Thomas which described his life and work. It also announced that Hodder and Stoughton were preparing language courses in Spanish, French, Italian (known as the Romance languages) and German based on his pioneering methods. Michel Thomas had finally agreed to commit his unique approach to teaching foreign languages to audio recordings, both cassettes and CDs. Several months later, four pairs of students were each taught their chosen language over a single weekend in a small recording studio in London. The students worked intensively over two days with few breaks and were rewarded through learning the crucial skills that Michel Thomas believed would provide all they needed to know to fully master a foreign language.

A condition for being selected to participate in the recordings was that students were expected to have no, or minimal knowledge of the language they were about to be taught. Michel Thomas wanted to replicate on his audio recordings the experience that all his past students had undergone in person. Listeners are invited to be a third participant in the teaching and learning process and so engage with the courses as naïve students. Each language is taught through a

9

Foundation course of eight one-hour recordings that have become a publishing phenomenon, selling almost a million units worldwide. They have been followed by five-hour Advanced courses and Vocabulary Builders.

In the autumn of 2007, two years after Michel Thomas's death, further language courses were published in Arabic, Russian and Mandarin Chinese. These too are to be followed with Advanced Courses and Vocabulary Courses. Additional courses in Japanese, Polish and Greek are also now in preparation. These new recordings all rigorously adopt the methods that Michel Thomas developed and incorporate the instructional principles described in this book. They illustrate the generalisability of the methodology and that it can be applied to languages which have little in common with English. They also demonstrate that the success of Michel Thomas's approach is based on the analysis of *what* and *how* to teach and not the personality or charisma of the teacher.

The original Foundation courses in Spanish, French, Italian and German were published as they were recorded, warts and all, and were subjected to very little editing, mostly reducing the length of the gaps where students paused to think. Most student errors, hesitations and mispronunciations have been retained, in complete contrast to conventional practice where published language courses present accomplished actors in well-rehearsed scenes learning at a pace that would defy the linguistic equivalent of an Einstein. Michel wanted to demonstrate to listeners how learning occurred and that, with the right teaching, the fundamentals of each language could be mastered over very short periods.

It is clearly impossible to teach every aspect of a language, particularly vocabulary, within a few hours so the goal was to give students a detailed appreciation of how each language worked through providing a thorough grounding in the structures underpinning their use. The recordings enable students to reach a level of understanding whereby they can develop their skills and vocabularies in the future. Through making the links between teaching and learning transparent, Michel hoped that listeners would acquire an awareness of how we learn that could be generalised to any context and ultimately any subject.

At the time of the recordings Michel Thomas was 86 years old yet he taught without a script, notes or prompts. Clearly he was using a methodology he knew inside out, displaying astonishing enthusiasm, determination and patience. He also demonstrated, for the first time publicly, the comprehensive and broad range of teaching methods and instructional techniques that he had developed and refined over many years. They are highly systematic, innovative and effective but have rarely been encountered in the same form in any schools or institutes of further and higher education. Although originally designed over 50 years ago, Michel's methods incorporate techniques that only now are the focus of psychological research exploring the relationship between teaching and learning. As an educator he was, in many respects, years ahead of his time.

MICHEL THOMAS'S EARLY LIFE

Michel Thomas's life and war-time experiences have been documented in detail in Christopher Robbins's authorised biography, *The Test of Courage*. It charts the truly devastating impact of two world wars on his life. The First World War caused him to have a disrupted childhood where he had to make his own way in the world from a relatively early age. During the Second World War, family and friends were murdered in concentration camps, he witnessed the most horrific events, was tortured by the Milice – a French paramilitary force similar to the Gestapo – and was involved in numerous high-risk military operations. That he survived was fairly miraculous when everyone that mattered to him perished. Yet he emerged with an unparallelled determination to make a difference to the lives of the most vulnerable, and ultimately turned his war-time experiences to his advantage. Less resilient individuals would have been overwhelmed and undermined by comparable events.

His recordings are much more than self-instructional language courses to enable listeners to master a basic vocabulary for their summer holiday or sight-seeing weekends. For Michel, teaching foreign languages was a by-product of his primary purpose which was to demonstrate that anyone could be taught anything with the right teaching. He wanted to show that everyone was capable of learning and that education enables people to think for themselves and to resist overtures to follow the crowd. Michel's war-time experiences made this a priority. His primary purpose was to prevent the atrocities that he observed during the Second World War from ever occurring again and he believed that education had a fundamental role to play in doing this.

Michel Thomas was born Moniek Kroskof in Lodz, a part of Russian Poland, on 3 February 1914, an only child born into a prosperous Jewish family. Christopher Robbins paints the portrait of a multi-talented, hugely principled, fiercely independent, insightful but wary young man; a perfectionist who never expected of others what he did not aspire to himself. Michel Thomas was very much indulged by the three significant women in his life: his mother, her younger sister, Idessa, and his grandmother. He recalled in his biography, 'I was surrounded by love. It was like air. Love was so much a part of my life, it was like breathing. The security of love was very strong. I am sure that is where I have drawn my strength over the years.'[1] Michel spent much of his early life in the company of adults, particularly women. Interestingly there is little mention of his relationship with either his father or uncle or close childhood friendships. What emerges is a person who when faced with obstacles had an ability to overcome them, take control, find solutions, and regain a sense of purpose and direction.

There were two significant aspects of Michel's early life that had a lasting impact on the person he became and ultimately on his decision to teach foreign languages. The first was that through growing up in Poland, Michel became profoundly aware of his Jewish identity, in part as a consequence of childhood pranks that had overtly anti-semitic overtones, but also of the more general treatment of Jewish citizens in Poland. Being the direct target of anti-semitism shocked Michel and alerted him to its insidious nature and devastating consequences. It left him with a very powerful desire to leave Lodz and escape its oppressive atmosphere.

The second was that Michel Thomas's mother noted that he was psychologically scarred by the anti-semitic childhood bullying to which he had been subjected and as a result of which had become a much less biddable child. He also experienced prolonged bouts of ill health that resulted in him spending extended periods with his mother as he travelled with her on business trips. Over time his mother felt that Michel would recover more quickly, physically and psychologically, if he lived outside Poland, which was still struggling to come to terms with the destruction caused by the First World War. At the age of six Michel went to live with his aunt Idessa and her new husband in Breslau, Germany. Although this may seem a strange decision for a mother to make given attitudes towards parenting in the 21st century, it was less unusual in the 1920s. It was not uncommon for children to live away from their parents during periods of ill health wherever an alternative healthier environment could be located. For example, it was often a recommended form of treatment for a range of respiratory and lung-related illnesses. It was also not uncommon in close-knit Jewish families and communities for children to live either in the same house with aunts or uncles or for immediate relatives to live in close proximity to each other. Michel's aunt had been a constant presence as he was growing up, someone he came to regard as a second mother. Equally he did not feel that he was apart from his mother. He saw her regularly and she cast a psychological presence which he found comforting and reassuring.

The move to Germany certainly had an immediate and beneficial impact on Michel. He quickly began to learn German and had a rich and invigorating life, learning to ski, visiting the opera and attending concerts. Despite a growing love of music, Michel showed little aptitude for playing the piano, and later recalled that lessons taught him more about how *not* to teach than they did to play this instrument. Significantly, he never felt German or totally accepted by German society although he spoke the language fluently and very much enjoyed living there for well over ten years. This theme permeated Michel's life both socially and academically, as we shall see, when he sought academic acceptance and verification of his methods.

It is questionable whether Michel could ever have felt accepted at any point in his life. There were numerous significant occasions when he felt let down by family, girlfriends, friends and colleagues which increased his sense of isolation and self-reliance. This also extended to organisations of which he was a part. No matter how successful his contributions to various campaigns during the war there always came a point at which total acceptance eluded him. Even though he was awarded the Silver Star for Valour, one of the American military's highest decorations, in May 2004, and was recognised at the US Holocaust Memorial in a ceremony to honour the liberators of the concentration camps, there was always a sense in which Michel felt extremely wary and sceptical of others; and as his life drew to an end there were very few people, if any, whom he felt that he could really trust.

The legacy of growing up in war-affected Poland had a profound impact on Michel and he was acutely aware of the growth of Nazism in Germany in the 1930s and the factors that contributed to its emergence. As a young Jewish man he sensed the impending danger, and after being warned by friends of his imminent arrest owing to his vocal opposition to the Nazis he left Breslau and his aunt and uncle at the age of 19 in May 1933. He moved to France and stayed with family friends and while there decided to go to university. This posed something of an initial dilemma as his French was poor and he had to become fluent quickly in order to take up the place that he secured. He therefore set about learning French, which he did with impressive speed, by applying his existing grammatical knowledge to this new and unfamiliar language. Although he was living in France and was in a perfect position to improve quickly, there was a considerable amount of knowledge to acquire as he wished to not only become fluent conversationally but also read and write to university standard. When he looked back he recognised that this was his first step in developing the methods that underpin his language courses.

Michel graduated in Philosophy from the University of Bordeaux shortly before moving to Vienna. This followed a visit home to Poland in 1937 to see family, relatives and friends. It proved to be the final time he saw them. They were all murdered during the Holocaust with the exception of one uncle, his mother's brother, Abraham, who had left to live in the United States before the war.

Vienna, despite the unsettling events all around, was in many ways an ideal place for Michel to live. It was intellectually exciting and the home of Freud and psychoanalysis, just the right environment for Michel to explore his interests in psychology, the origins of human behaviour and its relationship to unconscious mental processes. Michel took a post-graduate course in psychology and philosophy, again putting another piece of the jigsaw in place in terms of the body of knowledge that was being acquired that would ultimately provide the inspiration for teaching languages.

Michel's itinerant lifestyle was honing his survival skills and instincts. Every move required Michel to turn his hand to a new occupational venture to secure finances so that he could live. This demonstrated his extraordinary capacity to adapt, act decisively and survive. For example, in Vienna Michel worked for a jeweller making miniature gold chains, he read to a blind man and he painted pictures on glass. In Paris in late 1938, after fleeing Austria, he arranged and hosted musical evenings and sold his own paintings.

AFTER THE WAR

During the war Michel Thomas fought with the French Resistance and the US army, was captured by the Germans and held in a concentration camp, was present at the liberation of Dachau and after 1945 pursued Nazi war criminals. By the end of the war Michel had lost all sense of normality. His family members were dead and his life had been dominated by anti-semitism and conflict. He did not feel that his future lay in Europe and so left for the United States in July 1947. He arrived in Galveston, Texas and made his way to Los Angeles where his uncle now lived, having established a successful business there. In a poignant exchange between nephew and uncle, Michel was handed a bundle of letters received by Abraham from relatives in Germany and Poland. It is doubtful that Michel ever came to terms with the deaths of his family and the manner of their demise. He often said, as a cautionary note, 'never underestimate the finality of evil', a statement which perhaps hints at the depth of hurt and feelings that Michel struggled to conceal.

Within a relatively short time after arriving in California, Michel Thomas, who was now in his early thirties, embarked on a new life and career teaching foreign languages. The knowledge, understanding and expertise that had served him so well during the war now provided a passport to a new life in the USA, a life largely devoted to demonstrating how education might enable societies to address social inequalities and extremist propaganda. Michel Thomas's war-time experiences taught him that a free society was based on an education system that was available and accessible to all to produce informed, independent-thinking individuals. A statement from Thomas Jefferson had particular resonance for Michel, 'If a nation expects to be ignorant and free, in a state of civilisation, it expects what never was and never will be.'

Michel Thomas opened the Polyglot Institute in Beverly Hills in September 1947; it was later renamed the Michel Thomas Language Center. His methods were developed and refined over a 25-year period, by which time they had effectively reached the form in which they are now being published. He attracted considerable attention from the media, academics and Hollywood celebrities. The latter helped to pay the bills and enabled him to create the non-profit Foundation for Better Learning to raise funds for a Demonstration School which he hoped would pioneer innovative educational approaches. It was a source of considerable regret to Michel that the school never materialised, largely as a result of the educational establishment's unwillingness to support the venture. In the end Michel moved to New York in 1982 and opened a second language school.

Despite the upheavals in Michel's early life he was very proud of his origins and his family, and his work established a degree of continuity between his new life in America and his past in pre-war

Poland and war-torn France. Learning languages enabled him to survive and prosper during the constant upheavals before the outbreak of the Second World War. His knowledge of languages helped him to fit in and display chameleon-like qualities as he assumed different identities during the war. Clearly his survival instincts, his ability to think logically and analytically, even when faced with the most horrendous situations, served him well in his new life in America. Christopher Robbins notes that Michel depended on his intuitions because doing so had saved his life on numerous occasions. Ultimately, he recognised that the only person he could trust and rely on was himself; to do otherwise, he had learned, placed him at risk. Thus, Michel was very sure of himself and, through backing his hunches, was invariably convinced that his way of doing things was the right way. Similarly, whether it was because of his war-time experiences or some other factor in his family background, he did not like leaving things to chance. And so it was with Michel Thomas's language courses. They are meticulously planned and structured in his desire to show that what finally determines what students learn is the quality of teaching they receive, not their family background, the school they attend or their general academic ability.

WHY TEACH LANGUAGES?

Christopher Robbins states on more than one occasion in Michel Thomas's biography that 'for Michel the war can never be over. The memories from those years remain as real and emotionally powerful as events in the present'. Michel himself was quoted as saying 'in a way I saw education as a continuation of the war. Democratic countries had fought not just to defeat the Nazis but to preserve free societies'.[2] He attributed the rise of Nazism to the German education system which he believed was designed to produce a highly educated elite and largely disregard the vast majority who were cast in predominantly subservient roles with limited expectations and a generally unquestioning mentality. Michel saw that the masses accepted their fate, that they were to be ruled by a super-elite minority, who in turn allowed Hitler to rise to power and were seduced by his rhetoric. His biography quotes the mantra from his university professors justifying making graduation from high school difficult: 'We want an elite – we don't want an educated proletariat.' Although he recognised that being well educated could not guarantee independent thought, he felt it would potentially create a climate where people were less vulnerable to extremist propaganda.

Whether or not he was right is less significant than his broader aims, the legacy of which resides in his language courses.

Michel believed it was critical to give everyone a good education so that they could be informed and think independently. He wanted to demonstrate that this was achievable and that anyone could be taught anything. However, he became aware that there were few who would share his belief about the power of teaching. The conventional wisdom was that children's learning was limited by their ability or motivation and that teachers' effectiveness was crucially dependent on their personality and capacity to inspire.

Michel Thomas chose to teach languages because he regarded them as 'alien' to the majority of pupils he planned to teach, not because they are inherently difficult but because students would know very little when starting. Michel commented:

> I needed to find out how humans learn so I could discover how to teach. And I felt that the most alien thing for somebody to learn was a foreign language. Not the most difficult, but the most alien – simply because you know nothing when you begin.

Michel began to teach French to recalcitrant, disadvantaged, teenage students in downtown Los Angeles because it was the most irrelevant subject that he could imagine teaching them and because he always felt that he learned most from working with what were generally perceived to be 'difficult' students. On one occasion Michel asked a class if anyone knew where French was spoken to which there was a single reply, London. When asked why, the response was because London is in Paris.

Michel Thomas did not dispute the importance of students' motivation, the need to give them meaningful, purposeful and relevant activities nor the personal qualities of teachers. He wanted to show that students could make significant progress even when taught topics that were of no apparent interest. What could be less meaningful or motivating to children living in the poorer quarters of Los Angeles than learning a European foreign language? Very few of them had visited a Californian beach, let alone Spain, Italy, France or Germany.

MICHEL THOMAS'S EDUCATIONAL PHILOSOPHY

Michel Thomas believed that the student was never wrong and that he as the teacher was responsible for what they learned. He would have to put things right if they made errors or failed to learn. He also wanted learning to be stimulating and effortless. Woody Allen, when interviewed about Michel's course in the BBC documentary, 'The Language Master', likened learning French to the effortless way in which every baseball enthusiast remembers key statistics. He said:

> Every kid that likes baseball knows the batting average of every ball player and every statistic. You know it without putting in any effort. So it was with learning with Michel, it was effortless. Michel claimed that he could teach me French over a weekend and I thought why not. This was years ago and it was a very nominal fee and I thought what have I got to lose. Either the guy is crazy and I lose a couple of hundred bucks or it's some kind of miracle. So I gave it a try. He was amazing.

Michel Thomas's educational philosophy was ultimately derived from three core ideas: the first, that behaviour is learned rather than innate; the second, attributed to the influence of a maths teacher, that there was nothing so complicated that it could not be made simple; the third, that he wanted to take learners from knowing nothing to reach the highest levels of achievement, not as a result of any perceived ability on the part of the learner or motivational qualities of the teacher, but purely and simply as a consequence of the quality of teaching the fundamental building blocks being the way knowledge was organised, structured and presented to students. Each of these areas is explained, discussed and revisited throughout this book.

Michel's approach to teaching reflects a series of paradoxes and contradictions. He wanted to demonstrate that anyone could be taught anything with appropriately designed instructional programmes, yet he is only recognised as a teacher of foreign languages. Equally he wanted to ensure that disadvantaged and minority groups were as well educated as everyone else, but initially he attracted attention through teaching celebrities and the relatively affluent.

Michel wanted students to understand how each language worked so that they could generalise and apply their knowledge. More generally Michel wanted students to appreciate the full potential of his methods, their origins and rationale so that the nature of the teaching and learning process could be more fully understood. However, he did so through structured methods that are more commonly associated with learning by rote. He believed his methods were highly replicable and would have the same impact if delivered by any teacher, but was very guarded about their use and was unwilling to share them or make them available publicly lest they be misused or misinterpreted. Although Michel had a strong sense that his analysis of language structures and his teaching methods were broadly correct, he was willing to adapt and change when faced with feedack that this was necessary. For him the most powerful evidence came from students when they made errors. He was less sympathetic to the criticisms that emerged from the educational community, which he thought lacked substance and reflected defensiveness, prejudice and conventional wisdoms.

The existence of these paradoxes obscured Michel Thomas's true goals from some of his detractors. He wanted to retain absolute control of all he did professionally because he had so little control of so many events in his early life. Many aspects of the language courses and the way he protected them could be traced back to Michel's family background and formative experiences.

THE INFLUENCE OF FAMILY BACKGROUND ON MICHEL THOMAS

Christopher Robbins notes in his introduction to the biography, 'The more I learned about Michel, the more interested I became in the connection between the experiences of his life and the revolutionary system of teaching languages that has evolved from it'.[3] It is clearly not necessary to understand Michel Thomas's background to appreciate and learn from his courses, any more than it is necessary to know the intimate family details of a composer or author to appreciate their music or novels. In his own teaching Michel sought to provide the principles and understanding so that students would know how languages work. As the courses are so radically different from the way languages are usually taught it is felt that an awareness of some of the key influences on Michel's life will help readers to appreciate their rationale, structure and content. The most significant of these were his family, being an only child and his Jewish background.

It is hard to imagine how Michel Thomas must have felt arriving in the USA alone, knowing the fate of his parents and being unclear about the future. His family instilled in him a powerful sense of his own identity and capacity to survive. He recalled his mother saying 'What you are and what you know – these are the only things that count.' His values and beliefs, his resilience and determination, his desire to prevent the atrocities he had witnessed occurring again were all a reflection and reminder of his parents, aunts and uncles and his family history.

Michel Thomas's decision to emigrate to the USA and his motivation to teach languages required enormous self-confidence and self-belief. These were not qualities that he lacked and revealed something that was essential to Michel's personality. His life led him to the conclusion that an individual's destiny is in his own hands rather than being dependent on external influences. He always believed that he had control over his own future and never accepted the notion that fate might have dealt him a losing hand from which there was no escape. Despite the traumatic impact of two world wars on him, his family and his friends, he never asked, 'why me?' To do so would have handed power to his enemies and denied him his autonomy and capacity to act decisively and to shape his own fate.

In many respects Michel displayed all the characteristics frequently associated with being an only child. Studying the impact of birth order on personality and career choice is a growing area of psychology. Frank Sulloway in *Born to Rebel: Birth order, family dynamics and creative lives* and Joy Berthoud in *Pecking Order: How your place in the family affects your personality* both construct portraits of the impact of birth order on personality and career path. Sulloway examined the birth order of those who have become recognised as having made the most significant scientific breakthroughs in recent times. First-borns and only children are seen to be highly motivated, sometimes ruthless, ambitious and invariably successful. Their ambition is typically attributed to a desire to please parents; '… the tendency for firstborns to excel in school and in other forms of intellectual achievement is consistent with their strong motivation to satisfy parental expectations'.[4] Berthoud also characterises the first-born or only child as being more conventional and less likely to take risks than their brothers and sisters and notes their ambition, social maturity, self-confidence, and self-sufficiency.

Robin Skynner, the psychiatrist, has written about the link between family background and our choice of profession and behaviour in the workplace. Skynner became well known through his collaborations with John Cleese, the comedian and actor. In *Families and How to Survive Them* they explore the impact of family influences, particularly the early role of parents on our subsequent emotional and psychological development. In *Life and How to Survive*

It Skynner and Cleese develop the ideas presented in their earlier book and relate styles of parenting to our career choice and the individual needs that are potentially met. 'Let's take someone who has grown up in a family where people don't trust emotions, and where relationships are rather distant; they'll be more comfortable working in data processing ... Take someone else from a home where control and order and tidiness are the essential things; they'll fit naturally into a job as an accountant or civil servant. Someone from a family where there's quite a lot of anger, but open aggression is frowned on, will be at home working as a barrister where aggressive questioning is essential, but where it's all within a framework of rules and under the control of a father-figure.'[5]

Michel's Jewish background very much encouraged a questioning philosophy. Sir Jonathan Sacks, the Chief Rabbi, stated that Judaism is 'a questioning, argumentative and wrestling faith'.[6] He could have been describing Michel Thomas. This description certainly helps to explain Michel's questioning of orthodoxies to understand their origins and rationale rather than to directly confront or challenge their advocates. If Michel's life had been different he might have been more patient when debating with those whose views were different to his own. But for Michel, time was finite and he preferred to direct his energy into teaching the students who would benefit most from his methods rather than debate issues with staff from university language departments, who in his view, were very unlikely to change.

The general issues are less whether these portraits are accurate than the possibility that birth order and family behaviour have a potentially enormous impact in areas of our lives of which we may not be aware. As far as Michel is concerned, he was perfectly equipped in terms of family history and dynamics, intellect and personality to devise a new teaching methodology and ensure that it achieved world-wide recognition and acclaim.

The importance of family background is multi-dimensional. To a considerable degree it creates the template for our ability to change and adapt to new circumstances and ideas. Michel Thomas's methods will challenge many firmly held beliefs of teachers, parents, educational academics and readers of this book. Our willingness to change previously held beliefs and convictions is not only related to the merits or limitations of any arguments but is also rooted in our formative experiences. Psychologically speaking one of the most difficult challenges we face during life is how to negotiate all the changes we are forced to undergo. Any parent who has lived with either a toddler going through 'the terrible twos' or teenagers for any length of time will have a sense of the extent to which they resist change (which is how many psychologists interpret the tantrums of the two-year-old and teenager).

Accepting or appreciating Michel's methods will involve changing, amending, or at the very least temporarily suspending previously held views about the nature of teaching and learning. Teachers and parents often have strong beliefs about how students learn and should best be taught and it is likely that the full implications of Michel Thomas's methodology will not lead to immediate change but to firmly held attitudes and values being questioned. Adam Philips, the psychotherapist and author, suggested that 'change is the infidelity we fear most.' Michel's philosophy asks many of us to change the way we look at teaching and learning; reactions to his approach may say more about how we contemplate change than anything about Michel Thomas and his way of teaching.

THE LEARNING REVOLUTION

Those who have been most impressed with Michel's methods, and those for whom they have been designed, are the many students who have participated in his courses either directly, through being taught by Michel, or indirectly through the recordings. Their impact is indiscriminate and has been recognised by not only the well-known but also a significant number of failing students whose self-perceptions as effective learners have been restored.

So why have Michel's methods not been used more widely in schools or adopted by those responsible for training teachers how to teach? The educational community is not renowned for open-mindedness and a willingness to accept new ideas. As will be discussed in Chapter 16, Michel Thomas's philosophy, if embraced more widely, would demand a dramatic overhaul of not just how foreign languages are taught but how secondary schools are organised. Educational academics have been reluctant to debate Michel Thomas's theories assuming all too readily an implied criticism of their own methods. They have often attributed any success that Michel might have achieved to his charisma and personality and have rarely exploited the potentially rich vein of research opportunities that are present to evaluate how foreign languages might best be taught.

However, Michel's methods were not universally rejected by the academic world. Herbert Morris, the Dean of Humanities at the

University of California (UCLA), Los Angeles, in the early 1990s, was approached to see if he was interested in adopting Michel's methodology to improve language teaching at the university. An initially sceptical Morris agreed to spend a weekend with Michel learning Spanish. He reported:

> It was extraordinary. I had acquired a competence in Spanish after three days! A remarkable achievement. People ask me how it came about and I don't know how to answer them. It's a mystery to me. Michel has a charismatic quality, an intonation of voice, accompanied by extraordinary patience and self-assurance. I think he has managed to survive and achieve what he has done by having a degree of self-confidence that matches that of anyone I've ever known.[7]

Despite having earned the enthusiastic support of an influential figure within the University, the language department itself was unwilling to adopt or trial any of Michel's methods. University politics and the conservatism of those responsible for teaching foreign languages ensured that Michel's methods were rejected. It is interesting, not to say ironic, that when faced with anything new, academics will invariably reject innovation on the grounds of lack of evidence to support change. They will nevertheless continue to employ traditional approaches even though they are similarly lacking in supportive evidence as to their efficacy. This is a theme that will be explored in more detail in Chapters 2 and 3.

It was a source of considerable regret to Michel Thomas that the claims he made for his methods were generally ignored and all too often dismissed by the educational establishment. The conventional wisdom was that in so far as his methods could be shown to 'work' this was largely attributable to his forceful personality and quirky strategies rather than in recognition of their theoretical rationale and methodological rigour. He was disappointed and at times frustrated that he became well known primarily as a result of *whom* he taught rather than *what* and *how* he taught. He always maintained that his methods would work with *any* students and would be equally effective if implemented by *any* teacher. He was adamant that their success was not dependent on the magnetism of the teacher. He saw this well-worn criticism as nothing more than the educational establishment's unwillingness to attribute academic success to anything other than the ability of students or the personality of teachers. He felt that those working within the system had a blind spot as far as recognising that students' progress could be the result of a well-designed, systematic programme of study.

Michel devised a way of teaching that was based on questioning educational orthodoxies. He sought a logical, analytic rationale for structuring knowledge for students and wanted to present this in a systematic, coherent manner where there was a gradual progression in the skills taught. His mother laid the foundations for critically reviewing established practices through sharing her belief that the only true wealth was knowledge. Michel was inevitably going to be sceptical and questioning of a teaching approach that did not have theoretical rigour. This was evident in his meetings at UCLA with members of the language department. Michel immediately queried their methods, calling them obsolete and ineffective, a less than persuasive approach to getting members of a department to consider the merits of an alternative teaching methodology.

It is true of most fields, for example medicine, that it takes many years before research outcomes find their way into everyday practice. There are many reasons for this which include trialling and testing new treatments or interventions. It is only within the last ten years that Michel's methods have come to the attention of a wide, international audience. It is unrealistic to think that conventional practices will be replaced by anything as dramatic as Michel's approach overnight. Michel would not have wanted teachers to adopt his programmes just because they were told to do so; he would have wanted them to understand why they would be more effective and gather appropriate evidence to support his claim.

The real cause of tensions between Michel and traditional language teachers was that they were actually talking about different things. The latter were only addressing how to teach foreign languages. Michel, however, had invested his language courses with more ambitious aims. 'I wanted to show what could be achieved with learning by removing the heavy lid and opening the mind. I wanted to demonstrate that anybody can learn. I didn't devise my system to teach languages quickly. I did it to change the world'.[8]

SUMMARY

This chapter has provided an overview of some of the significant events in Michel's life and has explored their links to the development of his language courses. The courses, in almost every respect, challenge existing theories about how we learn, they challenge accepted practice in teaching not just languages but most subject areas, and they challenge traditional views about where the responsibility for students' learning lies. Michel, in his introduction to each course, asks students to leave behind preconceived notions about how to learn and reminds them that he is responsible for their learning. The extent to which they, or those who have used the courses, are able to do so is a reflection of how firmly wedded they are to traditional teaching approaches. Finally there appears to be a number of distinct influences on Michel Thomas's language courses, and this chapter has identified some of the psychological pieces in the jigsaw that shaped his professional life and chosen career.

PART 2

Teaching and learning: What do we already know?

Figure 1 on page 29 shows the potential influences on students' learning: the school, the teacher, the family and the student. Part 2 of this book takes each of these areas in turn and looks at what the research says about their impact on students' learning. Although an enormous amount of research has been conducted into child development and what makes schools effective, far less has addressed the areas of greatest concern to Michel Thomas: what and how to teach. He concentrated exclusively on certain features of schools, which although acknowledged to be critical factors in determining what students learn, have nevertheless not been the focus of the kind of research that can indicate whether certain ways of teaching are more effective than others.

This crucial area has been addressed to some extent through the government's National Literacy and Numeracy Strategies that have now been subsumed under the National Primary Strategy. Although it is claimed that they draw on research (for example see *The Literacy Game* by John Stannard and Laura Huxford), they were never trialled in such a way that they were shown to be more effective than other approaches to teaching literacy and maths. It is argued that the available evidence indicates that what students learn at school is directly related to family background, parental income and where they live. Currently it would appear that what and how you are taught, the areas on which Michel Thomas focused, are less relevant and that family circumstances appear to inoculate students to the impact of their schools, teachers, curriculum content or teaching methods.

Will Hutton[1] writing in the *Observer* newspaper on the way social class determines educational opportunities and access to the best universities, draws attention to the 'good society test' set by John Rawls, the American political philosopher. Rawls states that a society should aim for a condition in which a preborn individual would be indifferent to which home and family he or she was born into because they would still be able to fulfil their potential. This goal would be a fitting outcome of the kind of education system that Michel Thomas hoped would evolve from his language courses.

The four chapters in Part 2 provide a starting point for recognising where Michel Thomas's methods reside within current thinking about teaching and learning. This background is essential if Michel's broader goals are to be realised, as it highlights the kind of changes that would need to occur in how we think about teaching and learning, school organisation and educational practice.

Chapter 2 looks at the ways in which we judge schools to be successful. Chapters 3 and 4 discuss the elements of school life and characteristics of teachers that it is thought enable students to succeed or fail. Chapter 5 looks at our understanding of the factors that facilitate learning. These factors exert a powerful influence over our expectations, not only where students are concerned, but also how we approach learning new skills as adults. The conventional wisdoms may lead us to have unrealistic expectations about how we learn and create barriers to accepting new and innovative approaches to teaching.

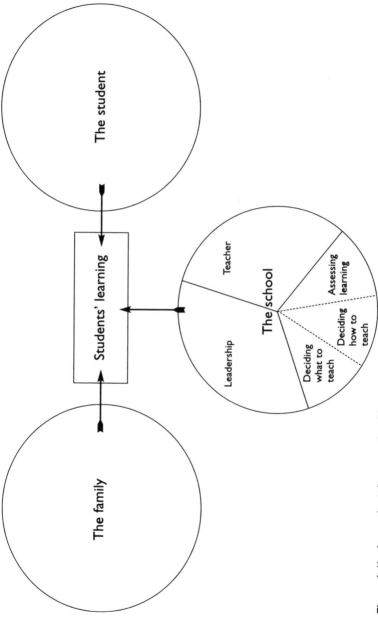

Figure 1 Key factors that influence students' learning

CHAPTER 2

HOW DO WE DETERMINE THE MOST EFFECTIVE WAYS OF TEACHING?

OVERVIEW

All those involved in education want to determine the most effective ways of teaching. Certain methods are more successful than others and we are dependent on research to investigate which ones are most likely to help students to learn. This chapter looks at the different ways in which research could be undertaken into the most effective ways of teaching foreign languages that will help readers to appreciate how little is known about how best to teach.

When we talk about teaching we are referring to the behaviour of teachers and the steps that they take to try to help students learn. Teachers organise the learning environment, plan what and how to teach and monitor students' progress. All of these activities describe what teachers do and define the process of teaching. We hope that the ultimate outcome of teaching is learning. This would be evidenced by students being able to do something that they had been unable to achieve prior to any teaching. It sounds fairly straightforward but can be problematic as it is not always easy to establish a direct link between what is taught and what students learn. There are a number of explanations for this. Learning takes place over time and progress may not be immediately apparent. Even when students learn, progress can be limited and hard to observe. Although we hope that learning results from what teachers do, student learning is influenced by many other factors which are not under the direct influence of teachers, such as personal relationships or through a multitude of other past-times like reading or watching television. Sometimes there is a change in behaviour and evidence of learning but it is the result of these other factors rather than the efforts of the teacher.

The purpose of any research is to address these issues and establish a direct link between teaching and learning through demonstrating that the specific activities organised by teachers result in student achievements. The main reason for conducting research is to demonstrate the generic nature of the teaching methodology so that it can be shown to work for a variety of teachers with a variety of students. Any effective methodology should work for all teachers and all students irrespective of the social, ethnic or academic background of the students or teachers. This is what Michel Thomas claimed for his methodology, that its impact would be the same for every teacher and every student, every time.

There is very little research that demonstrates conclusively that some teaching methods are more effective than others. There are occasions when researchers have shown that certain features of what students are taught are very important to future learning, as are some teaching methods. However, research of this type tends to be conducted under highly artificial conditions as the teaching is done by researchers rather than teachers and over very short time periods with students being taught on a one-to-one basis. There is little convincing evidence that research carried out under these circumstances transfers to other contexts, particularly schools, where teachers work with much larger groups and over long time-scales.

Despite the difficulties in conducting research we nevertheless want to know which factors have the most impact on students' learning. Some say it is the school, others that it is family background, and in the case of foreign languages, many believe it is down to the ability and aptitude of the students. Most would agree that it is a combination of all three. The more we know about effective teaching the greater the likelihood of teachers adopting successful strategies in the future. Unfortunately where the teaching of foreign languages is concerned there is a distinct lack of evidence on which methods are the most effective. Yet we probably all have a sense of how to teach through our own school experiences.

The knowledge and awareness that non-professionals acquire of the teaching profession and education system is unique. Between the ages of 5 and 16 we spend approximately 15,000 hours in school, during which time we develop a more intimate, in-depth knowledge of teaching, teachers and schools than we acquire about any other profession. A significant part of our lives is spent absorbing a variety of messages about the nature of teaching and learning over a period when we are at our most impressionable and vulnerable. Some of these messages are conveyed in a highly explicit manner, others less so. Regardless of whether we were successful within the formal education system we probably have a pretty strong sense of how schools work and how learning takes place, which is underpinned by our own unique experiences of school life.

Irrespective of our own first-hand knowledge of schools and teachers, we revisit those formative experiences as parents when our own children begin school. Parents are regularly alerted to their roles and the choices they can make about their children's education. They are now given a greater say in how schools are run than ever before and are constantly reminded of their responsibilities to ensure that children attend school regularly and are supported in their learning at home.

All of this encourages us to believe that we have knowledge about how schools function. We are given a wealth of data about our children's progress in the form of test results and school league tables. The annual debates that ensue when examination results are published about whether standards are rising or declining reinforces the impression that there is hard evidence available about what works in education and which schools and teachers are most successful. In fact, contrary to the impression created, we know very little about what leads to successful learning in education; what is known is depressing as it offers a potentially deterministic view of who will succeed and fail.

Education has been high profile in recent years and debates have conveyed clear messages about the factors that contribute to success and failure. However, our understanding of what works is rarely based on convincing evidence. Instead it invariably reflects educational folklore and the conventional wisdoms that shape behaviour and mould expectations to learning that are extremely powerful.

Martin Powell and I in *Teachers in Control* refer to the conventional wisdoms in education as *myths*, a word that has come to be understood as applying to a story or account of the world that has developed without needing proper evidence. In everyday language, myths contain a grain of truth, but have a tendency to assume greater veracity than is justifiable. For social anthropologists, however, the term has a technical meaning that refers to the process whereby stories or accounts develop within a culture. What is important about myths is not that they are right or wrong but that they become the accounts invoked to explain behaviour; they function as mechanisms of control, a means of regulating what is known and accepted and what is rejected. Significantly, much of what educational researchers believe they know, the myths they invoke to explain how teaching succeeds or fails, stops short of investigating how best to structure knowledge, how best to present that knowledge or how best to ensure that it is mastered, generalised and applied to new contexts. These are the crucial aspects of teaching and learning that were regarded as critical by Michel Thomas in designing programmes for teaching foreign languages but have largely been ignored or dismissed as unimportant or irrelevant by the majority of educational researchers. Instead, as was discussed in the introduction to Part 2, researchers have focused on identifying the features of improving schools, the characteristics of effective teachers or the attributes of successful learners.

To fully appreciate the unique character of Michel Thomas's methods and why they are seen to be so successful by those who have taken his courses it will be helpful to see how educational researchers have traditionally gone about trying to establish how to teach effectively. The fact that they rarely focus on the areas that embody Michel's methods possibly explains why his methods were not accepted by university-based teachers of foreign languages in the USA.

FINDING OUT WHAT WORKS: CONDUCTING RESEARCH

When children are unwell we would not dream of giving them medicine which has not been adequately researched. We assume that any medication has undergone the appropriate tests and has been shown to be an effective remedy for our children's ailments. We expect there to be a direct link between the child's illness, the medicine administered, and their recovery. It would be natural to think that the same happens within education, that the teaching programmes that students follow have been shown to work and result in greater learning. Unfortunately this is not the case; we are constantly exposing students to methods for which there is little evidence of their efficacy.

Drugs are tested through what are known as 'randomised controlled trials'. This involves selecting participants to act as guinea pigs to try out the drugs. The participants are then placed in one of two groups, either *experimental* or *control*, on a randomised basis. The experimental group is given the drug to be tested whereas the other group, the control group, is given a placebo which looks the same as the tested drug but contains no medicine whatsoever. Participants do not know which of the two groups they have been placed in; neither do those administering the drug. The impact of the drug and placebo on the volunteers can then be monitored to establish whether or not the drug is working. Experiments of this type enable researchers to examine the effects of the drug because in all other respects the two groups are treated identically, the only possible exception being the contents of the drug and placebo.

The gold standard for educational research is also experimental and involves randomised control trials where the aim is to investigate the relative impact of different teaching approaches. For a variety of reasons (such as expense, difficulty in maintaining methodological rigour and the level of expertise required) this methodology has rarely been used, researchers preferring instead to opt for methodologies (such as questionnaires, interviews, classroom observation and case studies), which are invaluable when researching different questions (for example, what are the attitudes, values, beliefs and opinions of teachers, parents or students?) but which in reality cannot indicate whether some teaching methods are more effective than others. For example, questionnaires and interviews allow us to get teachers' opinions about what they believe is effective. They are an extremely useful starting point for experimental research which takes teachers' views a little further and tries to establish whether or not their opinions translate into success for their students. Classroom observations have an immediate appeal and logic. However, as will be discussed in Chapter 3 they also have inherent limitations largely because they are rarely underpinned by theory. Case studies involve in-depth analyses of a single or small number of schools and generate a wealth of data. However, the relatively small number of schools involved makes it difficult to generalise findings to other contexts. Thus, whatever the benefits of these methodologies they stop short of providing clear evidence of how best to teach. This can only be achieved through experimental studies and although conducting experimental research is potentially difficult and not without numerous obstacles, it is, however, possible, and can show whether some teaching methods are more effective than others. Their significance is increased when they are part of a series of studies which systematically build upon each other.

In order to be absolutely sure about which schools, teachers or methods are effective we would have to run experiments along similar lines to those conducted in the natural sciences. In an ideal world all children would arrive at school with identical knowledge levels and pre-literacy and numeracy skills. No matter what their home background or pre-school experiences there would be a level playing field where everyone would start school at exactly the same point. After beginning school all children would have the same facilities, resources and money spent on their education, both at school and at home, so that these too could be ruled out as contributory factors in children's learning. The only difference between the children would be in the way that they are taught. Two groups of students would be taught through different methods and their learning monitored which would enable comparisons to be made between the effectiveness of the approaches.

Clearly this is impossible to achieve because we cannot control the backgrounds and previous knowledge of children to this degree. Children do not share a common starting point when beginning school any more than they experience equivalent educational opportunities once their formal education begins. Equally it is almost impossible to say that the progress that children make is exclusively attributable to the input from their schools. Learning is not something that only takes place between 9.00 a.m. and 4.00 p.m. Younger children talk to and read with their parents while older students have access to different resources, facilities and opportunities. Through day-to-day living children acquire considerable knowledge, quite independently of their formal education in school, and some of which will be reflected in their examination results. So the results from school-based experiments will always be less clear cut than those in the natural sciences. These variables can be mitigated to an extent by selecting schools which are comparable on a range of significant criteria, for example, social class, ethnicity and academic attainment, but never completely overcome. However, a huge amount of research, employing a range of non-experimental methods, has been conducted and it might be thought that some of it would help us to find out what works best in education.

David Hargreaves highlighted numerous limitations in much educational research[1]. His most trenchant criticisms targeted the (i) lack of experimental evidence to support teachers' classroom practice where 'there is rarely any scientific basis for what the teacher chooses to do', and (ii) government's reluctance to test out educational policies before implementing them.

In the late 1990s two influential reports were highly critical of most of the research conducted within the field of education. A report for the Department for Education and Employment (DfEE)[2] concluded that policy and practice are insufficiently informed by research. Where the research does address these issues it tends to be (i) too small scale to generate reliable and generalisable findings and (ii) not sufficiently grounded on existing knowledge to be capable of advancing understanding. A second report published by the Office for Standards in Education (Ofsted), was equally damning of educational research and its impact on practice[3]. The report reviewed 41 studies published in five high quality educational journals. Not a single study reported any experimental research, investigated effective teaching methodology or focused on foreign language teaching.

In England, the government's National Literacy (NLS) and Numeracy (NNS) Strategies have been used with just about every primary-aged child (children aged between 5 and 11) since 1998 (1999 for maths) amid claims that it was based on extensive research. Their estimated cost between 1998 and 2003 was £2.3 billion yet they were never trialled experimentally to see if they were more effective than any other approaches to teaching literacy or maths. In fact a review of the research underpinning the methods used in the NLS was not commissioned until November 1998, two months after its introduction, and was not published until February 1999, five months after its introduction![4]

Despite claims from the government about the success of the strategies, there is little evidence to suggest that they have had the desired impact. The official evaluations have not involved comparisons with other ways of teaching reading so there is no way of knowing whether pupils' improvements were down to the way they had been taught or some other factor. This was noted in a report on standards in English which comprises part of the Primary Review, the most comprehensive analysis of primary education conducted since the Plowden Report over 40 years ago. Since the introduction of the NLS, there has been 'almost no impact on reading levels'. The impact might have been greater had it been trialled more thoroughly before its release[5].

In the absence of any appropriate research and in the face of mounting criticism, the original version of the NLS was withdrawn and replaced with an alternative framework in October 2006. Of particular interest is that the theoretical framework underpinning the original version, which was never supported by any research, has been replaced with a new model that shares many common features with the theories underpinning Michel Thomas's language courses. However, and significantly, the new strategy has been launched with further substantial financial investment but without any experimental research to support its methods.

What educational researchers claim to know therefore, about what makes schools or teachers effective, is not based on experimental research. It is not implied that what is known is invalidated because it has not been trialled experimentally. It just means that we cannot have the same confidence that what appears to work for students in one context with one school and its staff will generalise to other schools, teachers and students.

WHAT DO WE KNOW ABOUT HOW TO TEACH FOREIGN LANGUAGES?

Teaching foreign languages has not been subjected to anything like the same amount of research as how children learn to read, for instance, and so we can have even less confidence in the efficacy of the methods that are traditionally used. Everything that we know about teaching foreign languages is derived either from non-experimental research or represents the conventional wisdoms that have built up over time as experienced teachers share expertise that then gets embedded in classroom practice. Chapter 13 summarises recent trends and current approaches to teaching foreign languages. Michel Thomas did not accept that these methods were the most effective as they failed to demonstrate the crucial link between what was taught and what students learned.

It was a source of regret to Michel Thomas that his methods were not researched experimentally and compared to other methodologies. In part this is due to the fact that university departments in the USA with whom he discussed researching his methods were unwilling to do so through experimental studies. For Michel the ideal would be to teach comparable groups of students through rigorous experimental conditions to evaluate the impact of his methods with the various alternatives. However, Chapters 9 and 10 refer to programmes to teach reading, spelling, English language skills and mathematics that are derived from the same theoretical perspectives and use almost identical methods to Michel, and have been shown to have clear benefits for students. (Chapter 8 summarises the instructional principles that underpin Michel Thomas's teaching methodology which again have been the subject of extensive psychological research and have been shown to have clear implications for how best to teach.)

Where research has been conducted which has compared different teaching methodologies studies have shown that programmes that embrace the same instructional principles and methods as Michel Thomas have invariably been more successful than those with which they have been compared. These methods and the research into their effectiveness will be discussed further in Chapter 7 and Part 3.

SUMMARY

This chapter has briefly looked at the way research is conducted into finding out how best to teach. Educational researchers rarely conduct experimental studies, preferring instead methodologies which cannot demonstrate that any one method is more effective than any other. Indeed there is no evidence that the methods conventionally used are the most effective. At the same time there is no experimental evidence, either way, on the effectiveness of Michel's methods. The main reason for the US educational establishment's suspicion and hostility to his approach was that it was different from conventional practice. However, there is strong evidence that the psychological principles and methods on which Michel based his approach have a very powerful influence on students' learning.

The reality is that we know very little about how best to teach. Everyday teachers experiment in their own classrooms with methods for which there is no evidence of success. It is the equivalent of treating our children's illnesses with medicine that has never been trialled. This means that we live in an educational culture where decisions about what works are based on opinion, personal preferences and conventional wisdoms; long-standing debates are never resolved and teaching methodology is subject to whims and fashion, reflecting a swinging pendulum where different practices come and go like high street fashions.

This is the context in which Michel Thomas's courses will be discussed.

CHAPTER 3

HOW DO SCHOOLS MAKE
A DIFFERENCE?

OVERVIEW

Michel Thomas spent his life refining ways of teaching so
that every student experienced success. He focused on
three areas: what to teach, how to structure knowledge
and how to teach. However, these are not the areas that
have occupied the attention of teachers, government,
researchers and others in trying to improve educational
standards. Instead they have largely focused on the nature
of schools, leadership and the characteristics of effective
teachers. This chapter explores what we have learned
about schools that make a difference to students' learning.
If there is overwhelming evidence that schools and
teachers make a significant difference to students' learning
rather than what is taught or teaching methodology there
will be a less persuasive case for considering the wider
applicability of Michel Thomas's methods.

Michel Thomas was interested in the fine detail of the teaching and
learning process. He wanted to know how to structure knowledge so
that it could be presented sequentially and systematically. He defined
effective teaching in relation to whether students learned what he set
out to teach rather than whether teachers were dedicated, motivated
or worked hard but had no discernible impact on students'
attainments. Education professionals might argue that, at best, he was
addressing issues of secondary importance when set alongside the far
weightier issues of school effectiveness, improvement and leadership.
Unfortunately, there is little that the individual teacher can do about
these areas, whereas any teacher can change the way in which they
teach overnight and have an immediate impact on students' learning.
This is what makes Michel's methods so exciting, radical and innovative.

HOW DO WE KNOW WHICH SCHOOLS ARE SUCCESSFUL?

Some parents go to considerable lengths to try to ensure that their children receive the very best possible education. Some move into a catchment area where there is a school with a good reputation, others suddenly become 'religious' and opt for a place in a faith school, while others pay for private education with its guarantee of small classes and promises of examination success. Some occupy the middle ground and move house and pay for private tutoring in key examination subjects while sending their children to a local secondary school. Certainly when places at good schools are at a premium, and are based on some form of 'selection', it is very common to find such practices.

Uppermost in parents' minds are often the results that schools achieve. We are led to believe that the public examinations that pupils take during their school careers are the most important measures of effectiveness but can we rely on them to tell us the whole story about which schools and teachers are best? National newspapers regularly print lists of the top performing schools and we might assume that the schools at the top of the league tables are the most effective. Can we assume that those lower down the tables are less effective or poorer schools? Do schools at the top reflect the best practice in teaching or do they tend to recruit the students most likely to succeed?

Initially it was crudely envisaged that effectiveness could be determined merely by looking at outcomes of the tests pupils take. It was thought that the schools that achieved the best results must have done so because they had the most effective teachers who employed the most effective teaching methods. However, such assumptions are largely misplaced. Taking exam results as the indicator of success is highly misleading as the schools that regularly achieve the best results are usually those schools in the more affluent catchment areas or those that administer their own admissions policy. These schools are vastly over-represented in the top 200 comprehensive schools in England and are much more likely to be highly unrepresentative of their local areas than schools whose admissions are controlled by the local authority[1].

Consider this as a comparison. At the moment what happens is more akin to the race for the premiership football title. In football there is a clear winner at the end of each season, when one team is crowned champion. The question is whether the team that wins the most premiership titles (or the World Series in baseball for those living in the USA) does so because of the quality of coaching and the ways in which clubs are managed or because it has the financial muscle to recruit, buy and select the best players. Merely looking at the premiership table at the end of any season does not tell the whole story about how the success of the leading team has been achieved. So looking at school league tables tells us more about the social make-up of schools than about what leads to effectiveness. Where football teams and schools are similar is that those that do best are the most affluent and well resourced.

IS THERE ANY EVIDENCE THAT SCHOOLS MAKE A DIFFERENCE?

The central issue here is whether or not schools minimise the impact of family background. Can schools reduce the advantages that some students have before they start school and render them less pronounced? To do so to any significant degree would indicate that schools are making a difference. A failure to address such advantages, for whatever reason, would suggest that, irrespective of the quality of teaching offered, schools are failing to make a difference to students' potential life and career opportunities.

As a result, it was suggested that a more sensitive indicator of success was required that reflected not just final outcomes but progress made as well and the extent to which schools were contributing to a reduction in the gap between the more and less advantaged students. The indicator became known as Value Added and is now published alongside all the other information about school pupils at 11 and 16. Measures of Value Added reflect what schools add to pupils' learning. They tell you how the school has helped students to achieve more than might have been predicted in the light of their previous learning. However, although an excellent idea in principle, it has proved enormously difficult to establish a way of calculating Value Added measures that takes into account the differences in school admissions in terms of pupils' ethnic, social and financial backgrounds.

A further difficulty concerns the way that Value Added scores at 16 are calculated. They are based on pupils' test results at 11 but these reveal not only the quality of teaching pupils have received within their primary schools but also the extent to which teachers have prepared pupils for the national assessments. For example, it has been found that schools spend almost half their available teaching time between January and May in any academic year preparing students for these tests[2]. Other problems with calculating Value Added measure at 16 concern how to take into account inflated scores of the type just discussed at age 11, teacher expectations and the ways in which pupils' progress is measured. Value Added scores, just like the examination results themselves, have to be treated with caution and can not tell the whole story about whether schools actually make a difference.

SCHOOL EFFECTIVENESS AND IMPROVEMENT

Researchers have recognised for some time that exam results and measures of Value Added have proved to be somewhat ambiguous and failed to reveal what it takes to be a successful school. As a consequence they have tried to identify the features of schools deemed to be effective, to look at the way they operate in a bid to try to uncover common policies or teaching approaches which account for their success. Originally this area of research became known as 'school effectiveness research'. There appears to be a consensus that effective schools focus on teaching and learning, benefit from effective leadership, set high expectations, create a positive school culture, give additional help to lower-achieving pupils, involve parents and external support services and relentlessly use data to evaluate students' progress.

However, the identified practices of effective schools were too general and superficial and so did not always offer insights into how best to help a school improve. Hence there has been a gradual shift to researching school improvement which tries to unlock the practices of successful schools. Here the focus is on the ways that schools respond to their specific contexts through enhancing their knowledge of the teaching and learning process.

One particularly interesting piece of research in this area focused on 'schools in exceptionally challenging circumstances'. These schools are characterised by low attainments and a socially and financially disadvantaged location. The research is significant because these schools invariably fail to improve through the models of school improvement that researchers have found to have an impact elsewhere[3]. If such models fail to impact on schools in the most challenging circumstances it begs the question about how robust and valid such models are. What we are looking for is a model that is generalisable and works in all settings, including those in the most disadvantaged areas. The issue is whether interventions that specifically target schools in challenging circumstances can generate a more effective model of school improvement.

Researchers worked with schools in exceptionally challenging circumstances over time and monitored the impact of several interventions through examination results and interviews with headteachers. A distinctive feature of the programme was that each school selected the interventions (e.g. use of interactive whiteboards, data analysis) that they felt were appropriate to meet their needs and many of them also received training in delivering a highly prescriptive phonics programme. Past school improvement projects have offered schools ready-made programmes which require that they are implemented as intended if they are to have any effect. Here each school put together their own unique cocktail of interventions of what they thought would be most relevant to their communities.

This research is significant because it targeted pupils that Michel Thomas had also focused on in his work in Los Angeles. More importantly, these are the students that Michel felt that would ultimately benefit most from his methodology. It is therefore of interest to compare the conclusions of a major research project (that received substantial funding) with Michel Thomas's recommendations for raising standards which are relatively cheap to implement. If it can be shown that there are ways of increasing the attainments of students from the most disadvantaged backgrounds that are *independent* of the areas addressed by Michel Thomas there would be implications for teaching foreign languages and a less pressing case for the use of Michel Thomas's methods to teach foreign languages or to consider their wider applicability.

Although the researchers claimed that the project was a success in terms of examination passes they also conceded that they could not be sure what led to any gains made by the students:

> How much these improvements can be claimed by the project is difficult to ascertain as the schools were involved in many other initiatives and developments.[4]

Nevertheless, the researchers identified three major characteristics of improving schools: focusing on teaching and learning, setting high expectations, and developing what is termed a 'learning community', a fairly ambiguous concept that refers to schools regularly reviewing existing practices and undergoing a continuous process of change. As will become apparent in Parts 3 and 4 of this book, Michel Thomas's teaching approach very much addresses our understanding of teaching and learning and sets the bar extremely high in relation to what he anticipates students will achieve as a result of following his courses.

If we are interested in generating clear guidelines for future teaching three criticisms can be levelled at projects of the type just summarised. The first criticism is that the features of improving schools are too broad and vague to produce replicable interventions. The second criticism is that researchers working with the schools in exceptionally challenging circumstances emphasised the importance of teaching and learning, but did not at any time relate this observation to psychological theories of teaching and learning or instructional theories. The third criticism is that the non-experimental nature of the research means that it is not possible to say with any confidence what led to any student gains. It is therefore extremely difficult to generalise and apply the findings from the research to new contexts and there is little convincing evidence from the school improvement research that this is achievable.

CHANGE BY LUCK OR DESIGN?

Undoubtedly some schools do improve dramatically and are very successful with students in challenging settings, but it is not clear whether this is achieved by implementing practices based on research findings or serendipity, whereby the right people are in the right place at the right time. Psychological literature indicates that improvement is due to the latter rather than the former. It is a far more difficult and complex process to change the behaviour of teachers in failing schools than is acknowledged by researchers in the field of school improvement. A number of psychologists have likened the functioning of schools to those of families and have drawn on their knowledge of systems theory and applied it to the workplace. It is suggested that as with any organisation, the behaviour patterns exhibited by teachers are well established, difficult to change and potentially reflect family dynamics.

Research indicates that failing schools are characterised by an unwillingness to accept evidence of failure, blaming others for failure, fear of change, goals that are not relevant or plausible, improvement strategies adopted but not properly implemented, inconsistent teaching quality, low levels of pupil-teacher interactions, negative feedback from teachers, teachers perceived as uncaring by pupils and having low expectations of students' progress[5]. This suggests that turning round unsuccessful schools is not an insignificant task.

A culture in which blame, fear, inconsistency, negativity and lack of care are the defining features is likely to be resistant to change as

Robin Skynner and John Cleese, who were mentioned in Chapter 1, have discussed. They have applied principles derived from family therapy to businesses and explored the various outcomes when emotionally healthy individuals are employed by unhealthy organisations and vice versa. It is possible that in low-performing schools unhealthy individuals are working in an unhealthy organisation and embrace those attitudes and beliefs that are in part responsible for low attainments and which confer an aura of resistance when attempts are made to introduce change. Just as families encourage its members to behave in ways that are familiar and comfortable, so do organisations such as schools.

The status quo is therefore ensured when senior teachers select new staff who will invariably be similar to themselves without even being aware that they are doing so. The result is that teachers select new colleagues in their own image, irrespective of any rhetoric to the contrary, as there is an overwhelming desire to appoint people who it is sensed are in some ways similar to those making the appointments. Schools attempt to appoint new staff that will 'fit in' and it is this process of 'fitting in' that can lead to stagnation and the maintenance of the status quo. Teachers and students behave as they do in schools for very good reasons even if it is not always obvious to an observer what those reasons are. For example, many of us will be familiar with the 'attention-seeking' pupil who would rather have the attention of teachers through misbehaving, even if that attention is largely negative and critical, than have no attention at all. In other words, psychologically speaking, low-achieving schools operate in the way that they do for very sound psychological reasons and an appreciation of these reasons can contribute to change and their ultimate improvement.

CAN SCHOOLS LEARN ANYTHING FROM BUSINESS ABOUT HOW TO BE EFFECTIVE?

The research on school effectiveness, school improvement, and schools in exceptional circumstances has failed to describe the features of improving schools in terms of generalisable principles, particularly the psychological dynamics underpinning school life, an understanding of which is critical to changing how organisations function. Literature on school effectiveness, improvement and leadership fails to draw not only on systems theory in psychology but also on the literature and experiences of successful, improving businesses. Although schools are not businesses, psychologically speaking, they function in ways that are directly comparable.

Tom Peters in *Crazy Times Call for Crazy Organisation* argues that the healthy business employs people who are curious, people who are different, and people who do not fit stereotypes. He says of such individuals that they are more likely to do something exciting and unexpected for any company they work for. Equally he suggests employing a few 'weirdos' on the grounds that they bring originality into the workplace for the benefit of the company. Peters believes that employing people who do not initially appear to 'fit in' keeps everyone on their toes and thinking about how to improve. What gets discussed is ideas, not personalities.

In *From Good to Great* Jim Collins, with a team of researchers, traced the fortunes of companies that made the transition from what he termed 'good' to 'great'. There were three particularly interesting features of these businesses that have rarely surfaced in the school improvement literature. The first is that leaders of the companies that made the transition were not individuals with 'big personalities' but were generally seen to be self-effacing, quiet, reserved and shy. They were ambitious – but less for themselves than for the company – and did not rely on lay-offs and restructuring as primary strategies for improvement.

The second interesting finding was that the success of companies was achieved over time rather than being achieved instantly through one or two specific initiatives. Company leaders did not try to cut corners but built up the company systematically over a number of years. In other words, there are no quick fixes, and genuine change and improvement, to be sustainable, does not occur overnight. The third notable finding was that the response of the most successful companies to failure was to view this constructively as a learning opportunity. This mirrors the views of Tom Peters, who also talks about the 'relentless pursuit of failure' which acknowledges that learning from what *does not* work is almost as important as finding out what *is* successful. The successful company develops in response to its failures almost as much as in response to its successes. Similarly, Sally Bibb notes that 'enlightened' companies exude a positive atmosphere free of fear where employees are rewarded according to their contribution rather than status, and are encouraged to take risks and make mistakes as these themselves are viewed as opportunities to learn.[6] Michel Thomas saw a student's failure to learn as *his* failure in teaching and regarded errors as essential information that helped him to develop and refine his teaching methodology.

Rob Goffee and Gareth Jones in *Why Should Anyone Be Led By You?* address two areas that are pertinent to the present discussion.

The first is that they reflect the thinking of Skynner and Cleese and Tom Peters when they argue that:

> Organisations desire leaders but structure themselves in ways that kill leadership. Far too many of our organisations – in business, in the public sector, and in the not for profit-sector are machines for the destruction of leadership. They encourage either conformists or role players with an impoverished sense of who they are and what they stand for. Neither makes for effective leaders.[7]

Goffee and Jones imply that organisations get the leaders that they deserve. Not only does their style of leadership affect those *within* the organisation but those on the *outside* as well and it is this fact that potentially reveals why the universities that Michel Thomas approached had difficulties with his ideas. Michel was neither a conformist nor lacking in self-belief, two characteristics which, according to Goffee and Jones, would destabilise any organisation.

The second area of significance raised by Goffee and Jones concerns the search for the characteristics of effective leaders. They suggest that this creates the belief that leadership has a strong psychological bias and reflects individual qualities, creating the impression that leadership is something that is done to other people rather than reflecting a relationship between the leader and the led. Although some of the educational literature on leadership continues to focus on the characteristics of effective leaders, it now also addresses a number of broader issues and reflects recent trends in the business research on leadership which recognises:

- that leadership is situational and what works in one place at one moment in time might not work elsewhere;
- the importance of shared values and
- that the individuals within an organisation share the responsibility for initiating change.

The final point endorses the wider applications of Michel Thomas's methodology (see Chapter 15), which, it is argued, enable individual teachers to change the way they teach and so in turn affect changes to the schools in which they work.

Goffee and Jones have identified a number of specific behaviours that reflect effective leadership which very much endorse Michel Thomas's way of trying to change aspects of the education system which have yet to appear within the educational literature. They highlighted the need for what they term 'authenticity' which involves: (i) displaying consistency between what you say and how you behave; (ii) consistency in behaviour in different contexts (i.e. not changing the message to suit different audiences) and finally (iii) what they term 'comfort with self' which refers to the consistency between beliefs and values, what is said, behaviour and the ultimate goals of the organisation. Goffee and Jones discuss some of the ramifications of developing authenticity. This involves taking personal risks and revealing weaknesses which imply a clear sense of direction and a willingness to show vulnerability in pursuit of specified goals. The notion of 'authenticity' could have been based on direct observations of Michel Thomas and his behaviour and efforts over many years in both developing his language courses and demonstrating their wider relevance.

Schools are not businesses. However, Jim Collins in *From Good to Great and the Social Sectors* argues that the work that he and his colleagues have done is not fundamentally about running a business; it is about what separates the great from the good. The principles that enable a business to excel and progress from being merely good are generalisable and will work for any organisation, whether it be a private sector business or a service within the public sector such as a school. Finally, Collins reiterates the importance of individuals within an organisation feeling that *they* can make a difference. Through the clarity of their views they are able to exert an influence on the organisation rather than waiting for the right leader or for proposed change to resonate with their own beliefs. Collins identifies three characteristics of the most successful organisations and the individuals who work for them. They are: (i) knowing what they are deeply passionate about; (ii) being aware of their strengths and (iii) being aware of what motivates them. Michel Thomas could have ticked each of the boxes by these traits; he not only cared passionately about teaching but was absolutely clear why he focused on foreign languages and that this was an area in which he truly excelled.

Overall a picture emerges from writers who have studied improving businesses that is quite different from those that write about school improvement. If schools were to incorporate what has been learned from the most successful improving businesses they would embrace change, accept responsibility for pupils' learning and exhibit confidence and openness in how they work with pupils and parents. In so doing they would be more likely to select new teachers who display these traits and who will, in turn, contribute to developing a positive ethos.

SUMMARY

This chapter has looked at how schools try to make a difference to the lives of students and the ways in which we judge whether schools actually achieve this. The research on school improvement has been summarised for two reasons. The first is to illustrate the wide gulf that exists between the areas it addresses in trying to improve students' learning and the areas prioritised by Michel Thomas. In many respects Michel attempted to improve schools in ways that were potentially accessible to every teacher, simply by trying to change what and how pupils were taught. This is a very different starting point from the conventional view within education where change has often been dependent on the leadership style of a dynamic innovator coming along and making sweeping changes.

The research on schools in challenging areas demonstrated how those in education have tried to improve the educational outcomes of pupils from the kind of disadvantaged backgrounds that Michel worked with in California and for whom his methods were originally intended to benefit. However, this research is not based on any theories of instruction and has failed to generate any generalisable principles.

The second reason for discussing school improvement is to illustrate the disparity that exists between what educational researchers have addressed and what those researching in the business field have learned about successful businesses and effective leadership. This has relevance in relation to Michel Thomas's long-term goal to contribute to a learning revolution. The ideas on leadership expressed by Collins, Peters, Goffee and Jones and Bibb give a sense of direction for those who share Michel Thomas's aspirations.

CHAPTER 4

HOW DO TEACHERS MAKE
A DIFFERENCE?

OVERVIEW

This chapter reviews the research that has been conducted into teacher effectiveness. The differences between the areas addressed by much of this research are highlighted and contrasted with the topics of interest to Michel Thomas. The lack of research in the areas of concern to Michel Thomas suggests that they are not regarded as the critical factors in raising standards by researchers, and begins to explain why Michel Thomas's teaching methods have not been widely accepted.

We are inspired and engaged by some teachers and often become drawn to, and excel at, the subjects that they teach. The column in the *Times Educational Supplement* 'My Best Teacher' reports the influences of key teachers in the lives of public figures in shaping their later careers. For understandable reasons there is no comparable column on those teachers who had the opposite impact on the subjects they studied. Yet many of us have less positive, but equally powerful, memories of teachers who deterred us from studying any further the subjects that they taught. What exactly is it that successful teachers do that marks them out as exceptional?

In contrast to the extensive research on school effectiveness and improvement, relatively little research has been conducted to identify the distinctive skills of effective teachers. At first sight this is surprising given the central role of teachers in helping students to learn, but researchers using complex statistical analyses have looked at the factors that seem to be most influential in determining what students learn.[1] They found that the pupils, their background and prior attainments accounted for a considerable part of the variation in performance between students. Only 25% of the variation between pupils was attributable to the schools and teachers but, significantly, 80% of this variation was teacher rather than school generated.

It is perhaps to be expected that researchers have concerned themselves less with teachers than schools. Until fairly recently teachers have had considerable autonomy in their own classrooms and have been free to teach through whatever methods they felt were appropriate. The introduction of the National Curriculum in England in 1988 was seen to signal an end to this freedom. However it was not the straightjacket that teachers feared and although it outlined in very broad terms what students needed to learn, it did not go as far as telling teachers how to teach. It was only after the introduction in England of the National Literacy (NLS) and Numeracy Strategies (NNS) that there appeared to be central control over choice of teaching methodology, with the implication that some ways of teaching were more effective than others. Until this point it was generally thought that one method was very much the same as any other. What was critical was that teachers felt comfortable with their chosen methodology.

Even after the introduction of the national strategies it was generally thought that their success was down to the quality of individual schools and the merits of headteacher leadership in ensuring that recommended methods were successfully implemented. Despite considerable central control over what students should be taught in literacy and maths, teachers still have substantial autonomy in *how* they teach. The prevailing view remains that there is no definitive way of teaching. This is in direct contrast to the views of Michel Thomas who believed that students would be far more successful in learning through the methods that he developed than many of the potential alternatives. However, we are currently moving further away from the idea that one way of teaching is better than another. For example, when the NLS was launched all schools were expected to teach phonics in the same way. The revised strategy has currently sanctioned the use of 35 different commercial programmes to teach phonics and although they are all supposed to share similar features, they are actually vastly different.[2]

DOES TEACHING STYLE MAKE A DIFFERENCE TO WHAT STUDENTS LEARN?

The research that has been conducted into teacher effectiveness has steered well clear of the areas of greatest interest to Michel Thomas. Michel focused on structuring knowledge so that students were taught what was most useful through a gradual progression from easier to more difficult skills and concepts. Instead the research on teacher effectiveness has tended to focus on the characteristics of successful teachers and their style of teaching. During the 1970s debates focused on whether teachers adopted formal teaching styles where the teacher's role was to impart clearly defined knowledge largely through whole-class teaching. This could be contrasted with less formal, 'child-centred' approaches where teaching was individualised under the assumption that pupils learned in different ways, would progress at their own rate and would be taught within small groups or on a one-to-one basis. Teachers did not set out to impart prescribed knowledge or skills but acted as facilitators, helping pupils to construct and develop their own understandings. As you will see in Chapter 14, debates about these contrasting styles are highly relevant today in the teaching of foreign languages in general and the use of Michel Thomas's methods in particular.

The role of formal and informal teaching approaches polarised thinking within the educational world and the early research in the 1970s into teacher effectiveness reflected the tensions and debates of the time. Neville Bennett and his colleagues at the University of Lancaster looked at 'teaching style' in a highly controversial study published in *Teaching Styles and Pupil Progress*. They identified three teaching styles – 'formal', 'informal' and 'mixed styles' – and found that those who used the 'formal', traditional, teacher directed, whole-class style of teaching were more effective than those using the progressive, highly individualised, 'informal' methods which were very much favoured at the time and had been given added impetus through the influential Plowden Report on primary education which was published in 1967. Pupils taught by a mixed approach fell somewhere between the 'formal' and 'informal' on the basis of their performance in tests. This study was criticised primarily because of the difficulties in defining different categories and the way teachers identified the style that most adequately represented their method of teaching.

Classroom observation has become the main methodology through which researchers have studied teacher effectiveness. The main focus of the observations was, and still is, the nature of the interactions between teachers and pupils and the extent to which they addressed the whole class, groups or individual students. Irrespective of the way teachers interacted with students, special attention was devoted to the types of questions teachers asked and whether they were closed (i.e. involved students giving a specific 'correct' answer) or more open ended (i.e. did not require a 'correct' answer but invited students to discuss and consider different responses). Establishing effective methods through classroom observation and examining teaching styles is often problematic and complicated by the fact that teachers rarely adopt the same style or strategies for all subjects and may be more directive when teaching some topics than others.

WHAT METHODS HELP STUDENTS TO LEARN?

Two further well regarded studies were conducted during the 1980s which researched the impact of schools on pupils' learning and looked at a broad range of factors that influence what students learned. Both were conducted in London schools, the first in junior schools (pupils aged 7 to 11), led by Peter Mortimore from the Institute of Education in London, and the second in early years settings (pupils aged 5 to 7), led by Barbara Tizard from the Thomas Coram Research Institute. Neither study looked specifically at teaching style but highlighted a number of features of teachers' professional practice that have a bearing on Michel Thomas's approach to teaching foreign languages. Students tended to make better progress when teachers had higher expectations of what students might be able to achieve and taught a limited number of concepts at any one time. The implication was that students' learning was teacher directed. The findings from these and other studies[3] were influential in attempting to identify some elements of common practice between teachers who could be seen to achieve success with their pupils. They confirm that:

- teachers often use a range of teaching styles depending on the nature of the activity not educational ideology;
- improving schools and effective teachers are seen to retain high expectations for students' learning and that
- students make better progress when taught a small number of things at any one time.

These conclusions endorse essential components within Michel Thomas's teaching methodology. The majority of teachers would agree that high expectations influence students' progress, yet it is a phrase that means different things to different people. For Michel Thomas however, it meant only one thing, that he would achieve 100% success with every student.

CAN WE IDENTIFY GENERALISABLE PRINCIPLES
OF TEACHING?

When researchers have looked in more detail at the methods employed by effective teachers they have found it difficult to identify shared strategies that could generate generalisable principles of teaching and learning. For example, Ted Wragg and his colleagues at the University of Exeter asked teachers to identify the factors that enabled pupils to learn to read effectively. The responses could be divided into two categories: the first describing characteristics of teachers and the second characteristics of pupils. Where teachers were mentioned, the majority of responses highlighted aspects of their personality, subject knowledge and enthusiasm. Success was rarely attributed to the specific teaching methods, patterns of classroom organisation or the way knowledge was structured, organised and presented. When these aspects of classroom practice were investigated, researchers were unable to identify common, generic principles of teaching.

Headteachers and local authority advisors were asked to nominate teachers whom they regarded as effective and these subjective judgements were then supported by a number of more objective measures of effective teaching. After observing these teachers in the classroom, Wragg and his colleagues were no nearer to being able to identify any common teaching strategies that they all employed.

> [...] each teacher was unique, bringing her own individual experience of what worked well to her teaching of reading. Their approaches to reading, the materials they used, the authors they favoured, the structure of the day, the context in which they taught, their views of pedagogy and of their pupils, were very different.[4]

Experienced classroom researchers and experts in effective teaching had been unable to identify any common strands in the practice of their selected good practitioners. Instead what they identified as the common features of effective classroom practice were aspects of teachers' personalities and attitudes, such as their motivation, expectations and professional knowledge. The question remains, why, over a period of so many years, have educational researchers failed to identify generalisable principles of teaching despite their best efforts?

Establishing best practice through questionnaires, interviews or observing classroom practice has one major flaw which is highly problematic in terms of thinking creatively about identifying new teaching approaches. The research is limited by the knowledge and expertise of the chosen sample and does not acknowledge the possibility that there may be more effective ways of teaching than those known to, or displayed by, the teachers involved in the research. Part 3 of this book describes the way in which Michel Thomas analysed each language to determine what needed to be taught and incorporated a number of core instructional principles into his teaching methodology. Chapter 8 describes how these principles are applied to teaching each language. It is unlikely that the content of these chapters would have emerged from either questioning expert teachers or observing them in the classroom. Their origins are theoretical rather than existing practice and this reflects the more general concern that very few attempts to articulate principles of effective teaching are derived from theory.

THEORY AND EFFECTIVE TEACHERS

One piece of research that was an exception to the general perception about the role of theory was a study conducted by Neville Bennett and his colleagues who related tasks that students were given to a theoretical model of learning. The model suggests that there are different areas of learning (for example accumulating new knowledge, problem solving, applying knowledge) which are facilitated by different types of tasks and activities. Whether teaching was teacher or pupil directed was not determined by teachers' preferred teaching styles but the kind of learning that was being encouraged. This added a new dimension to understanding teacher effectiveness through shifting the emphasis from observing teacher-pupil interactions to assessing whether students were set appropriate tasks given the areas of learning that were being promoted. When looking at effective teaching in this light, Bennett and his colleagues found that students were only given appropriate tasks 40% of the time and that the incidence of mismatching was especially marked for higher achieving pupils since 75% of the tasks they received underestimated their existing level of achievement.

Neville Bennett's research into teacher effectiveness suggests that successful teaching involves engaging students in a range of tasks, some of which involve them being taught skills and knowledge explicitly and directly and some that extend students' initial understanding with more complex tasks. These are less teacher directed and involve pupils in generalising and applying what they have learned to different contexts. Bennett's research on matching tasks to areas of learning reflects a key component of Michel Thomas's approach to teaching which also emphasises that the nature of the task determines the degree to which students' learning is teacher directed. Overall however, very few of the areas addressed by Michel Thomas have been investigated in the educational research on teacher effectiveness through either experimental or non-experimental methods.

There is still little consensus about the most effective ways of teaching apart from the suggestions that it involves a degree of whole class, directed activities and requires teachers to have high expectations for students' learning. More worryingly there is very little research that sheds light on the matter. The conventional wisdom remains that there is no one method that will work for all pupils. Equally, a method that is successful for one teacher may not be effective for another, the assumption being that teachers have got to feel 'ownership' and commitment, and believe in the strategies that they are using.

CURRENT RESEARCH ON TEACHING AND LEARNING

A major initiative was launched by the Economic and Social Research Council (ESRC) in 2000 to conduct more research on teaching and learning to address this lack of consensus while at the same time bridging the gap between theory, research and practice. The high-budget programme covers research from pre-school settings right through to post-compulsory, higher and work-place education. Two things stand out from the projects that have been funded. The first is that only one appears to address the content of what is taught. The rest of the projects focus on different areas of teaching and learning such as the role of parents, developing group work, promoting inclusive education, and consulting students about the teaching and learning process. The importance of these areas is readily acknowledged and they are deserving of extensive research. However, it is unfortunate that there is little experimental research into any of the areas addressed by Michel Thomas such as what and how to teach.

The second is that only one project appears to be using experimental methods to determine the impact of different ways of teaching on students' learning. Again, the areas of prime importance to Michel Thomas remain immune from empirical research. As previously stated, one possible reason for this is that these areas are not seen to be of sufficient importance to be worth researching.

Alternatively it may be that their impact is too difficult to research and that the process of teaching is too complex to be subjected to systematic analysis. Either way it suggests that Michel's approach to teaching will not be readily embraced by the educational community.

A teacher's guide to the completed research and its outcomes has been published within the Teaching and Learning Research Programme.[5] The guide presents ten principles of effective teaching and learning which reflect major findings into what makes a difference in the classroom. For example, it is recommended that effective teaching and learning:

- equips learners for life in its broadest sense;
- engages with valued forms of knowledge;
- needs assessment to be congruent with learning;
- promotes the active engagement of the learner;
- demands consistent policy frameworks with support for teaching and learning as their primary focus.

These points, from Michel Thomas's perspective, are very general. They read more like desired aims as it is not immediately apparent how they would translate into common instructional strategies, in very much the same way that it is difficult to translate the general outcomes from the school improvement research into classroom practice.

In summary, research conducted over many years has rarely addressed curriculum content or teaching methodology as major contributory factors in facilitating students' learning. It has invariably been assumed that one way of teaching is pretty much like any other and thus, that ultimately a 'one size fits all approach' can never work. The argument continues that teaching is an art rather than a science and that what really matters is that teachers work in ways that suit their own personalities and with which they feel comfortable.

IS TEACHING A SCIENCE OR AN ART?

Michel Thomas's approach to teaching and learning differs from conventional practice in the extent to which the emphasis is on the teacher rather than the learner. Michel Thomas focuses on the teacher and aims to derive key generalisable principles that would work for any teacher in any context and enable him or her to become more effective and have a positive impact on students' learning. Michel Thomas worked out what to teach from a logical analysis of how languages are best taught, which was in turn informed by psychological theory. The more traditional emphasis on the learner arises from the belief that successful learning is based on having a thorough understanding of the ways in which students differ, an appreciation of their strengths and weaknesses and insights into how they construct knowledge and make sense of what they have been taught. In many respects the differences and resulting tensions between the two approaches is encapsulated in the question, *Is teaching a science or an art?* Michel Thomas would reply that it is a science. For Michel whether students learn is logical, predictable and determined purely and simply by the way knowledge is structured and presented to them. Do it the right way and they will succeed, do it the wrong way and they will fail. For the majority of those in the teaching profession, teachers, administrators, politicians and teacher educators, teaching is an art.

The caveat is that Michel would probably have added that 'science frees the art'. In other words there is a core framework that if followed will give students the necessary skills and knowledge which will then create opportunities for them to be innovative, spontaneous and achieve to higher levels than would be possible without this prerequisite knowledge. Michel Thomas's ideas and educational philosophy reflect those of the historian, Brian Simon, who was a hugely influential figure in the educational world during the latter part of the 20th century. He played an important part in the campaign for the introduction of comprehensive education and was a highly articulate critic of the use of intelligence tests to select students for secondary education.[6]

Simon argued for a change in emphasis in understanding how to teach effectively, he wanted to see a shift from the traditional focus on the individual differences between students to identifying principles of instruction. In his criticisms of individualised views of teaching, he argued that it is impossible to develop a science of teaching if each student is unique and so requires his own specifically designed teaching programme. Principles of teaching, Simon claimed, could only be developed through looking at what students have in common. The aim was to develop a pedagogy which, for Simon, was the science of teaching that embodies both the curriculum and teaching methodology. However, he did not underestimate the enormity of such a task:

> The concept of pedagogy is alien to our experience and
> way of thinking. There are, no doubt, many reasons why
> this is so; among them wide acceptance of the unresolved

dichotomies between 'progressive' and 'traditional' approaches, between 'child-centred' and 'subject-centred' approaches, or, more generally, between the 'informal' and 'formal'.[7]

Simon concludes that the gulf between proponents of different views is so vast that developing a science of teaching 'may seem to be crying for the moon'.

The situation has changed little over a quarter of a century later and reflects the gap that exists between the educational establishment and those like Michel Thomas who were trying to introduce an alternative way of seeing the teaching and learning process. Robin Alexander in his 2003 paper *Still No Pedagogy?* explored why we are still floundering to establish a pedagogy and generalisable principles of teaching and learning. He revisits Simon's original arguments and dissects current educational philosophies, policies and practices to interrogate whether there has been any movement towards developing a science of teaching. He concludes that the position now is not very different from Simon's time and has actually been exacerbated by the government's attempt to impose curricula on schools. Thus, we are seemingly no nearer to reaching a situation where the educational community will be wholly receptive to the design and content of Michel Thomas's programmes for teaching foreign languages.

SUMMARY

This chapter has reviewed the research and debates about effective teaching. Attempts to identify the most effective ways of teaching have created tensions between contrasting philosophies that vary in where the responsibility for learning lies. Overall, research has failed to identify core generalisable principles of instruction that would prove effective for all teachers with all students. The debates offer insights into why educationalists almost invariably have difficulty with teaching approaches like those of Michel Thomas where he assumes the responsibility for students' learning through the quality of the curriculum and nature of the teaching methodology.

CHAPTER 5

HOW DO STUDENTS LEARN?

OVERVIEW

Psychology has explored the individual differences between students to explain why some learn more effectively and efficiently than others. Some explanations have persisted over many years, such as the view that more intelligent students will do better than less intelligent ones. The role of intelligence in human learning has been hotly contested and the subject of much discussion. The ideas behind the concept are resilient and keep reappearing in different guises. This chapter explores the most frequent explanations that account for students' learning and explains why they were of little appeal to Michel Thomas. The chapter concludes with data from recent studies and surveys which indicate that family status and background are major factors in determining students' future learning. This finding appears to be robust and highlights the importance of Michel Thomas's methods for enhancing students' learning opportunities and raising academic standards.

Just as we have a sense of what makes a school or teacher effective, we have intuitive feelings for why some students are more successful learners than others. In the research discussed in the previous chapter conducted by Ted Wragg and his colleagues, teachers were asked what would help to improve standards. School ethos and classroom atmosphere were mentioned most frequently, followed by parental involvement. Lack of parental support was cited as a major factor constraining pupil progress, after lack of resources, funding, extra classroom support and having too many other subjects to teach. Paul Croll and Diana Moses conducted research into teachers' perceptions of the causes of students' difficulties in learning. Students' general ability and home background were frequently cited, as was their intelligence, as major causal factors accounting for their difficulties. Significantly as far as our discussion is concerned, few teachers mentioned the nature of *what* was taught or *how* it was taught.

Students' ability, intelligence and home background would come top of most people's list of factors that enable students to make good progress in school. The terms ability and intelligence are often used interchangeably. They both refer to the idea that students who are of higher ability and intelligence possess a greater capacity to learn, and will learn more quickly and to a higher level than those of lower ability and intelligence. Yet the extent to which evidence of ability in any area at an early age allows us to predict how well these children will do in the future is questionable.

HOW IMPORTANT IS IQ?

Following the 1944 Education Act, the use of intelligence tests in the UK was widespread in assessing whether pupils had difficulties in learning. If pupils had a measured Intelligence Quotient (IQ) of 70 or less (the average being 100) they were thought to have learning difficulties and would benefit from a placement in a special school, as they would learn more slowly than their peers. The figure of IQ 70 was recognised for many years as the cut-off for special education and it was therefore assumed that the figure must have been based on research indicating that children of different IQs learned at different rates or had different learning potentials (i.e. how much they will learn). However, the figure of 70 was derived from an unexpected and less than scientific source. It emerged from the work of Cyril Burt, who was the first educational psychologist to be appointed in the UK when he took up a post with the London County Council in 1913. Burt wanted to employ an objective measure for determining which children would benefit from a special school placement. The Council had places for approximately 1.5% of the school population and Burt found that this figure could be met by using an IQ of 69.4 as the cut-off point. Over time this was rounded up to 70. This number, which became firmly fixed in people's minds as a convenient criterion for selection for special education, and which has had such a widespread, pernicious influence on the lives of many children, was originally adopted on purely pragmatic grounds to fill the number of available places in London schools.

Since the late 1980s there has been a wealth of research showing that IQ is a very poor predictor of how well children will learn to read.[1] It has been demonstrated on numerous occasions, and to a high degree, that there is now agreement amongst the majority of psychologists that IQ is a very poor way of determining who will and who will not succeed in learning to read. The evidence now indicates that children of average and below average IQ are able learn to read at comparable rates and through similar methods. Keith Stanovich, a leading researcher in this area, has reported that there is no evidence at all in terms of aetiology, cognitive profile or brain mechanisms related to reading individual words to show that children of high and low intelligence who are behind their peers are in any way different.

PHONOLOGICAL AWARENESS: THE NEW IQ?

Psychologists have subsequently turned their attention to another core skill known as *phonological awareness*, which refers to being able to manipulate sounds in the absence of print. A perfect and well-known example of this skill is the game 'I Spy', where participants take it in turns to spot objects around them that start with a given sound. Two further examples of phonological awareness tasks are known as *synthesis* and *segmentation*. With synthesis pupils are given the separate sounds in words and then have to pronounce the word that they make when put together. For example, children would be asked what word is represented by the sounds '/c/a/t/ (k/æ/t)'. This is seen to be the critical skill in learning to read. The second key phonological awareness task is segmentation, which is a critical skill in learning to spell and is the reverse of synthesis. Here pupils are given a word, for example 'man', and have to state the individual sounds in the word, which in this case would be '/m/a/n/ (m/æ/n)'.

A seminal study from the late 1970s conducted at the University of Oxford[2] demonstrated that children who arrive in school with good phonological awareness skills generally make better progress in learning to read by the time they are seven. Phonological skills are so important that they appear to be a better predictor of success in learning to read than IQ scores. In many respects phonological awareness is the new IQ. Instead of psychologists administering IQ tests to determine what kind of progress children might be expected to make, teachers are encouraged to give assessments of phonological awareness so that similar judgements can be made. But even with phonological awareness can we be sure that it is children's phonological skills *per se* that are critical to their future progress or do they conceal the significance and impact of home background on children's learning?

Research has shown that phonological awareness does not develop in a vacuum.[3] It needs to be taught directly and one way of achieving this is through hearing stories and sharing books. Imagine the different starting points of the child who hears stories and shares books with parents and carers from an early age, perhaps from the time he or she can sit up at around six to nine months, and the child who does not see books until they start school at four or five years of age. The former will have a three- to four-year head start which will potentially be enormously advantageous and give children an unassailable lead in learning to read. The critical issue therefore, is the extent to which early success in any subject or activity reflects genuine ability as opposed to early exposure and training in a particular area.

WHAT HELPS STUDENTS TO LEARN?

What else do educationalists think enables students to learn? One theory that has received considerable attention is that of 'learning styles'. Here it is argued that students have preferred ways of learning. Some learn through written information, others are seen to be auditory learners and prefer to hear new information. One of the most popular manifestations of this approach is by those who argue for multi-sensory approaches, in other words, those who support simultaneous visual, auditory and kinesthetic (movement/touch) inputs. One of the potential concerns of advocates of this theory about Michel's Thomas's courses is that the emphasis on the spoken word may well suit the auditory learner but disadvantage visual or kinaesthetic learners.

The problem is that a recent review of learning styles commissioned by Demos, an independent think tank that analyses social and political change, suggested that there is little evidence to support the 'learning styles' theory. The authors of the review concluded that the research evidence for these styles is highly variable; there was even less evidence that schemes emphasizing different learning styles enhance teaching so that learning is improved; and that in their view the evidence for learning styles is profoundly unsatisfactory and needs attention. They noted that:

> Some teachers are using learning styles in ways that constitute poor professional practice, for example, when claiming that learning styles are largely fixed and innate. This belief leads teachers to 'label students as having a particular learning style and so to provide materials and

sources that are appropriate to that style'. A good education does not limit them to that style or type, but ensures that students have opportunities to strengthen the other learning styles.[4]

The Teaching and Learning Research Programme produced a commentary on the evidence connected with learning styles. It stated that:

There is a considerable scarcity of quality research to support the value of identifying learning styles. A recent psychological investigation of the VAK (visual, auditory or kinesthetic) principle concluded that attempts to focus on learning styles were 'wasted effort'.[5]

Susan Greenfield writing in the *Times Educational Supplement* in July 2007 concurred with these findings. She wrote:

Unfortunately, from a neuroscientific point of view, it is nonsense. Humans have evolved to build a picture of the world through our senses working in unison, exploiting the immense interconnectivity that exists between the senses in the brain. It is when the senses are activated together that brain cells fire more strongly than when stimuli are received apart.[6]

Another popular theory concerns 'Brain Gym' which involves giving students various exercises in the belief that this will impact directly on their achievements. The programme claims that neural mechanisms can be influenced by particular types of physical activity. However, this is refuted in the Teaching and Learning Research Programme commentary:

The pseudo-scientific terms that are used to explain how this works, let alone the concepts they express, are unrecognisable within the domain of neuroscience.

Finally there has been considerable publicity for the capacity of Omega 3 to improve examination results. The Teaching and Learning Research Programme was also not convinced of its merits:

[…] to date, there have been no published scientific studies that demonstrate Omega-3 supplements enhance school performance or cognitive ability amongst the general population of children.[5]

PREDICTING FUTURE LEARNING AND THE
SELF-FULFILLING PROPHECY

At best the jury is still out on Brain Gym, Omega 3, multi-sensory approaches and learning styles – at worst they have little educational validity. However, our understanding of the roles of intelligence and ability are far more credible and durable particularly when coupled with our curious obsession with trying to predict how well students will do so that we can feel confident that they have fulfilled their potential. The belief that we can predict future learning based on existing achievements probably does more to undermine our aspirations for students' learning than any other.

Predicting what students will learn has a vice-like hold on politicians, administrators, researchers and teachers alike and is promoted with a rare determination and iron will by politicians and local authority administrators. As we shall see shortly, even when the hypothesised predictors are revealed to be without foundation, they are rapidly replaced by alternative measures. We may change the words but rarely the tune. Michel Thomas recognised these preoccupations and considered that they presented formidable barriers to effective teaching. They are challenged explicitly through his teaching approach which implies that the only effective predictor of future learning is the analysis of what is to be taught and how this knowledge is organised, structured and then presented to students.

The desire to predict future learning has a long history in education and was fundamental to the Warnock Report, a landmark report on special education.[7] The report was published in 1978 and estimated that approximately 20% of pupils would have difficulties in learning at some point during their school careers. Since the Warnock report was published, the figure of 20% has been a benchmark for the proportion of pupils who are expected to have learning difficulties. The apparent permanence of this percentage is potentially an illustration of the damaging nature of another well researched phenomenon, 'the self-fulfilling prophecy'.

The 'self-fulfilling prophecy' refers to the tendency of pupils to perform and achieve in ways that are consistent with our expectations. The pupils we expect to do well more often than not do better than those we expect to do less well and our expectations are invariably based on a range of beliefs that potentially cannot be substantiated. Pupils are more likely to be seen to have a difficulty in learning if they come from a lower socio-economic group, an ethnic minority or are male. For the last 25 years teachers have been encouraged to believe and accept that 20% of pupils will not reach the standards expected for their age as a result of having a difficulty in learning; we should not be surprised to see that 20–25% of pupils have failed to achieve Level 4 in English at age 11 which is close to Warnock's predicted figure.

Our predictions and expectations about pupils' learning are conveyed in numerous and frequently subtle ways, but particularly through the language used to describe pupils' learning. The way references are made to pupils' 'ability' is a potentially insidious form of discrimination. Although IQ tests have been shown to be unreliable in terms of making predictions about the progress pupils make in learning to read, the language of the intelligence tests still abounds in the references made to ability and learning potential. Think of all the euphemisms used to describe pupils with ability: bright, quick, able, etc. Equally, think of all the far less appealing epithets used to describe those perceived to have low ability: slow, thick, stupid, etc., although it is not assumed for one minute that these terms are ever used explicitly by anyone involved in education. However, it is interesting to note that there are terms that we would also never dream of using to describe pupils who make poor progress such as 'idiot', 'imbecile', 'defective', 'feeble-minded' or 'educationally subnormal'. They have become terms of abuse, but it is salutary to remember that they were all, at one time, an accepted part of everyday educational discourse and were enshrined in government legislation[8]. The current term to describe those with low ability, 'special educational needs', was introduced in the Warnock report and at nearly 30 years has survived longer than most.

In 'The Language Master', the BBC documentary about Michel Thomas's teaching approach, all the children had failed to master a foreign language in the past, with one student in particular recalling how she had been told to give up trying as she obviously had no aptitude for learning a foreign language. Similarly, the head of French who monitored students' progress reported at the beginning of the programme that children had different aptitudes for learning to speak other languages. She stated that:

> I think that there are different aptitudes for languages. I think it requires quite a lot of things like attention to detail that kids really don't want to be bothered with. Language, the way it is taught at the moment requires a lot of hard graft, repetition, a lot of things that students find boring.

The implications are very clear. We should not expect too much from certain students owing to their lack of ability, unwillingness to attend to detail and reluctance to work hard. We may change the language but our underlying conceptual frameworks have remained resolutely the same for well over 100 years.

WHAT DOES PREDICT FUTURE LEARNING?

There are fields, particularly in sport and music, where experts have spent an enormous amount of time trying to identify child prodigies who could progress and reach the highest levels of performance as adults in their chosen fields. For every success there are far more who do not make the grade. For example, football clubs invest enormous amounts of money in academies where exceptional children are given special training and opportunities to increase the likelihood of them becoming outstanding players. Unfortunately, despite all the expertise that is available very few actually emerge from the process to become successful professional footballers. The teenage tennis prodigy, driven by the ambitious tennis parent, yields similarly unimpressive results. In a recent interview, John McEnroe was talking about how difficult it was to predict which young players would become champions of the future. He said 'there are kids out there but it's not necessarily easy to find the diamonds in the rough. If people knew how to do that there would be countries all over the world doing it. It's not easy. It's very difficult to get the best coaches to find the best players.'[9] In sport one possible explanation is that only one tennis player can win Wimbledon and only 11 players can be in the football team that wins the Premiership. The system imposes limits on how many can succeed. But if we cannot identify future champions in sports, where their skills are highly visible, how likely is it that we can do so with confidence in academic areas where the workings of the brain remain largely unseen?

Education, in theory, should be very different and it was Michel Thomas's firm belief that every student he taught *would* succeed. It is easy to see why Michel Thomas's approach does not sit comfortably alongside standard educational practices. He would have regarded attempts at predicting who will succeed and fail as insidious, irrelevant endeavours better left to clairvoyants, mystics and bookmakers. Any predictions Michel made would be based on a logical analysis of what was being taught. Success could be predicted easily and with complete confidence in the light of the methods and programmes being adopted by teachers. It never entered his mind that a student would not learn through his courses. The only unknown was how long it might take rather than how much they would learn. This was not arrogance on Michel's part, but the logical consequence of the theories and assumptions underpinning his methodology. When challenged about whether everyone could achieve he was always absolutely clear that if they were taught in the 'right way' then every student would learn. However, the notion of there being a 'right way' to teach, as has already been discussed, is a concept that is anathema in the world of education.

Ideally, publicly funded education should create opportunities for students and mitigate the influence of home background. Everyone should be able to succeed. That they do not says a lot about the system and the potentially harmful impact of our beliefs, expectations and the self-fulfilling prophecy. If we can predict what students will learn on school entry, it could be argued that there is little point in devoting resources to their education if they are likely to learn very little. Similarly, being able to predict accurately who will succeed and fail implies that the education they receive has a negligible impact on their achievements and life opportunities. It is disheartening for those students, and their parents, who are expected to learn little and pass few exams, that the 12 years they spend in school make so little difference. What students learn and the standards they achieve should be predicted solely on the basis of the quality of teaching they receive. Good quality teaching can overcome any initial disadvantages and inspire students to achieve, whatever their starting points.

Many of the students that Michel Thomas taught in Los Angeles, like those in the BBC documentary 'The Language Master', had a history of failure where foreign languages were concerned. They probably absorbed subtle messages in the past about their lack of ability in learning languages. This is one of the reasons why Michel gives students a different starting point for their learning, which begins with trying to erase all understanding of how they think learning takes place, so that they start his courses with a positive attitude and high expectations. The way the courses are structured gives students early success, but perhaps more importantly, immediate feedback on their progress so that they can appreciate that they are learning very quickly.

FAMILY BACKGROUND PREDICTS ACADEMIC SUCCESS

The earlier discussion on prediction looked at characteristics of pupils and their individual differences. However, various measures of family background do appear to be accurate predictors of success or failure in learning. Research shows that the strength of the association between poor results and poverty grows during a student's school career.[10] Similarly, research shows that the association between income and attainment has increased in recent years, with students from higher-income backgrounds experiencing greater improvements in attainment relative to students from lower-income backgrounds.[11] The gap between the educational performance of students from different socio-economic groups is wider in the UK than elsewhere. Furthermore, it has been found that young children with similar levels of competence diverge as they progress through school according to their socio-economic background.

Research has also indicated that school performance can be predicted with a high degree of accuracy from no more than the social profile of its intake.[12] Most schools currently regarded as successful have a large proportion of pupils from middle-class backgrounds, whereas those at the bottom of the league tables take pupils from less affluent and more deprived backgrounds. Of particular interest is the finding that pupils from lower-income families do better when attending schools with a middle-class intake, implying that peer group is more influential in raising standards than the quality of teaching available.

The best predictors of success in learning appear to be parental income and family background and the schools that achieve the best examination results, not surprisingly, are those within the private sector.[13, 14] What is worrying is that the most successful schools within the state sector are also those in the most financially affluent catchment areas, or, as discussed in Chapter 3, those schools that have control over their admissions, thus exerting a degree of selection over their intakes. As a result, it is extremely difficult to determine how well schools would perform on a level playing field, that is where each school had pupils drawn from a variety of backgrounds where the mean income per family was the same.

The students that Michel Thomas was most concerned to teach were those who came from the most disadvantaged backgrounds, many of whom are currently failing within the present systems. It remains to be seen whether Michel Thomas's philosophy and methods could succeed where traditional approaches are failing, but his assumptions, the instructional principles on which his teaching methods are based and the way knowledge is structured do offer grounds for optimism.

SUMMARY

It has been suggested that many of us intuitively believe that our learning potential is down to our own determination, motivation, intelligence and ability. Surprisingly, it appears that in the majority of instances our progress is less dependent on these factors than we are aware. Instead, it seems to be closely related to our family backgrounds. Attempts to discover our potential, ascertain our ability, identify our learning styles and predict future progress all seem to be questionable activities based on dubious evidence. The areas that Michel Thomas thought were most important in facilitating students' learning have rarely been the focus of detailed and sustained research, which could be seen as a reflection of their lack of general worth within the educational community. It is clear that recent attempts to raise standards amongst the lowest achieving students are not bringing about the desired result; this implies that an alternative approach to helping students to learn and raise standards is warranted.

PART 3

The theory and practice of teaching foreign languages the Michel Thomas way

Part 3 of this book examines the theories and instructional principles underpinning Michel Thomas's methods. They question many accepted practices within the field of education and suggest that how knowledge is taught has more to do with trends and fashions than with what has been shown to work and to have a direct impact on learning. Michel Thomas adopts a particular philosophy towards teaching, learning and assessment, which is also reflected in instructional psychology. It was first formally expressed by the American psychologist, Robert Glaser, in 1962, within a framework called 'assessment-through-teaching' (see Figure 3.1). Within this framework deciding what to teach, deciding how to teach and assessing students' learning are interrelated. Michel Thomas's analysis of each area is discussed in detail in Part 3.

Figure 3.1 A framework of 'assessment-through-teaching' based on Glaser (1962)

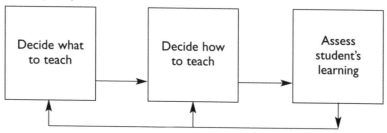

Chapter 6 locates the theoretical origins of Michel Thomas's approach to teaching foreign languages within instructional psychology which offers an analysis of how the environment influences the way we learn. Instructional psychology draws on three different but overlapping theories: rational analysis, behavioural psychology and Direct Instruction. Chapter 7 explains how these theoretical perspectives have generated a number of key instructional principles which inform the teaching and learning process adopted by Michel Thomas. Chapter 8 relates these principles to specific examples within Michel Thomas's Spanish and French language courses to illustrate how they are put into practice. However, it should be made clear that Michel did not explicitly draw on these theories. Having studied psychology, he would have been aware of behaviourism, although not necessarily its application to teaching. It is less likely that he would have been familiar with Direct Instruction or rational analysis, although this cannot be discounted.

Throughout Part 3 the instructional principles that underpin Michel Thomas's approach to teaching foreign languages are illustrated with examples from teaching reading and maths. The reason for this is four-fold:

- The first is that it is easier to explain the principles in relation to subjects that everyone has a degree of familiarity with.
- The second is that many readers may well have children at school now or who have recently been in primary schools and will have direct first-hand experience of how reading and maths are currently being taught. Equally, GCSE students picking up this book will also be familiar with much of what is said about how things are typically done in schools.
- The third is that the instructional analyses that are described have a much longer history and research tradition in relation to these subjects than teaching foreign languages.
- Finally, the history and debates surrounding the teaching of reading and maths have many parallels with those associated with teaching foreign languages.

CHAPTER 6

A STARTING POINT FOR TEACHING

OVERVIEW

This chapter describes the theoretical origins of Michel Thomas's approach to teaching foreign languages. Most applications of psychology to education have been based on developmental psychology and the theories of Piaget, Vygotsky and Bruner. These theories are summarised and contrasted with instructional psychology which informs Michel Thomas's methodology. Instructional psychology focuses on the learning environment and suggests that the most important factor in determining students' learning is the analysis of what is to be taught and the way this is structured for learners.

Michel Thomas never took the easy option in life. After the many upheavals during his childhood, adolescence and the Second World War it would not have been unreasonable to think that Michel had endured enough conflict and battles for one lifetime. He could have developed and taught his language courses, and enjoyed the considerable recognition and acclaim for their impact. He would have been more than comfortable financially and could have had a relatively stress-free life. However, this is not what happened when Michel settled in America and embarked on a career teaching languages. He didn't court controversy, it just had a way of finding him, largely because he stood by his principles and was unwilling to compromise them, no matter what the cost.

His language courses are underpinned by a philosophy that questions conventional thinking about how we learn and the nature of the teaching and learning process. It is a philosophy that has been anathema to those in the teaching profession for a number of reasons that will be explored in this chapter. Michel Thomas's courses open with the following declaration:

You are just about to experience a new and different approach to learning and to language learning that will give you practical and functional use within 10 to 12 hours of learning time. All this is achieved, and will be achieved, without memorising … without learning by rote; without drill; without textbooks; without taking notes and without homework … It is very important for you to be relaxed, to take off, to leave off, any form of tension, any form of anxiety that is usually associated with learning and traditionally also particularly with language learning. And any form of anxiety, any form of tension inhibits true and effective learning.

Never worry about remembering and therefore never try to remember, because this is a method where the responsibility for your remembering is in the teaching and not with you, not with the learner. This is a method where the responsibility for retention is in the teaching and not with the learner. Therefore, there is no homework, not even any mental homework. It is very important not to review, even mentally, what you have learnt. Let it be absorbed and internalised to become knowledge and what you know you will not forget.

There are two significant implications to be drawn from these assertions. The first is Michel's request to learners that they put to one side past experiences of learning foreign languages. Preconceived notions that success is based on trying to memorise vocabulary through rote learning or doing lots of homework, the bane of most students' lives, are misplaced. The second, and probably more controversial of the two, is that responsibility for learning lies with the teacher, not the pupil. Typically we think that learning is dependent on the learner's ability or motivation and although the role of the teacher is critical in challenging and stimulating students, it is nevertheless assumed that the capacity to learn is ultimately determined by overall ability and learning potential, as discussed in Chapter 5.

For Michel Thomas, the role of the teacher was quite different. He acknowledged that motivated students were more likely to learn than disaffected, disinterested ones. He also recognised that it was the responsibility of the teacher to build up interest and enthusiasm in the learner. However, he did not accept the conventional view of 'ability' as a fixed characteristic that predicted a student's capacity to learn or what they could achieve. On the contrary, he believed that there were no limits to what individuals could learn, other than the attributes of the teacher and the teaching environment that they created. Michel's language courses are based on the premise that everyone can master their content. For Michel there is no such concept as a student with learning difficulties, only teachers with teaching difficulties. This topic will be revisited and discussed in more detail in Chapter 13 when considering whether indeed certain students have an aptitude for learning a foreign language.

There are three critical components of the teaching environment:

- The first is the analysis of the material that has to be learned. If the analysis is correct, teaching is easier and the subsequent learning of the pupil ensured.
- The second is isolating and structuring the most useful information to teach so that there is a logical progression in the skills, knowledge and concepts taught. Easier skills are taught before more difficult ones and useful information taught before less useful information. In this context useful information is defined in terms of its generalisability and wider applicability.
- The third component of the learning environment is determining the best way of presenting skills, knowledge and concepts to students so that learning is facilitated. Chapter 8 describes the instructional principles that inform the way material is presented to learners.

To fully appreciate the radical nature of the principles underpinning Michel Thomas's language courses, it will be helpful to look at what psychologists have said in the past about how we learn. Although various details of these theories have been criticised, they reflect the conventional wisdom about human development and how this has impacted on our understanding of the factors that lead to successful learning. Their tentacle-like reach pervades every aspect of the education system and educational thinking. Challenges to the orthodoxies that they have inspired are invariably resisted and dismissed.

THEORIES OF CHILDREN'S DEVELOPMENT

The theories of Jean Piaget, Lev Vygotsky and Jerome Bruner have been highly influential within the field of education. Their legacy is still very evident in the teaching of foreign languages. The theories and implications for teaching are now briefly summarised.

Piaget

The most familiar theories about how we learn are based on the ideas of Jean Piaget. He was a biologist but became preoccupied with the nature of children's learning, initially though systematically and painstakingly documenting the progress of his own children. Unfortunately, such observations, no matter how interesting, do not provide a sound basis for a 'scientific' theory of children's learning. This is not to say that his observations are not insightful, just that it is difficult to generalise them to all children. It may be helpful to regard them as hypotheses which needed to be tested rather than hard, proven facts, which is what the educational community was a little too willing to believe.

Piaget proposed that children progressed through four stages of development: *sensori-motor, pre-operational, concrete* and *formal.*

- During the sensori-motor stage (birth to two years) children learn primarily through sensory experiences which are mediated through their emerging motor abilities. The stage is characterised by children manipulating objects and acquiring an understanding of the physical properties of the world.
- During the pre-operational stage (two to seven years) children move beyond a physical exploration of their world and begin to internalise features of the environment. Thinking is largely literal and egocentric as they see the world from their own perspective, and 'animistic' where human characteristics are attributed to non-living objects.
- Logical reasoning emerges during the third stage, concrete operational (seven to 11 years). Children become less egocentric, begin to see the world from another's point of view and start to represent the environment with concrete materials which are also used as an aid in problem solving.
- During the fourth stage, formal operations (11 years plus), children begin to think abstractly, can problem solve without representing the world in a concrete form and generally display a wider range of abilities (logical thinking, considering different perspectives on a problem or issue). Development occurs as a result of children assimilating new information into existing representations of the world (referred to as *schemas*) and then adapting to the environment through modifying existing schemas or creating different ones when required.

Piaget's theories were widely adopted and applied by educationalists. They were the perfect antidote to the highly formal and didactic methods of the post-war years described in Chapter 5. In contrast to these methods, Piaget did not believe that knowledge could be communicated to students in a rigid manner where they remained largely passive recipients and were seen to be empty vessels waiting to be filled. For Piaget, acquiring knowledge was an active process requiring students to engage directly and purposefully with their surroundings, often through play. Over time, Piaget believed they would construct their own knowledge and develop their own unique understandings of the world.

This gave rise to the principle of 'learning readiness' which exerted a powerful influence in the 1960s and 1970s. It was thought that children would learn at their own rate and only when they were ready to do so as determined by their stage of development. Children would progress through each stage in a fixed manner and at a pace reflecting their overall development. The principle that took hold in the educational world was that learning was a reflection of an individual's level of cognitive development and could not be unduly influenced by environmental factors. This view has largely persisted and when aligned with beliefs about intelligence (discussed in the previous chapter) it is easy to see why there is an almost universal acceptance that an individual's ability is the major factor in determining how much is learned.

There have been numerous criticisms of Piaget's theories.[1] Recent studies have indicated that babies and young children have a more advanced understanding of the world than Piaget suggested. Furthermore, cognitive development and the acquisition of knowledge do not appear to emerge in the strict stages that Piaget suggested. Children learn from each other in a range of social contexts rather than in isolation as implied by Piaget. Nevertheless his ideas have had a huge impact on educational thinking although it was others, rather than Piaget himself, who were responsible for translating his theories into classroom practice.

Vygotsky

As psychologists became more sensitive to the importance of the way that the process of development could be influenced by various types of intervention from adults, the theories of Lev Vygotsky received considerable attention. Vygotsky was born in Russia in 1896 and died at 38 in 1934 but in his short life wrote persuasively and impressively about children's learning. Until the 1950s his theories were deemed reactionary and bourgeois by government authorities. They were translated into English in the 1950s and 1960s after which they have exerted a growing presence and achieved widespread popularity. There are perhaps two features of the theories that have received considerable attention. The first is the 'Zone of Proximal Development' (ZPD), which refers to the gap in achievements between what a student can do now without help and what the student will be able to achieve with appropriate guidance from a teacher. The anticipated achievement is described in terms of the student's 'potential' for learning and the help that enables students to reach their potential relates to the second key concept, that of 'scaffolding.' Students are guided with appropriate prompts from their teacher rather than being explicitly told how to master new skills, knowledge and concepts in a didactic fashion. Scaffolding is a concept that has been adopted by many teachers of foreign languages and is seen to be an effective teaching method within conventional approaches to language teaching.

Vygotsky saw that the purpose of education was not the mere learning of specific knowledge and skills, but the development of students' learning abilities, their capacity to think clearly and creatively and to communicate their understanding in a variety of ways through the numerous symbol systems associated with a given culture (for example, language, numbers and maps). Language was seen as particularly important. It was related to students' capacity to think which, in turn, was dependent upon students' socio-cultural experience.

The ZPD is seen to be the place where the child and adult meet. In developing children's abilities, teachers guide them towards performing actions or tasks which are just beyond their current capacity and ability – within certain limits. Play is also critical in this process, as it was for Piaget, in facilitating children's understanding of their culture and its rules. It provides a context for them to test out their newly acquired knowledge and skills.

Bruner

Jerome Bruner drew on the work of Vygotsky and was particularly influential during the 1970s. He identified three phases of development:

- In the 'enactive' phase children learn to take action for themselves, move and manipulate objects and learn through play.

- In the 'iconic' phase children represent the world in a variety of forms, for example, pictures, diagrams, letters, drawings and numbers.
- Finally, during the third phase, the 'symbolic' phase, children learn to think abstractly.

Whereas Piaget regarded his four stages as sequential, Bruner emphasised that each phase was available throughout people's lives, although any one might be dominant at a particular point of development.

Bruner also articulated a theory of instruction in which learning was seen to be an active process where knowledge is constructed from past and present experiences. Learning is seen to be very much dependent on children's interactions with the environment, which results in their own constructions, interpretations and understandings. Bruner believed that the key to learning was stimulating students' interest rather than focusing on the goals of teaching and the benefits that may arise from it. Bruner's instructional theory accepted the premise that any subject could be taught effectively to any student at any stage of development but ultimately saw that knowledge was a process rather than a product. As a result he believed that topics and themes could be revisited as students develop (through what he termed the 'spiral curriculum'). What students learned at any particular moment in time was less important than *how* they learned.

The three theories (Piaget, Vygotsky and Bruner) despite their differences, have a number of common features. They are all attempting to articulate what happens developmentally when students learn, in particular the mental processes that characterise different aspects of learning. They highlight the stages or phases in children's development, the importance of play, learning as a cultural phenomenon and the role of adults in facilitating, stimulating and scaffolding learning rather than teaching factual details and knowledge. Theories of development largely create our expectations for what students will be able to achieve. We recognise that children develop in different ways and at different rates and generally accept that some children will learn more quickly and to higher levels than others. As a result the extent to which children succeed or fail is largely explained by their rate of development, individual attributes and overall ability rather than *what* and *how* they have been taught. Developmental theories give rise to particular ways of interpreting the teaching and learning process and are largely responsible for promoting the ways we conventionally think about how students learn. In particular the concept of intelligence and its euphemisms are an integral part of the stories that are told to explain differences in students' attainments. Some of the misconceptions about the role of intelligence and ability were exposed in the previous chapter but it needs to be recognised that such beliefs are so firmly established in the national psyche that they will not readily give way to alternative perspectives.

It is not too difficult to speculate and see why a developmental philosophy rests more comfortably with teachers, parents, educational administrators and politicians, in fact with almost everyone except the students. The cause of low achievements and learning failure are located within the students rather than all those aspects of the education system that we can adapt and improve. It is easier and less threatening for all concerned to see the cause of failure lying with the students instead of with those responsible for controlling the curriculum and organising and providing educational services. It serves as a powerful psychological defence mechanism which is rarely challenged. Conventional practice to meet the needs of failing students is to offer small-group or one-to-one teaching which is enormously expensive and, given the evidence, not terribly effective. In 2007 the British government announced that a hefty £35 million would be spent on funding one-to-one teaching for failing pupils, a considerable outlay, much of which could have been prevented by providing alternative better researched teaching approaches in the first instance. More crucially however, as will be discussed in Chapter 15, there is no evidence that one-to-one or small group teaching has the desired impact if students continue to be taught the same things on an individual basis that they had previously failed to master in a larger group.

AN ALTERNATIVE PERSPECTIVE

Michel Thomas adopted a completely different approach to teaching and learning. He believed that it was possible to teach without any knowledge of a student's background, interests or motivations. For Michel what determined whether or not students learned was how successfully he was able to organise what needed to be taught through a logical progression of skills and knowledge and where learning earlier skills facilitated the acquisition of later, more difficult skills. Michel's introduction to the language courses give a clue as to how he was thinking. In the Spanish course he reminds students that:

If I think of one of the major newspapers in the New York area, years ago they tried to establish how many words they use in a whole newspaper, in a thick newspaper, and they came up with 600 words – just to give you an idea about the *limitación* (the limitation) *del vocabulario activo* (of the active vocabulary) which we use in our everyday language.

The key point here is that our written vocabulary on a day-to-day basis is relatively limited. Thus, learning a small amount of information could be highly cost effective and go a long way. Michel illustrates how the same principle applies to spoken language and draws students' attention to the vocabulary in English and other languages that is either the same or very similar. For example in relation to Spanish he says the following:

First, a few words about the Spanish language in relation to English, to show you how to get acquainted with the language. It is not entirely foreign, alien to English but there is a broad, common basis of familiarity between both English and Spanish, so much so that there is a large percentage of *su vocabulario inglés* (of your English vocabulary) that is very similar to Spanish. Thousands of words and, *para comenzar*, ('to commence' or 'to begin with'), I am going to give you a few keys to show you how you can *inmediatamente* (immediately) *transformar* (transform) *su vocabulario inglés* (your English vocabulary) into Spanish.

So that you will have a starting *vocabulario* of well over 2,000 words, which is not bad to begin with, *especialmente* (especially) if you *considera* (consider) how *limitado* (how limited) the *vocabulario* is, which we use in our active language. Our *vocabulario activo* (our active vocabulary) is quite small in any language. It may vary between 500 and 1,500 words, that's all we use in any language.

I'm going to give you a few examples of how to *transformar* (how to transform) *su vocabulario inglés* (your English vocabulary) into Spanish. For instance, the words in English ending in 'ible', like 'possible', or 'able', like 'probable' or 'acceptable' and so on, are the same in English and in Spanish except for the *pronunciación* (the pronunciation).

There's a *diferencia* (a difference) in the *pronunciación* (in the pronunciation) because 'ible' in Spanish is pronounced '*ee*ble' because the letter 'i' in Spanish is always pronounced '*ee*'. And 'able' in Spanish is pronounced '*ar*ble' because the letter 'a' in Spanish is always pronounced '*ar*'. So we have '*ee*ble' and '*ar*ble'. So if you want to say 'possible', it would be 'pos-ee-ble' and 'probable' would be 'prob-*ar*-ble'.

In relation to French, Michel also states that an active vocabulary is somewhere between 500 and 1,500 words and that over 60% of English vocabulary comes from French.

Michel Thomas's starting point was to ask what is the most useful information for students to learn? As was mentioned in Chapter 1, Michel's thinking about teaching and learning was very much influenced by his own experiences. Despite his love of music he experienced little success as a pianist and felt that this had as much to do with the way he was taught as it did with any lack of aptitude on his own part. This is not about blaming teachers for our failures but confirming their importance and potentially hugely significant role in our lives when they get things right.

Michel's explanation for his failure to become an accomplished pianist would have run something along the lines that his teacher had not found a way of making the learning easy for him. There is a huge amount of information to absorb and there are a substantial number of skills to acquire when learning to play any musical instrument. The role of the teacher is to make informed decisions about how to organise a vast body of knowledge so that it is acquired quickly and almost effortlessly. The process starts with the decision about what to teach first.

Most readers of this book over the age of 17 will have learned to drive a car at some time in their lives, clearly with varying degrees of success. Some of us pass our tests first time, within weeks of our 17th birthday, others take considerably longer and on some occasions it is a task that is never mastered. Irrespective of the speed with which we learn, driving a car for the first time is a daunting experience. There is so much to attend to simultaneously. We have to steer, change gear, accelerate, manoeuvre the car, be aware of other traffic, co-ordinate hands, eyes and feet, etc. The effective driving instructor knows that it would be futile to teach a novice driver too many things at once and so has to make informed decisions about the most useful skills to teach first. Despite the obvious complexities of driving, and the anxieties surrounding those early lessons, the majority manage the task eventually. Over time we look back and recognise that we drive so instinctively that it then becomes difficult to analyse exactly what we do. As a result, because we cannot analyse how we drive, it becomes difficult to identify key principles which could underpin our explanations to others about how to drive. It leads to those caricatured scenarios beloved of comedy writers where one family member tries to teach another to drive. It is a recipe for disaster for many reasons but the one critical factor is that the teacher has not been able to analyse the task and structure the skills to be learned in a coherent and manageable progression.

Being an extremely capable performer or highly skilled in a particular field is not an adequate qualification to become a successful teacher. The top tennis coaches have rarely been the top tennis players. Brad Gilbert, who has coached Andre Agassi to six grand slam tennis titles and an Olympic gold medal, though a highly competent player, did not win a grand slam final. Fellipo Scollari, who managed Brazil to World Cup success in 2002 never represented his own country, Portugal, at football. David Leadbetter, one of the most successful golf teachers of all time, and who has established golf clinics throughout the world, never won a professional golf title. John Buchanan, the coach to the dominant Australian cricket team, which has won three successive world cups, likewise did not represent his country. Of significance however, was his background as a teacher and a university lecturer, which was perhaps a more appropriate qualification for becoming an outstanding coach. In the UK, England won the World Cup in 1966 for the only time. Just one member of that team, Jack Charlton, went on to become a successful manager. Finally, Sir Simon Rattle, the principal conductor of the Berlin Philharmonic orchestra, and past conductor of the City of Birmingham Symphony Orchestra, is perhaps the most celebrated conductor of his generation and yet again, although an impressive percussionist with the National Youth Orchestra, did not perform as a concert soloist on any of the instruments which he conducts in the orchestra or on which soloists perform.

There are countless other examples of excellent practitioners in various fields failing to become effective teachers, and the reverse, where outstanding teachers were not necessarily gifted practitioners. Why should this be the case? Possibly those who are most talented in any area have never had to examine in any detail how to ply their trade. It is second nature and comes so easily and effortlessly that they have never had to think about *how* they play or perform. When it comes to helping others they are either not able to analyse their skills in sufficient detail and clarity or perhaps not able to explain how current performance can be improved in a gradual, step-by-step fashion.

Michel Thomas was an exception to the rule. He was not only a highly talented linguist but also an outstanding teacher. Underpinning his skills as a teacher was his in-depth knowledge of languages and how to make learning easy for students. Past pupils talk about learning with Michel being 'effortless' and this was achieved, in part, through the way he structured knowledge as well as his capacity to present it in small, incremental, cumulative steps so that it almost took students by surprise how quickly they had learned.

ANALYSE WHAT TO TEACH

The starting point in the teaching process was Michel's analysis of each language so that students are taught what is most valuable and most generalisable. His decisions about how best to teach were not informed with reference to how students learn but by his in-depth knowledge of several languages, their common features and what would be most useful to learners, irrespective of their perceived ability to learn a new language. The critical question that Michel asked was 'what is the most effective way to teach?' rather than the more conventional 'how do children learn?' The latter question is the one that understandably dominates the thinking of psychologists and teachers and is a legacy of the impact of the developmental theorists discussed earlier. It seems to be the obvious and logical starting point. Work out how children learn and then fit what has to be taught around their apparently natural way of acquiring new skills and knowledge. It was this way of thinking that ultimately underpinned, and scuppered, Michel Thomas's attempts to have his methods accepted by the educational establishment.

Many readers of this book will have either tried Michel Thomas's courses or will be considering using them in the future. For some, this will be a consequence of either not being given the opportunity to learn a foreign language in the past or having failed to reach a desired level of fluency and mastery in a chosen language. It is extremely likely that many readers falling into these categories will have seen themselves as poor linguists or at the very least as lacking in any natural talent for languages, unlike high-flying friends who seemed to master them without any apparent effort. Similarly, when English politicians, from Ted Heath to Tony Blair, have embarrassingly stumbled to converse with their European counterparts in a foreign language their attempts have been resoundingly mocked and ridiculed. When everyone else in Europe speaks English with such fluency we are left to conclude that they have a natural talent for languages whereas our difficulties or reluctance to master foreign languages are attributed to our absence of such ability as a nation.

The implication of Michel Thomas's starting point, that any inability to learn a foreign language has less to do with natural talent and inherent linguistic abilities than the quality of teaching, is unfamiliar, with potentially enormous consequences for how we look at our past successes and failures. We are not well disposed to having such conventional wisdoms undermined. By starting with the question, 'what is the most effective way to teach?' Michel was opening the door to a new way of thinking about teaching and learning.

Michel Thomas's analysis of how best to teach foreign languages was inspired, to a degree, by the thoughts of his maths teacher who had impressed upon him the notion that there is nothing so complex that it cannot be made simple. Michel's reference to our active vocabulary and the word usage in a well known New York newspaper focuses attention on the idea that learning a small amount of carefully selected information can be highly useful through its generalisability and its wide application (and therefore usefulness). Michel recognised that students did not need to know everything in order to have a good working knowledge of a language. Instead, the judicial selection of a small number of core skills could be extremely powerful and give students an excellent working knowledge of a language.

PARETO'S LAW

The idea that it is possible to teach a small amount of information that is highly useful reflects *Pareto's Law* which is often referred to as the *80/20 principle* and has been described in detail by Richard Koch in his book, *The 80/20 Principle: The secret to success by achieving more with less*. Named after Vilfredo Pareto who was born in 1848 in France, Pareto looked at patterns of wealth in 19th century England and found that a small minority of the population in the samples he studied acquired the major share of income and wealth. Approximately 20% of the population acquired 80% of the wealth. This principle is much used in the world of business and proposes that 'a minority of causes, inputs or effort usually leads to the majority of the results, outputs or rewards'.[2] It implies that 80% of what we achieve at work is the result of only 20% of the time and effort involved. Thus, a major part of our working lives is not productive in relation to its impact.

It is perhaps easiest to illustrate this principle with some examples:

- It is said that a small number of earthquakes, approximately 20%, account for 80% of all earthquake damage. A small number are powerful with devastating consequences, whereas the vast majority are responsible for a very small percentage of the damage caused.
- The Post Office ran a series of radio adverts a number of years ago claiming that it could help businesses identify their most profitable customers. The advert stated that for the majority of businesses approximately 80% of their profits would be generated by approximately 20% of their customers. Knowing the 80% of customers who use a store but generate little in the way of substantial income can be helpful as customers' spending patterns could be examined and lead to ways in which their expenditure could be increased. More generally in business 20% of products account for 80% of sales.
- 20% of criminals account for 80% of the value of crimes, 20% of motorists cause 80% of accidents and generate 80% of speeding fines identified by motorway cameras, 20% of those that marry are involved in 80% of divorces, indicating that it is the same individuals that keep getting divorced. As far as school life is concerned, 20% of pupils appear to cause 80% of behavioural problems.

Similar percentages to Pareto's 80/20 split represent the location of wealth in the USA. Figures based on the findings by a Federal Reserve study showed that the top 10% of Americans owned 70% of the country's wealth. A further example can be found in the usage of words in the English language, although the figures do not fit the 80/20 principle quite so neatly. Nevertheless, they do illustrate the more general assertion about the usefulness and utility of a small amount of information that has significant implications for teaching children to read.

APPLYING PARETO'S LAW TO TEACHING

Unlike German or Spanish, English is not a phonically regular language. This is what makes it so difficult for some children when learning to read. In German and Spanish the same written symbol (known as a *grapheme*) represents the same sound (*phoneme*). In written English, the letter combination 'ea' can represent up to eight different phonemes (i.e. t<u>ea</u>, b<u>ea</u>r, b<u>ea</u>utiful, d<u>ea</u>r, h<u>ea</u>d, h<u>ea</u>rd, br<u>ea</u>k, id<u>ea</u>) and of the 100 most frequently occurring words in written English only 39 are phonically regular (e.g. am, in, him, on, went, too, three). The general consensus is that reading English is difficult because of the inconsistent mappings between print (letters) and the sounds that they represent.

However, the problem looks a little different when we apply Pareto's Law to an analysis of written English. Research that I have carried out with two colleagues, Ellie McNab and Janet Vousden at the University of Warwick shows that when you actually look at written language usage it is far more consistent, regular and predictable than we have assumed. Our analysis showed that the 16 most frequently occurring words (a, the, I, in, was, to, and, it, my, that, he, went, of, is, then, with) account for approximately 25% of all written English, and the 100 most frequently occurring words account for approximately 50% of all written English.

The knowledge that 100 words account for such a high proportion of written English is not new and was the basis for the Ladybird Reading Scheme published in the UK in the early 1960s. It has naturally been assumed that because learning 100 high frequency words is so useful that learning the next 50 most frequently occurring words would be equally valuable. However, our understanding of Pareto's Law suggests that such confidence is misplaced, which is borne out by our research. Being able to read a further 50 words enables children to read no more than approximately 6–7% additional words. Learning to read the first 100 words in terms of their frequency gives a very good pay-off whereas learning extra high-frequency words is of increasingly limited value.

It is possible to speculate on a scenario where, in the absence of knowledge of how Pareto's Law applies to written English, children become labelled as having a difficulty in learning to read. Take the child aged between six and seven years old who has taken a couple of years to learn the first 100 high frequency words. She takes great pleasure in having done so. Her motivation is maintained and transfers to learning the next 50 words she is presented with. Although she learns these quickly and feels pleased with herself, her teachers, in contrast, are extremely apprehensive as there does not appear to be any difference in how well she reads new books. Her teachers and parents attribute this to continuing literacy difficulties. However, the pattern in the child's reading is both perfectly understandable and highly predictable. Although the child can read more words, which is commendable and undoubtedly confidence boosting, there is not a commensurate improvement in reading books because the words that have been learned appear with such relatively low frequency as to be effectively redundant. They do not occur often enough in any written material to be useful to the beginning reader.

Two further points need to be made about written English which shed more light on how best to teach reading but also have enormous implications for teaching foreign languages. The first is a real bonus as far as teaching reading is concerned because Pareto's Law applies to all written literature, irrespective of whether you are examining reading scheme books that are prepared specifically for beginning readers, children's 'real books' (i.e. the kind of books most parents read to their children which are selected on the basis of quality and enjoyment and are not part of a series of carefully graded texts with artificial, carefully controlled vocabulary) or adult literature. For example, our database of adult literature comprised a total of over approximately 850,000 words with more than 53% being accounted for by just 100 words. Our database of children's literature consisted of 66 books (e.g. *The Tiger that Came to Tea, Not Now Bernard, Daddy Can you Play with Me, Kipper, Whatever Next, Elmer, Dear Zoo*) and 29,000 words, 49% of them being one of the 100 high frequency words. One of the reading schemes analysed was The Oxford Reading Tree, which consisted of just over 30,000 words with 52% being one of the 100 high frequency words. The fact that the 100 high frequency words appeared more often in the adult literature than a specially prepared reading scheme was unexpected and counter-intuitive given the debates about teaching reading and the lack of consistency in written English discussed earlier.

The second point that needs to be made is that Pareto's Law also applies to teaching children phonic skills (i.e. the mappings between phonemes and graphemes). It has been calculated[3] that it is possible to teach a maximum of 461 different mappings between phonemes and graphemes. Our research showed that just 60 are highly useful and enable the majority of phonically regular words to be read. As predicted from Pareto's Law, the remaining 400 give a relatively limited return especially when set alongside the time and effort involved in teaching them.

Michel Thomas utilised Pareto's Law in designing his courses. He concluded that the way to address the question, 'what is the most effective way to teach?' was to find out what would be most useful to students new to each language that he taught. Hence his focus on the similarities between English and other languages. A further building block in Michel's approach is to give students an understanding of how a language worked through learning the rules of grammar but without ever having to resort to rote learning or memorisation activities. Michel, without explicitly doing so, was drawing on Pareto's Law in devising a system to teach foreign languages. He was acutely aware that a large component of everyday language usage was accounted for by a relatively small amount of linguistic knowledge and skills. The theoretical origins of Michel Thomas's programmes lie in a little-known area of psychology, *instructional psychology* which is introduced in the following chapter. The instructional principles derived from instructional psychology that underpin Michel Thomas's courses are explained in Chapter 8.

SUMMARY

This chapter has summarised the developmental theories in psychology that are typically drawn upon within the field of education to inform how best to teach. Their limitations were considered and contrasted with an alternative perspective which is reflected in Michel Thomas's language courses. The differences were explored in relation to Michel Thomas's references in his course introductions to engaging listeners in a new and different approach to teaching that does not rely on homework or learning by rote and where the responsibility for remembering lies with Michel, the teacher rather than the learner. The chapter concluded with a discussion of Pareto's Law which provides the rationale for working out what to teach.

CHAPTER 7

INSTRUCTIONAL PSYCHOLOGY

OVERVIEW

This chapter introduces *instructional psychology* that provides the theoretical basis for Michel Thomas's language courses. Instructional psychology focuses on the learning environment and the various ways that it influences our cognitive development and behaviour. The aim is to teach in a maximally effective way which is reflected in the Theory of Optimal Instruction that offers a rationale for identifying the most useful skills, knowledge and concepts to teach. The chapter also introduces the work of two other psychologists, B. F. Skinner and Ziggy Engelmann, whose work has been underpinned by the same rationale and theoretical principles as Michel Thomas.

Instructional psychology takes as its starting point, in any quest to determine how to teach effectively, the learning environment rather than the student. As was discussed in Chapter 5, the traditional route to thinking about how to teach is based on the assumption that this is best informed by knowledge of how students learn. It is thought that there are ways in which students learn that are independent of their home and learning environments. In contrast to this, within instructional psychology how students learn is a direct consequence of their previous, formal and informal learning experiences (for example, family life, attending play groups and nurseries as a child, playing with friends, etc.). The example in Chapter 6 of a child being taught new words but failing to make the expected progress in learning to read was the result of being taught the 'wrong' information. She learned words that did not appear with sufficient frequency in written English to impact on her overall reading. Her failure to improve was not her 'fault'. The responsibility for this lay with the teacher who failed to teach what was most useful. Students' perceived strengths and weaknesses, their perceived learning styles, what they do well and what they fail to master are all seen to be a direct response to the way in which they have been taught. Thus, within instructional psychology what and how students learn invariably says more about the teacher's strengths, weaknesses and preferences than it does about the students.

FOCUS ON THE TEACHING ENVIRONMENT

The teaching environment embraces all aspects of the context in which teaching occurs where teachers exert an influence. This includes the content of what is taught, the way it is structured, teaching methodology and the location where learning takes place. One of the first things Michel Thomas did in the BBC documentary, 'The Language Master', was to change the nature of the teaching environment. When he walked into the classroom he commented:

> I am looking forward to teaching you today but under better physical conditions because I don't think the way we are sitting is very comfortable and I would like you to feel comfortable so we are going to rearrange everything here.

He proceeded to remove the traditional chairs and desks where students usually sat and worked and replaced them with comfortable armchairs, carpets, softer lighting and plants to create a relaxing starting point for his teaching.

The focus on the teaching environment has its origins in areas of psychology that attempt to analyse its impact on human cognition (our perceptions, thoughts, language and memory). The conventional wisdom is that our abilities are determined by our genes, our hardwiring, and the traits we are born with. The environment is important in so far as it creates the contexts in which our abilities can flourish so we can fulfil our potential. We think of potential in very much the way Vygotsky defined it, as the Zone of Proximal Development. It is the level of achievement we can reach with the right kind of help from all available sources. It is the point at which we are performing at maximum capacity and just could not do any better given the skills we were born with. We are motivated, receive expert teaching and respond by learning to a level that we feel is unlikely to be surpassed. There is general recognition that whatever level we reach, the limiting factors determining just how far we can improve are our own abilities and attributes.

For many educationalists the 'holy grail' is to find a way of determining and measuring potential so that we know what to expect and the maximum levels to which someone might aspire. It is very much the British way to attribute what students learn to their abilities and learning potential and to then search for early indicators of success. Children are then channelled into different types of educational provision according to their abilities. All forms of academic selection are based on this premise from the '11 plus' examination, introduced after the 1944 Education Act, to awarding places at football academies, specialist schools and universities. The same assumptions inform educational policies to try to identify pupils who are gifted and talented or 'at risk' of academic failure. Such approaches in relation to those at risk of experiencing failure have had a chequered history and are based on the belief that it is possible to identify and teach critical skills that underpin learning more complex tasks, and which when acquired, prevent later difficulties. One example that emerged in the 1960s and 70s was associated with the learning disabilities movement.

It was thought that children would have difficulties in learning to read because of underlying visual, auditory, perceptual or motor problems. So they were taught to trace between parallel lines, pick the odd-one-out from visual displays, or catch a ball with the one hand and throw it back with the other hand. However, although their tracing, identification of the odd-one-out and catching and throwing skills improved dramatically, it was not matched with commensurate gains in reading. The implication was that if you want to improve children's reading, focus directly on skills used when reading, (i.e. high-frequency words, phonic skills), not underlying visual, auditory, perceptual or motor skills.

As discussed in Chapter 5, Michel Thomas regarded any attempts to identify potential as unethical and all attempts to do so were anathema to him. This was reflected on the commentary in 'The Language Master' which said, 'Michel doesn't believe in an aptitude for learning, only good and bad teaching'. For Michel, a failure to learn can always be traced back to some aspect of what or how students were taught.

The alternative to offering different learning opportunities based on perceptions of potential is to give all students equivalent, wide-ranging, high-quality educational experiences. Everyone continues to learn everything to the highest standards for as long as possible. Any decisions about potential are taken much later in the day and so give students longer to achieve and experience success. For example, every time England fail in any international sporting event, whether it be football, cricket or tennis, there is a lot of soul searching. This is accompanied by the inevitable calls for better systems to identify talented children, at increasingly younger ages, so that they can have intensive training to become superstars in their chosen sport. This philosophy was illustrated in a front page headline in the national paper *USA Today* in July 2007 which featured a five-year-old boy, Jan, who was being hailed as the next Roger Federer[1]. The family sold their cars and home in California to raise the funds to go and live in France where their son had been enrolled on a training programme designed to turn him into a champion. David Ornstein sought the views of a number of leading sports coaches in an article in the *Guardian* in June 2007 and asked them to respond to the question, 'does your child have what it takes to be the next Lewis Hamilton?', after disclosing that the Formula 1 racing driver's father had spotted his son's talent at the age of five.[2]

In his response Dave Collins, the Performance Director of UK Athletics, drew attention to the Dutch strategy known as '5-3-1' which refers to children playing five sports until the age of 12, three sports until the age of 14 or 15 and then one sport thereafter. The emphasis on coaching in a wider range of sports for longer gives children the opportunity to develop a broader range of skills that is seen to be essential for those wanting to reach the highest levels in any sport. The alternative to early identification, therefore, is to teach everyone for longer in the hope that late starters catch up with those showing early promise.

Within the field of instructional psychology the analysis of what is to be taught is fundamental to ensuring that students experience success. Clearly many students learn foreign languages without ever being exposed to the results of the analyses which are about to be described. However, it is also the case that there is a high failure rate which could potentially be overturned through exposing students to a different way of teaching.

The next section outlines the rationale for determining what to teach in any subject area. The initial examples will once again focus on reading because there are many similarities with the way Michel Thomas approached the teaching of foreign languages. However, there is an increasing evidence-base demonstrating the impact of instructional psychology in teaching reading that has yet to be established for teaching languages. The precise details of what children are taught when learning to read is far less important than the process through which it is determined.

RATIONAL ANALYSIS

Instructional psychology draws on one theory developed within the field of psychology known as 'rational analysis'. It shifts the emphasis from inducing what happens 'in the mind' to looking at the structure of the environment and how it influences cognition (Anderson, 1990). Anderson argues that what we learn mirrors the structure of the world and that we adapt to the environment in a predictable and statistical manner. For example, research has shown that the rate at which information in human memory is retained over time mirrors the probability that the same information is needed in the future. We remember what we need to know and forget what is less relevant to us. It is as if our memories work out what is useful and what is less useful based on how often information is recalled. The more often information is used the greater the likelihood of it being remembered and vice versa: the longer a piece of information goes without being used the greater the likelihood of it fading from our memories. Thus, the way our memory system works is highly efficient, remembering what is useful and forgetting what is not, which ultimately becomes invaluable when structuring teaching sessions for students. It is frustrating to forget things from time to time so we are seduced into believing our memory is not efficient as we do not always have immediate recall of all the information that we want at our fingertips. However, if we were aware of when we last required information we may find ourselves pleasantly surprised that we tend to forget things that are recalled infrequently but remember more commonly used knowledge. Within rational analysis forgetting can actually be viewed positively as it indicates that our memories are working efficiently and labelling useful and less useful information appropriately.

There is a suggestion within rational analysis that our memories function in this manner because it is a reflection of broader events in the environment. For example, researchers analysed how often words appeared in various information sources (e.g. newspaper articles).[3] They assumed that the occurrence of a word represented a need to retrieve some information associated with that word. The results of this analysis revealed that the probability that a word would appear in the present day's headlines decreased as the number of days since its last appearance increased, in a very similar way that human memory retention decreases over time. The same was also true of how often books were borrowed from a library. The probability that a book would be borrowed was directly related to the time that elapsed since it was last borrowed. A similar pattern was observed with how often children used words in their spoken language. The more often a word was used in the immediate past, the more likely it was to be used again in the future. These outcomes were taken as evidence of a rational memory system that has adapted to its environment. In other words, our cognitive system develops in such a way that it is very much shaped by many features that we observe within the environment but without ever being conscious of doing so. Thus, we are not aware of this happening any more than we register how we walk, or talk or digest our food. It is the unique relationship between the structure of the environment and cognition that provides the underpinning philosophy to effective teaching and Michel Thomas's approach to foreign language teaching.

The process described by Anderson resonates with Danniel Levitin's account of why certain songs are more memorable than others in *This is Your Brain on Music*. Levitin suggests a similar process of unconscious learning of musical structures through countless hours of listening to music. He proposes that memorable songs activate neural networks in our brains that register the rules and syntax of the music we listen to. Levitin argues that through our familiarity with music we gradually learn the statistical probabilities of which chords are likely to follow each other. We are more sensitive to certain sequences than others and composers manipulate these sequences in ways that are potentially unpredictable, stimulating and ultimately memorable.

Fundamental to Anderson's approach is the idea that learners represent the environment in a maximally efficient way. Thus, competent readers will develop skills in such a way that what they learn will be statistically optimal (i.e. the rate at which features of written English are remembered or forgotten will reflect their frequency of occurrence) in relation to the structure of written English and the frequency of occurrence of sounds (phonemes) and the letters that represent them (graphemes). We should therefore, be able to find evidence that the way we read as adults, and the skills that we acquire, has been influenced by the content of the material we read and how often various words and sounds appear. Reassuringly, there is a large body of evidence to support the proposition that adults are sensitive to the statistical properties (i.e. frequency of occurrence of words, graphemes and phonemes) of both written and spoken language, at many levels, for example, how often a word is used in the language.

In a variety of language and memory-based experiments, where adults are asked to read words or name objects, high-frequency words are named more quickly than low-frequency words and high-frequency objects are named more quickly than low-frequency objects.[4] Similarly, in tasks where participants must decide whether a presented string of letters represents a real word or not (i.e. ring vs. rnig), the frequency of a word is a good predictor of the time taken to reach a decision. High-frequency words also show an advantage in the recall of items from memory. When adults are asked to remember word lists, high-frequency words are recalled more accurately than low-frequency words. Finally, research in a number of other areas indicates that the adult reading system is indeed sensitive to the statistical properties of the language.

THE THEORY OF OPTIMAL INSTRUCTION

Perhaps the most important implication of the research in rational analysis relates to whether it is possible to identify an optimal amount of information to teach pupils. This question reflects the 'optimal reading hypothesis' where 'the process of learning to read is seen, in this view, as basically a statistical process in that it requires the learner to acquire a set of associations between written word forms and their pronunciations'.[5] In other words, how adults read will reflect the content of the literature that they encounter and the frequency of occurrence of graphemes and the phonemes that they represent. It follows that a key task in teaching reading is how best to characterise the (statistical) regularities in written English and represent these to those learning to read so that their performance becomes statistically optimal. The Theory of Optimal Instruction provides a theoretical framework for determining what to teach. It states that there is an optimal amount of information to teach which will lead to maximum generalisation. Too little information will not provide an adequate basis for generalisation. Too much information may require students to memorise information that is either not useful or confusing. Pareto's Law provides the basis for identifying the optimal amount of information to teach.

Chapter 6 explained how the books that children read correspond to Pareto's Law. The aim therefore, within instructional psychology is to design programmes and teaching approaches that enable students to adapt to, or learn, the structures in the books that they encounter. This means that the items that occur most frequently need to be learned because they will be most useful and if we want children to experience a smooth transition to adult books, the structure of children's texts should mirror the structure of adult texts. Children can therefore be taught to read through learning a relatively small amount of information.

MICHEL THOMAS'S APPLICATION OF THE THEORY OF OPTIMAL INSTRUCTION

Michel Thomas exploited the Theory of Optimal Instruction in teaching foreign languages. His in-depth knowledge of languages, his desire to teach, his awareness that even the most complex tasks can be simplified for students enabled him to appreciate that in numerous respects the similarities between languages were potentially more important than their differences. What he identified as similarities reflected Pareto's Law and there were two dimensions of each language that he highlighted: high-frequency vocabulary and grammatical structures. Michel recognised that in teaching any language there is an optimal amount of information to teach which will lead to maximum generalisation. Clearly there is a vast amount of vocabulary that could be taught, much of which is not generalisable and would be useful only in specific circumstances. So Michel provided a template for teaching any vocabulary and showed how it is used in each language. Grammatical structures represent the generalisable feature of languages and are the focus of the courses. They provide sufficient information to enable students to use each language in any context. Michel analysed each language and identified what is most useful, generalisable and crucially, optimal.

BEHAVIOURAL PSYCHOLOGY

Two other areas of psychology, although very different from rational analysis in a number of respects, have also focused on analysing the environment as the basis for understanding how best to teach. The first is behavioural psychology, which is closely associated with the American psychologist B. F. Skinner, perhaps best known for his work in researching the way reinforcement and rewards influence behaviour. It is inevitable that Michel Thomas's knowledge of psychology would have brought him into contact with the work of Skinner and there is clear evidence of his impact on the instructional philosophy underpinning Michel's courses. They were both firmly convinced about the responsibilities of the teacher and had a shared perception of the causes of a failure to learn.

Skinner represented a line of thinking that suggests that in order to understand behaviour it is necessary to examine the contexts in which it occurs. He set about trying to describe behaviour in clear, unambiguous terms which focused on what could be observed. For example, if someone describes themselves as happy or sad we can never know how that feels for anyone else. We do not know what internal states, emotions or feelings are being described when they say they are happy. We can relate it to our own feelings when we use the term to describe ourselves but we can never be sure that we are describing the same thing. All we can do is observe their behaviour and ask whether it is consistent with someone expressing feelings of happiness.

Skinner's thoughts on the subject were crystallised following the death of his brother. He was interviewed by Anthony Clare in the Radio 4 programme, 'In the Psychiatrist's Chair'. He was being asked about his feelings surrounding the sudden death of his brother. Skinner commented as follows:

> I don't know what they were and I don't think I could have put a name to them at the time. How do you put a name to feelings after all. This is a very important point. I wrote a paper in 1945 on the way in which we can learn words referring to our bodies from people who don't know about them. I can tell you what is red and what is green if you have colour vision, but how do I tell you what is diffidence and what is embarrassment, how do I hold these up for you and say this is diffidence and this is embarrassment? I have to guess what you are feeling and I can guess wrong. The language which describes feeling is by nature probably always inaccurate. When my brother died we were completely amazed. I had just come back from a trip in Europe. My brother and I were having a soda with a friend and then in five minutes he was dead. Well how can you feel at that time?

As a result of the difficulties in describing feelings and emotions, Skinner, while not ignoring their existence (as alleged by some of his harshest critics), saw their potential limitations and so focused exclusively on observable behaviour and the contexts in which it occurred. That is not to say that descriptions of behaviour are not also without difficulties. There are numerous features of observable behaviour that can be analysed at any one time, for example, degree of eye contact, hand movements, posture, physical proximity to others, etc. Nevertheless, in the context of learning new skills or a foreign language the focus will be on specific components of behaviour making direct observations more precise and less ambiguous. Skinner also developed a theory that was essentially optimistic in relation to children's behaviour and learning in a way that was highly consistent with the philosophy of Michel Thomas. In the same interview Skinner said:

> I think I can claim to have done more than anyone I can think of at the present time in exploring alternatives to punishment, ways of getting people to learn, behave well, treat each other well, which do not require punishment.

There are a number of implications of drawing on this aspect of behavioural psychology to inform the teaching and learning process which is clearly evident in Michel Thomas's teaching approach. The first is its essential optimism. Skinner developed his approach so that teachers could focus on the positive in their interactions with students. Skinner, like Michel, believed that there was no such thing as the ineducable student. Everyone could learn but only if the teaching was right. So he developed an approach to teaching that would enable all students to learn anything, irrespective of their social background, the financial status of their families, parental input or perceived level of ability.

In the late 1970s Yorkshire Television made a documentary, 'A Change in Mind: The autobiography of a non person'[6], about Skinner, in which he consented to a series of interviews. Skinner believed that the key to understanding behaviour was to understand the environment and based his approach on a statement of the philosopher Francis Bacon, that 'nature to be commanded must be obeyed'. In other words, nature tells you what is, and is not, possible. Skinner explains that before you can do anything in physics you must discover what physics will allow you to do. This very much influenced his philosophy towards students' learning, which he explained as follows:

> If you want to be a good teacher you have got to have the student teach you what to do. The student is always right. If the student isn't learning it isn't the student's fault it is the teacher's fault. If the student isn't learning the teacher has not created an environment in which students learn. You must let the student specify the conditions under which the student will then actually learn.

For Skinner, teaching is changing behaviour. The more effective you are as a teacher, the more effective you are at changing behaviour. Finding the right conditions for learning is the key to changing behaviour.

The second implication follows naturally from the first. If teaching concentrates on the positive and focuses on observable behaviour there will be little need to attach labels to describe students' learning. Labelling is widespread in the world of education. Current labels that are everywhere are ADHD (Attention Deficit Hyperactive Disorder), autism, autistic spectrum disorders, Aspergers, dyslexia, dyspraxia, discalculalia, and so on. Whatever the arguments in favour of such epithets and the potential relief that they bring to some of those to whom they are applied, they were no more a part of Michel's approach to teaching than Skinner's. For Skinner they were actually seen to say more about those using the descriptors than their recipients. The individual who describes someone as 'thick' or 'bright' is probably saying far more about themselves than the individuals to whom they are referring.

The curricula for teaching reading and maths derived from behavioural psychology, while optimistic and expressed clearly and unambiguously, had a number of limitations, most notably the way it was thought that students would generalise and apply their knowledge. Within behavioural psychology, as with cognitive psychology, it was assumed that students would develop this capacity through recognising similarities between any new tasks and previously taught ones and appreciate that they could be completed through existing skills and knowledge. The programmes resulting from behavioural psychology did not explicitly teach students how to generalise and apply their knowledge in new contexts. Direct Instruction addresses this limitation and demonstrates how such skills can be taught directly.

DIRECT INSTRUCTION

Direct Instruction was developed in the 1960s and 1970s by Ziggy Engelmann and his colleagues, initially at the University of Illinois and then at the University of Oregon. Engelmann studied philosophy at university and started his professional life as a self-employed investment counsellor before becoming the creative director and ultimately vice-president in various advertising agencies. He became interested in psychology when researching how children learn, on behalf of clients who marketed to children. He rapidly focused on designing mathematical programmes which were initially piloted on his own sons to find and research logical sequences for teaching maths. Engelmann gradually devoted more time to developing curricula that could almost be guaranteed to be successful because of the clear progression from teaching one skill to the next. Although similar to behavioural psychology in many respects, Direct Instruction differs largely because of the way it enables children to use their knowledge to good effect through showing them how to generalise and problem solve.

In the mid 1960s Engelmann began to work full-time in education. Engelmann, like Michel Thomas and Skinner, saw learners as supremely logical and believed that whatever they learned would be the direct result of what they were taught. A failure to learn is the result of faulty teaching. Errors, rather than being indicative of learning difficulty, were, rather more controversially, interpreted as the learner's way of providing feedback on the quality of teaching. Invariably students made errors on the programmes Engelmann designed; he saw these as design flaws which were to be welcomed as they enabled him to adapt and refine his programmes. The challenge for Engelmann and his colleagues was to eliminate, or at least reduce, ambiguity and to develop teaching programmes which were open to one, and only one, interpretation. Ultimately, within Direct Instruction programmes students learn that 'you work hard' and 'get smart'. Becoming 'smart' is the consequence of what you have been taught rather than being the determining factor of what is learned, which is the more conventional view.

The only full and coherent account of the instructional process has been provided in Engelmann and Doug Carnine's *Theory of Instruction* which was published in 1982. This work is unknown in the UK and yet it contains a full and complete analysis of how to teach a variety of core everyday concepts. It is surprising, given all the efforts on both sides of the Atlantic and the rest of the English-speaking world to improve educational standards, that Engelmann and Carnine's analysis is so little known. Of significance for this book is the fact that their analysis of how to teach was so similar to that of Michel Thomas. Although they were working in different fields, they came to similar conclusions about the nature of teaching and learning and how best to structure knowledge for students.

The impact of programmes to teach literacy and numeracy were investigated in one of the largest research programmes ever undertaken, known as Project Follow-Through[7], which began in the USA in 1967 under President Lyndon Johnson. Its express purpose was to study instructional methods that would lead to a reduction in the disparity between low- and high-performing students by improving the attainments of low-performing students. It was finally concluded in 1995; it cost approximately $1 billion and involved research on over 20,000 students nationwide. By far the most successful programmes were those based on Direct Instruction, with the next most successful being behavioural programmes. In fact these two programmes were often the only ones to show any positive effects on students' learning. A number of programmes actually had a negative effect with the students in the control groups making better progress than those following specific programmes. One of the non-effective programmes was based on the English primary classroom of the 1970s that reflected the discovery learning methods underpinned by developmental psychology (discussed in Chapter 6).

WIDER APPLICATIONS OF THE THEORY OF OPTIMAL INSTRUCTION

In this book the Theory of Optimal Instruction is illustrated in relation to an analysis of written English and teaching foreign languages. Michel Thomas focused his attention on the teaching of languages; Engelmann and Carnine on the core skills of reading, writing, arithmetic and vocabulary (as did Skinner). However, there are others, in entirely different fields, who have been captivated by the same idea, often with strikingly similar outcomes. One example is in the area of football, where Wiel Coerver devised the 'Coerver Coaching System' in the 1970s. Coerver aimed to improve individual football skills to develop more effective attacking players. He created a new way to teach football through analysing great players on slow motion video. He came to the conclusion that many of their one-on-one and control skills could be broken down and taught to most players. He identified what could be thought of as a relatively small number of optimal 'moves', all derived from outstanding players. He and his colleagues then devised a series of individual and group exercises and games to teach pupils how to play effective, attractive football.

The impact of Coerver's methods could be seen in the Holland teams of the 1970s. They pioneered a buccaneering, adventurous style of football known as 'total football'. Players were equally skilful and effective in all positions and they reached two World Cup finals in 1974 and 1978. Fundamentally though, the system was inspired by the same logical analyses of what would be most useful and generalisable as programmes derived from instructional psychology and Michel Thomas's courses to teach languages.

SUMMARY

This chapter has introduced instructional psychology and discussed the way in which it has drawn on rational analysis to appreciate the role of the environment in how we learn. Examples were given to illustrate how we are sensitive to the statistical features of the environment and adapt to it in any entirely predictable way. The Theory of Optimal Instruction capitalises on this understanding to give coherence to the teaching and learning process through identifying what is most useful to students to learn. The chapter concluded by illustrating how the theory can be seen to have been applied to analysing football skills to emphasise the generic nature of the teaching methods that emerge from instructional psychology.

CHAPTER 8

INSTRUCTIONAL PRINCIPLES

OVERVIEW

Part 2 discussed the research into what is known about effective schools and teachers and their impact on learning. It was suggested that much educational practice is based on myths and conventional wisdoms, and very rarely on theory or experimental research into what has been shown to be effective. The educational research has tried to articulate the features of effective or improving schools and teachers but rarely supplied any convincing evidence that outcomes from one project yield generalisable principles and methodologies that have been, or even could be, widely applicable and achieve comparable results beyond the initial research locations. Family background and financial circumstances appear to be major factors in determining what students learn rather than schools and teachers and there is little sign of this changing in the foreseeable future. A degree of familiarity with the evidence on which educationalists draw and the debates about what works is potentially helpful in understanding where Michel Thomas's philosophy fits into established ways of thinking. There are few instances of the type of analysis conducted by Michel informing how students are taught, largely because its rationale is so different from contemporary practice that its significance has rarely been fully acknowledged, understood or even appreciated.

This chapter describes the assumptions that Michel Thomas made about the nature of teaching and learning and the instructional principles on which his courses are based.

MICHEL THOMAS'S ASSUMPTIONS ABOUT
TEACHING AND LEARNING

What led Michel Thomas to many of his insights about how to teach effectively was his belief that the responsibility for learning lay with the teacher rather than the student. It has been noted previously that this philosophy is not widely accepted because it challenges the conventional wisdom about students' learning derived from developmental and cognitive psychology. It also threatens teachers' professionalism through implying that students' low achievements are down to the way that they have taught.

Understandably, there is a tendency for teachers to take the credit for their students' good examination results but to blame their students when things go wrong in less successful years. This can be illustrated through a report that one secondary school, in what is generally recognised as being in a leafy suburb and affluent area of England, sent to parents following less than positive GCSE results. The school had fewer than 50% of GCSE passes at the acceptable grades of A*–C, which was well below the national average for the year. The report started encouragingly before offering a damning comment on the children:

> This year's GCSE results represented an excellent all-round effort by the 236 candidates in Year 11. As a whole, the year group did not have the academic strength in depth of the record-breaking 2003 Year 11.

Poor results were attributed to the lack of 'academic strength in depth', effectively informing parents that their children lacked ability. However, in a more successful year the school's position is revealingly reversed:

> GCSE results represented an excellent performance by this whole Year 11 group of candidates. We substantially improved on last year's GCSE results in all the categories used by the DfES for analysing school performance. As a truly 'comprehensive', non selective school we can take great pride in the fact that we have done our professional best for all our students, whatever their ability, adding substantial value to their previous attainment.

The comments of the secondary school head teacher only mirror government rhetoric. Government is more than happy to claim credit for any perceived increase in standards but vehemently resists any notion that it might be equally responsible for poor results. Thus, a paper prepared on behalf of the government for a conference on the failure of the National Literacy Strategy (NLS) to raise standards as quickly as desired claimed that the main problems lay in the management of headteachers and the classroom implementation of the phonics programme by teachers rather than its content.[1] It stated:

> It is the contention of this paper that the design of the NLS
> is broadly correct and that the issues of improvement are
> more to do with its implementation than its design.

Four years later in 2007 the government finally acknowledged that the phonics programmes were in fact flawed and withdrew them. The government insisted that they were implemented over an eight year period before conceding, albeit indirectly, that the content of the programmes was a contributory factor in significant numbers of pupils failing to meet given targets.

The emphasis on teaching rather than learning, locating the responsibility for success with the teacher rather than the student and accepting errors as a form of feedback rather than suggesting the student has a difficulty, are potentially the most controversial aspects of Michel Thomas's language courses. Whatever image we have of learning a foreign language it is more than likely that it is bound up with having to learn vocabulary and verb conjugation by heart. It is often seen to be one of the features of language learning from which there is no escape and yet Michel stands years of traditional practice on its head when declaring that languages can be taught without requiring students to engage in learning by rote or memorising lists of vocabulary.

LEARNING WITHOUT MEMORISING OR FORGETTING

The summer months are a time of year that cannot come soon enough for many, when thoughts turn to holidays and a more relaxed pace of life. However, April through to July is also a period inextricably associated with the exam season, the time of year when futures are on the line and students are confined to home to spend hours revising. There was a time in England when public examinations were only taken at the ages of 16 and 18. They are now taken at 7, 11, 14, 16, 17 and 18 as England has become the testing capital of the world.

Schools spend hours drilling students for these examinations and the conventional wisdom is the harder they work the better the grades. Parents, teachers and carers convince us that the only way to achieve success is to lock ourselves away in our bedrooms, dispense with MP3 players, televisions or any other distracting sensory input and put in the hours sitting at our desks revising and accumulating huge quantities of facts, most of which we will never need again. Students exchange telephone calls and texts to compare the hours worked, the parental bribes offered for success and to make plans for post-examination celebrations. Given this background it may be hard to believe Michel Thomas's promise of success without hours of rote learning memorising vocabulary. Woody Allen, when interviewed in the BBC 'Language Master', described learning with Michel as effortless. If this can be achieved, as Michel promised, the obvious question is why doesn't everybody know about it? Perhaps because it takes time for findings from psychological research to be incorporated into classroom practice. So how does it work?

MIX THE OLD WITH THE NEW

A regular feature of primary school life is the weekly spelling test. Every Monday morning thousands of children are given 20 words to learn to spell. The test follows on Friday before children are given a new set of words the next Monday. Over a six-week half-term they will have learned to spell 120 words. The crunch comes when teachers assess how many of those words children can still spell when they are all checked at the end of the six weeks. Typically children will remember those they learned first (known as the *primacy effect*) and those that came at the end (the *recency effect*). Much of the rest is forgotten. Early experiments on forgetting, conducted in the 1880s by Ebinghaus, a German psychologist, found that one hour after learning, 56% of what was learned had been forgotten, after one day the figure was 66% and after a month 80%. Why do we forget under these circumstances?

'Catastrophic interference' is the term used to describe the way that we forget information presented to us under the conditions of the typical weekly spelling test. With enough effort just about everyone would be able to learn the 20 spellings presented in the first week. Similarly it is not unrealistic to think that the same will happen with the 20 spellings presented in the second week. The problem is how new information affects what we have learned previously. It effectively wipes out and erases old learning and our earlier memories of the first 20 words. This is always likely to be the case when new information is practised sequentially in chunks. It might be thought that if children had better memories everything would be all right.

The final scene in the Alfred Hitchcock film *The Thirty-Nine Steps*, based on the John Buchan novel, suggests that this would not be the solution. The film is set in England and Scotland during the Second World War and reaches its climax in a London theatre. The hero, Richard Hannay, has stumbled on to a plot to smuggle sensitive information out of England and realises this information has been learned by heart by one of the performers on the theatre bill that evening, Mr Memory. During the course of Mr Memory's act Richard Hannay crucially asks, 'What are the Thirty-Nine Steps?'. Mr Memory, who was programmed to answer this question, begins to reply 'The Thirty-Nine Steps is an organization of spies, collecting information on behalf of the foreign office of ...' Before he can speak the name of the country, Mr Memory is silenced with a gun shot that rings out from a box above the stage. He is taken backstage where wounded and dying he continues to proudly recite the complicated scientific mathematical formulas of the secret documents that he had painstakingly memorised. As the film closes he turns to Hannay and confides that memorising the secret formula was the biggest job he had ever tackled. He asks, 'Am I right, sir?' Hannay confirms that he is and in the final line of the film Mr Memory replies 'Thank you, sir. Thank you. I'm glad it's off my mind.'

This line signals the paradox and inherent dilemma of having a perfect memory. Remembering everything has a cost, namely that being unable to forget is a tremendous burden and potentially creates more problems than it solves. Luria, a Russian psychologist, describes the plight of one of his patients who is unable to forget in *The Mind of a Mnemonist*. Even if it were possible it would not be desirable to remember everything. There is some information that we want students to learn whereas we would not be too concerned if other things were forgotten. An efficient memory remembers what is useful and forgets what is irrelevant or redundant; Michel Thomas helped students to learn efficiently through the way he organised and presented material which effectively signals to students what needs to be remembered as well as letting students know what is less important. This can be illustrated by returning to the example of children learning to spell. How might children remember more without suffering the negative consequences of a 'perfect memory'?

INTERLEAVED LEARNING

Any improvement lies within an instructional principle known as 'interleaved learning'. It works along the following lines. In the first week students learn to spell 20 new words. However, in the second week only five new words are introduced which are then taught alongside the 20 original words. So in the second week students learn 25 words. In the third week five further new words are introduced which are learned alongside the previous 25. By the end of a six week half-term students will have learned to spell 45 new words in an incremental, cumulative fashion. The likelihood is that after a one-week holiday the majority of them will have been remembered, and perhaps even more importantly where spellings are concerned, students will be able to transfer their learning to spelling those words correctly in their everyday written work – a major problem commonly associated with the conventional way of teaching spelling. This process of mixing the old with the new ensures that what is already familiar is constantly revisited and so is less likely to fade from memory. The new information is then gradually and systematically integrated with existing knowledge which again helps to cement it firmly in our memories.

The traditional approach creates the illusion of rapid progress in contrast to an interleaved strategy: 120 words learned in six weeks compared to only 45 within the new, interleaved, system. The problem arises in mistaking the number of words presented as an indication of what students have learned. This is a common assumption that fails to recognise the need to constantly check whether what has been presented has been retained. Learning to spell, or learning the new vocabulary in a foreign language, is not a sprint but a marathon. There are no prizes for what we know after six weeks, only what we can remember over much longer time scales.

Chapter 7 introduced rational analysis where it was claimed that we are more likely to remember what we recall frequently. Interleaved learning incorporates this principle into a teaching strategy. Students are constantly revisiting previously encountered material, triggering their memories to recognise that this information must be important because it is encountered so often. Under a traditional system, irrespective of how frequently any of the 20 words are practised during the first week, they are not needed again until the test after the holiday, which is seven weeks after they were first introduced. Students' memories have drawn the conclusion that despite the initial onslaught these words are not particularly important as they have not been used again for such a long time. We have to keep returning to information we want to remember and this principle is adopted throughout Michel Thomas's language courses. Michel recognised that learning long lists of vocabulary is of limited value and so instead adopted the principle of interleaved learning to juxtapose new and old information to ensure that what we learn is retained over time.

MICHEL THOMAS'S APPLICATION OF INTERLEAVED LEARNING

The role of interleaved learning in teaching vocabulary is illustrated in Table 8.1. In this example new vocabulary is presented, 'I am going' (*voy*) and 'to' (*a*) which is then combined to produce 'I am going to' (*voy a*). This is then mixed with previously introduced vocabulary: 'to eat' (*comer*), 'to buy' (*comprar*), 'to tell' (*decir*), 'now' (*ahora*), 'it' (*lo*), 'you' (*le*), 'not' (*no*), 'because' (*porque*), 'very' (*muy*) 'it is' (*es*) and 'expensive' (*caro*). Students also revise verb endings when there are two consecutive verbs, and the use of pronouns. The new information is highlighted in bold.

Table 8.1 Interleaved learning: Mixing the old with the new (Spanish)

New information	**I am going**	**voy**
New information	**to**	**a**
New information	**I am going to**	**voy a**
Old and new	**I am going to** eat now.	**Voy a** comer ahora.
Old and new	**I am going to** buy it.	**Voy a** comprarlo.
Old and new	**I am** not **going to** buy it because it is very expensive.	No **voy a** comprarlo porque es muy caro.
Old and new	**I am going to** tell you.	**Voy a** decirle.

A further feature of the way learning is secured is through reviews of what has already been taught. At critical points, when suitable chunks of information have been presented on specific vocabulary or grammatical points, Michel revises past learning. An example is presented in Table 8.2. Michel starts with a review of Spanish verbs in the 'to' form, followed by examples of where the stress occurs when speaking (penultimate syllable) and concludes with verb usage with questions and pronouns which are all illustrated with the verb 'to understand'. Here the verb endings are in bold.

Table 8.2 Review of Spanish verbs in the present tense

Previously taught verbs revised (infinitive)	
to want	quer**er**
to be able	pod**er**
to speak	habl**ar**
to understand	comprend**er**
In the present tense, you push down (stress) on the penultimate syllable	
I want	quier**o**
you want	quier**e**
I can	pued**o**
I speak	habl**o**
I don't speak	no habl**o**
Different grammatical forms revised with the verb 'understand'	
I understand	comprend**o**
I don't understand	no comprend**o**
you understand	comprend**e**
Do **you** understand it?	¿Lo comprend**e**?
Do **you** understand me?	¿Me comprend**e**?
Don't **you** understand me?	¿No me comprend**e**?
Why don't **you** understand me?	¿Por qué no me comprend**e**?
they understand	comprend**en**

A LITTLE BUT OFTEN

The conventional wisdom is that the harder you work the better the outcome. During the examination season students are encouraged to draw up their revision plans well in advance and will be given a notional number of hours to work each day. Students can end up feeling guilty or inviting parental disapproval if they take too much time out to meet friends or play on their computers. The reality is a little more complex and subtle and doing well is not just about 'working hard' but 'working smart'. One of the most reliable findings in memory research is that a form of practice, known as 'distributed practice', is in general far more powerful when long-term retention is the goal than an alternative known as 'massed practice'. Put simply, it is better to do 'a little but often' than revise in one long extended session. The last thing the government would have done had they drawn on psychological principles was introduce daily literacy and numeracy hours to improve standards. This has been acknowledged belatedly where primary schools have greater flexibility and can teach for shorter periods, but as will be discussed in Chapter 14, this core principle has not yet influenced the thinking behind secondary school timetables.

One exception to the general finding that distributed practice is more powerful than massed practice is in relation to examinations. On the whole, much of the information that is stored in preparation for examinations is unlikely to be needed beyond the time that we are told to stop writing and put our pens down. As a result a potentially more useful approach when revising is massed practice. In effect cramming the day before an examination could be highly effective and cost-efficient in terms of time. It would provide very good short-term retention with the added bonus that a student would soon forget what had been revised after the examination. This could be extremely useful and would effectively wipe the slate clean so that preparations for the next examination could go ahead without being 'contaminated' by previous learning. Parents and teachers could transform themselves from villains to heroes by suggesting that revision is almost left until the last minute instead of insisting on weeks of social isolation and adherence to revision schedules.

Michel Thomas was concerned to make learning effortless and secure long-term retention so material is presented via distributed practice throughout his programmes. After concepts, vocabulary and grammatical structures are introduced, they are revised at various points during the remainder of the programme. This is done skilfully and subtly without any specific reference to the strategy being adopted. The power of distributed practice is enhanced through the way previously taught information is practised and revisited and this in turn is reflected in what is taught and the way the information in each course is sequenced and structured.

TEACHING MORE THROUGH LESS

A recurring theme in describing the instructional principles underpinning Michel Thomas's courses is that the ultimate goal is to enable students to *generalise* from what they have learned and apply their knowledge to new situations. *Generalisation* featured heavily in the discussion on rational analysis when the most valuable information to teach is defined in terms of its usefulness and wide applicability. It is at the heart of the teaching methods used by Michel in which students progress through a number of stages which start with accuracy and fluency and end with students being able to generalise and apply their knowledge. Many of the instructional principles introduced in this chapter (for example, the next section on contextual diversity) enable students to generalise their knowledge to different contexts. While most teachers aspire to this goal and declare that teaching students to generalise their knowledge is fundamental to their practice, the reality is that the way tasks are invariably presented to pupils rarely facilitates this process.

CONTEXTUAL DIVERSITY

The principle of contextual diversity suggests that students learn to generalise when they can see how newly acquired skills are used in different contexts. Children learning to read are able to generalise more effectively when they see newly acquired vocabulary in as many different and diverse contexts as possible. For example, if children have just been taught to read the word 'and' in one context, for example by being shown the word on a card, they then need to encounter the word in a wide variety of different books and settings, which could include the back of breakfast cereal packets, signs in supermarkets, newspaper headlines, comics, etc. The wider the variety the better. Children will then recognise that what gives 'and' its specific pronunciation is the sequence of letters, 'a, n, d' and no other factors such as font type, size or colour.

The alternative to presenting newly taught words in diverse contexts is to present them within a familiar and comfortable format such as the one found in reading schemes. This is where vocabulary is controlled and usually phonically regular so that books can be sequenced according to their perceived level of difficulty. They create the illusion of progress as children go from one book to another and they give parents a degree of reassurance as they associate the number of books read with improved reading standards. However, the crunch comes when children encounter books from other sources. In general, if two children have been taught exactly the same thing but one has been presented with a wide variety of texts to read and the other has not, it will be the former pupil who will be more likely to generalise and apply his knowledge. The child who races through a set of standard books that typically comprise a reading scheme may look as though he is making rapid progress (and the confidence that this provides is not to be underestimated), but he will nevertheless be less well equipped to use that knowledge elsewhere. When children see words only within a particular type of book it will be harder to help them to appreciate that the word is pronounced in exactly the same way when it appears in different contexts.

One very interesting and unexpected example of contextual diversity in children's lives comes through watching television. It is counter-intuitive, especially given all the press claims to the contrary, but there may well be some instances where watching a wide range of programmes is helpful, particularly in relation to children's reading. I have never met a child who after watching a soap opera or American television programme has ever declared that they would not watch it again because they were unable to understand the accents. Children appear to have little difficulty making out the same words when pronounced differently with Australian, American, London, Lancashire or Yorkshire accents. Watching television gives children the opportunity to hear the same words pronounced in a variety of ways. It introduces a degree of tolerance to difference and means that children can recognise the same word in different programmes, despite the varying accents. The programmes offer a range of contexts for children and are a perfect illustration of contextual diversity. Being able to work out what was said from a pronunciation that is slightly different as a result of a mispronunciation or unfamiliar accent is an invaluable skill in learning a foreign language. There is evidence to show that students make similar adjustments when reading, through a process known as self-correction.[2]

SELF-CORRECTION

Just as children are able to understand words spoken orally with different accents, when they are reading they are able to understand words which are decoded correctly but may lead to an incorrect pronunciation. For example, if children are taught that the letter combination 'ea' represents the sound '/ee/ (i)' as in 'see', they will pronounce the word 'break', as 'breek'. Research indicates that children are able to self-correct and articulate the correct pronunciation ('break') when the word in question is in their vocabulary. So if children read a sentence like 'I had been working all morning and didn't even have time for a break', the context and knowing the meaning of 'break' would enable them to self-correct an incorrect pronunciation (i.e. 'breek' instead of 'break') and then read the sentence correctly. The way in which children self-correct indicates that comprehension is a major factor in determining whether or not they ultimately read accurately. So it is when learning a foreign language with Michel Thomas. He emphasises the importance of understanding how a language is used, encourages students to monitor the responses of listeners to ensure that they have understood what was said and constantly emphasises the need to stress the correct part of a verb when speaking due to the meaning this conveys.

MICHEL THOMAS'S APPLICATION OF CONTEXTUAL DIVERSITY

Michel Thomas addresses the concept of contextual diversity through the course structure and through teaching skills and concepts that concentrate on how to use language. What students learn is practised and reinforced in different contexts. One of the first things students encounter in Spanish is where to position pronouns in sentences in relation to verbs. This is then revisited each time a new feature of verb usage is introduced (for example, present, future and past tenses). Every time something new is presented students have opportunities to practise previously taught skills in a new context that reflects what has just been introduced. As a result Michel Thomas teaches each language through a relatively small vocabulary but uses that vocabulary in many different contexts. This is preferable to developing an extensive vocabulary that is practised in a relatively limited number of situations.

There are recurring features in each course that focus on, for example, the use of (i) verbs; (ii) negatives; (iii) questions; (iv) stringing two or more verbs together consecutively and (v) use of pronouns which provide different contexts for students to practise what they have learned. This was illustrated earlier in the third section of Table 8.2 (Different grammatical forms revised with the verb 'understand') in connection with teaching pronouns and can be seen in Table 8.3 in relation to negatives. The negatives shown in

Table 8.3 are selected from the Spanish Foundation course and the clear pattern is that a negative is formed by placing '*no*' in front of a positive statement. This happens with sentences in all tenses and for all contexts. Showing a diverse range of negatives, as Michel does, teaches students the full range of contexts for constructing negative statements or sentences. The level of repetition, and showing students how skills are used in different contexts could lead to relatively competent foreign language speakers, who are using the courses to update their skills or refresh their memories, to feel a little frustrated. They may think that the key teaching points have all been covered and that the repetition is not necessary. However, for the new student, or one lacking confidence, seeing the same skill used in the same way, but in different contexts, is very powerful and a critical element in the teaching process that enables students to generalise their learning to new settings.

Table 8.3 Teaching negatives in Spanish through contextual diversity

it is It is not.	*es* ***No** es.*
It is possible. It is not possible.	*Es posible.* ***No** es posible.*
Isn't it acceptable for you? why Why isn't it acceptable for you?	*¿**No** es aceptable para usted?* *¿por qué?* *¿Por qué **no** es aceptable para usted?*
It is very good. It is not very good.	*Es muy bueno.* ***No** es muy bueno.*
I have I don't have	*tengo* ***no** tengo*
I have it. I don't have it.	*Lo tengo.* ***No** lo tengo.*
You have it. You don't have it.	*Lo tiene.* ***No** lo tiene.*
Do you have it? Don't you have it?	*¿Lo tiene?* *¿**No** lo tiene?*
I want to see it. I don't want to see it.	*Quiero verlo.* ***No** quiero verlo.*
I am busy. (masculine) I am not very busy. (masculine)	*Estoy ocupado.* ***No** estoy muy ocupado.*

I am busy. (feminine) I am not very busy today. (feminine)	*Estoy ocupada.* **No** *estoy muy ocupada hoy.*
I am going to buy it. I am not going to buy it.	*Voy a comprarlo.* **No** *voy a comprarlo.*
I am going to do it. I am not going to do it now.	*Voy a hacerlo.* **No** *voy a hacerlo ahora.*
I am selling it. I am not selling it.	*Lo vendo.* **No** *lo vendo.*
I understand it very well. I don't understand it very well.	*Lo comprendo muy bien.* **No** *lo comprendo muy bien.*
I understand it. I don't understand it.	*Lo comprendo.* **No** *lo comprendo.*
We see ourselves. We don't see ourselves.	*Nos vemos.* **No** *nos vemos.*
It will be possible. It won't be possible.	*Será posible.* **No** *será posible.*
I would do it. I wouldn't do it.	*Lo haría.* **No** *lo haría.*
He is sending it to me tomorrow. He wouldn't send it to me today.	*Me lo manda mañana.* **No** *me lo mandaría hoy.*

Table 8.4 opposite illustrates teaching negatives in French, also through the principles of contextual diversity.

Tables 8.3 and 8.4 reveal a further aspect of contextual diversity. All of Michel Thomas's language courses are structured in a similar way so a student who has followed one course will find similar patterns in the other courses. Negatives are taught at the same point in the courses as are many other language structures. These patterns create different contexts in which the same skills are being taught (i.e. use of negatives, pronouns, prepositions, two or more verbs in a sentence, future and past tenses, etc.). Further examples of the way the same kind of skill is taught in different contexts through learning a different language can be found in Chapter 9 (for example, see Table 9.1 for the initial steps in teaching Spanish and French to compare the similarity between the two).

Table 8.4 Teaching negatives in French through contextual diversity

it is It is not.	c'est Ce **n**'est **pas**.
It is for me. It is not for me.	C'est pour moi. Ce **n**'est **pas** pour moi.
It is possible. It is not possible.	C'est possible. Ce **n**'est **pas** possible.
It is possible for me. It is not possible for me.	C'est possible pour moi. Ce **n**'est **pas** possible pour moi.
It is very comfortable. It is very comfortable for me. It is not very comfortable for me.	C'est très confortable. C'est très confortable pour moi. Ce **n**'est **pas** très confortable pour moi.
It is like that. It is not like that.	C'est comme ça. Ce **n**'est **pas** comme ça.
I'm sorry but I'm sorry but it is not very comfortable.	je regrette mais Je regrette mais ce **n**'est **pas** très confortable.
It is acceptable. I'm sorry but it is not acceptable.	C'est acceptable. Je regrette mais ce **n**'est **pas** acceptable.
I can I cannot.	je peux Je **ne** peux **pas**.
to understand you I cannot understand you.	vous comprendre Je **ne** peux **pas** vous comprendre.

SUMMARY

This chapter has described a number of core instructional principles, derived from instructional psychology, that enable Michel Thomas to fulfil the promises he makes at the beginning of the courses about remembering without rote learning, mental rehearsal or doing homework. Michel creates the right atmosphere for learning by reminding learners that *he*, rather than the student, is responsible for what is learned. The assumptions that Michel makes and the instructional principles on which he draws are what lead students to feel that learning with Michel Thomas is effortless.

CHAPTER 9

DECIDING WHAT TO TEACH

OVERVIEW

Michel Thomas adopts the same rationale, principles and methods to teach all of his language courses. They are structured and sequenced in similar ways so students switching from one course to another will find familiarity and consistency in the teaching approach. This chapter illustrates how instructional psychology and the core instructional principles described in Chapters 7 and 8 underpin each course and contribute to deciding what to teach. This is the first stage in the process of assessment-through-teaching described in the introduction to Part 3.

Whatever approach is adopted to teaching a new subject there is always an enormous amount of information to be learned, more than can ever be taught at any one time. The problem is that students really need to know everything from the very beginning. If teachers and students were telepathic everything would be fine and students would learn all they needed to know in an instant. But of course they are not, so an informed decision has to be taken about what to teach first.

Michel Thomas's approach to deciding what to teach when arriving at suitable instructional sequences is unusual in education but not without precedents elsewhere. Ian Stewart in *Nature's Numbers* argues that we live in a universe of patterns and that the formal way in which they are recognised, classified and exploited is through mathematics. This is the system through which we bring order and identity to these patterns which Stewart sees as the 'vital clues to the rules that govern natural processes'.[1] Stewart discusses how behaviour that appears irregular and completely random to the untrained eye can actually be explained as we develop more sophisticated ways of observing and measuring the world.

So it was with Michel Thomas. He sought to bring the same sense of pattern recognition and order to the teaching of foreign languages. He could see links, similarities and differences between languages and wanted to make these explicit to students. There is an intuitive appeal in the idea that the patterns evident to the mathematician are present in spoken and written language, even if they remain largely undetected. Michel provided coherence through language structures and instructional sequences instead of through the more conventional approach of topics and themes (which are discussed in Chapters 13 and 14).

Michel Thomas talked about his approach to deciding what to teach in 'The Language Master'. He said that he dissected each language into its smallest parts and reassembled them in such a way that they could be understood. Courses are taught in a step-by-step fashion through sentences of gradually increasing complexity. Michel's aim was to enable students to express their own thoughts through applying what they had learned rather than through memorised phrases.

DECIDING ON AN ORDER FOR TEACHING SKILLS, KNOWLEDGE AND CONCEPTS

A critical feature of teaching programmes underpinned by instructional psychology is the order in which new information is introduced. It makes the difference between learning being effortless and seemingly incidental or being the source of difficulty and confusion. Chapter 6 contrasted the influence of developmental and instructional psychology on the teaching and learning process. Research in developmental psychology is motivated by a desire to reach a greater understanding about the way in which we acquire different skills and abilities. The fundamental error made by educationalists has been to assume that the order in which skills are acquired developmentally automatically makes the most appropriate teaching sequence. Michel Thomas was quick to recognise this error which is why he dissected languages into what he regarded as their smallest components before reassembling them in a revised order.

Chapter 5 discussed how phonological awareness is often regarded as a good predictor of later success in learning to read. Psychologists have researched how awareness of phonology develops and have suggested a clear development sequence in which phonological skills are acquired. Children find it easier to recognise whole words before syllables followed by onsets (initial consonants in the written word, e.g. c in 'cat'; pl in 'plot') and rimes (vowel plus any following consonants, e.g. at in 'cat'; ost in 'lost') followed by the sounds represented by single letters (known as grapheme-phoneme-correspondences, GPCs). At one time it was thought that this would make the best order for teaching phonological skills. However, research showed that this was not the case and that what was most difficult developmentally, (i.e. relating sounds to single letters) was in fact the most useful from a teaching point of view because of its generalisability.[2]

Janet Vousden in a recently published article in the journal *Applied Cognitive Psychology* has calculated the number of monosyllabic words in a database of written and spoken English, known as CELEX that can be read through the instructional strategy of GPCs and the developmental strategy of onsets and rimes. The database consists of over two million words that can be read by knowledge of 339 GPCs. In a dramatic contrast, children would need knowledge of over 2,100 onsets and rimes to read approximately the same number of words, which significantly increases the amount of information that has to be remembered. In other words GPCs are far more useful and generalisable than onsets and rimes because they are so widely applicable and do not make the same demands on children's memories. Thus, instructional psychology provides a more helpful starting point for deciding what to teach. There are four guidelines to consider when determining an order for teaching skills, knowledge and concepts (which will be referred to as 'instructional sequences').

TEACH WHAT IS MOST USEFUL

The first guideline is the usefulness of any skill. Chapter 6 discussed Pareto's Law and its role in determining which high frequency words and phonic skills to teach. Having identified which high frequency words it is worth learning, the order in which they are then taught is determined by their overall frequency. In the database of adult literature discussed in Chapter 6, by far the most frequently occurring word was 'the', which appeared more than twice as often as the second most frequently occurring word, 'of'. Just six words (the, of, and, to, a, in) occur so often that they account for a large proportion of the high frequency words that can be read in any database. The implication is that these words should be taught first and in order of frequency because of their high utility.

Carnine and his colleagues in *Direct Instruction Reading* also recommend teaching the sounds (phonemes) associated with the 26 letters of the alphabet according to their frequency in written English. This means adopting a frequency-based order (a, m, t, s, i, f, d, r, o, g, l, h, u, c, b, n, k, v, e, p, w, j, y, x, q, z) instead of the usual alphabetic one. The argument is that by learning the high-frequency letter sounds first children will be able to use this knowledge to both read and write simple three and four-letter words more quickly because of how often they occur in written English.

The debates about teaching reading have highlighted the tensions between the respective roles of developmental and instructional psychology in structuring instructional sequences. From an instructional point of view students are always taught what is most useful and generalisable. In contrast, a developmental perspective prioritises what students acquire first because it is generally seen to be easier.

Michel Thomas's analysis of what to teach is unique and the result of his knowledge of different languages. His major concern was to identify what was most useful and generalisable. However, instead of looking at each language separately and asking, for example, what students need to be taught to become competent in Spanish or what students need to be taught to become competent in French, he took a broader view and analysed the similarities and differences between languages. He wanted to establish what they had in common so that those features of languages could be taught in the same way. He anticipated that this would then make it easier for students to learn more than one language because the teaching framework would be the same irrespective of the language being taught.

MICHEL THOMAS'S APPLICATION OF THE GUIDELINE TO TEACH WHAT IS MOST USEFUL

Michel Thomas's introduction to his courses highlights the principles of high utility and generalisability. Michel gives students a sense of purpose through reminding them that what they are learning is extremely useful and although some of the early sentences might seem a little strange, their role is to convey a feeling of achievement so that within a very short period of time students are capable of translating increasingly long and intricate sentences into the target language.

Early on in each recording there is an audible gasp of amazement as students realise how much they have learned after only a couple of hours and the complexity of the sentences that they are being asked to translate, for example, 'I want to know at what time it is going to be ready because I need it and I want to have it today if it is possible.' Even though the students may never construct a sentence like this again, as their vocabulary grows they will have the necessary knowledge to form similarly structured sentences (i.e. use of present tense, future tense, two or more consecutive verbs, the verb 'to be', connectives, and pronouns with one and two verb phrases) that are geared to their immediate needs.

Table 9.1 shows the initial steps in the programmes for Spanish and French. Both are very similar and start with words that end with '-able' and '-ible' and which have the same meaning in Spanish and French but different pronunciations. Examples are provided of sentences beginning with 'it is' (e.g. 'it is possible', 'it is probable'). Michel then introduces 'for me' and 'for you' (e.g. 'it is possible for me', 'it is possible for you') before showing students how to make negative statements ('it is not possible for me', 'it is not possible for you'). The skills are sequenced identically in Spanish and French and include a number of examples to give students essential practice. These early stages in the programmes highlight the similarities between languages and illustrate how sentences are constructed using different grammatical structures (i.e. sentences with pronouns, verbs, adverbs, prepositions and negatives).

Table 9.1 Initial steps in teaching Spanish and French

Spanish		French	
Similarity between Spanish and English. Active vocabulary is small: 500–1,500 words.		French language: similarities to English. Over 60% of English vocabulary comes from French. Active vocabulary is small: 500–1,500 words.	
Key endings: words ending in '-ible' and '-able' pronounced differently from English but often have the same meaning.		Words in English ending with '-ible' and '-able' are the same in French.	
possible probable it is It is possible.	*possible* *probable* *es* *Es possible.*	possible table it is / that is It is possible. It is comfortable. good It is good.	*possible* *table* *c'est* *C'est possible.* *C'est confortable.* *bon* *C'est bon.*

		very	très
		It is very good.	C'est très bon.
		It is very	C'est très
		comfortable.	confortable.
It is probable.	Es probable.	It is probable.	C'est probable.
It is terrible.	Es terrible.		
It is acceptable	Es aceptable	It is acceptable	C'est acceptable
for me.	para mí.	for me.	pour moi.
for you	para usted	for you	pour vous
It is for me.	Es para mí.	It is for me.	C'est pour moi.
		It is for you.	C'est pour vous.
		It is very	C'est très
		comfortable for me.	confortable pour moi.
Use 'no' to make negative sentences.		**Use 'ne … pas' to make negative sentences.**	
It is not.	No es.	It is not.	Ce n'est pas.
It is not for you.	No es para usted.		
		Not for me,	Pas pour moi, merci.
		thank you.	
It is not for you;	No es para usted;		
it is for me.	es para mí.		
It is not possible	No es posible para mí.	It is not very	Ce n'est pas très
for me.		comfortable for me.	confortable pour moi.
It is possible for you.	Es posible para usted.		
It is acceptable for me.	Es aceptable para mí.		

At different points during the early stages of the courses students are told, (as with words ending in '-able' and '-ible') that there are a number of words with particular endings in English that have identical meanings in other languages but slightly different pronunciations and spellings. Again each time new words are introduced Michel gives several examples before providing opportunities for students to practise a number of previously acquired skills (i.e. asking questions, use of the definite article 'the' and the indefinite article 'a'). Table 9.2 lists words that are similar in English, Spanish and French with the following endings: '-ent', '-ant', '-ary', '-ance', '-ence', '-ition', '-ation', '-ic' and '-ical'.

Table 9.2 Similarities between English, Spanish and French

Spanish		French	
Key endings: English '-ent' and '-ant' endings become '-ente' and '-ante' in Spanish.		Words in English ending in '-ent' and '-ant' come from French. They have similar spellings and the same meaning.	
different	diferente	different	différent
important	importante	important	important
Key ending: English words ending in '-ary' end in '-ario' in Spanish.		Words in English ending in '-ary' become '-aire' in French.	
necessary	necesario	necessary	nécessaire
contrary	contrario	contrary	contraire
on the contrary	al contrario	on the contrary	au contraire
vocabulary	vocabulario	vocabulary	vocabulaire
Key endings: words in English ending in '-ence' and '-ance' end in '-encia' and '-ancia' in Spanish.		Words in English ending in '-ance' and '-ence' come from French.	
difference	diferencia	difference	différence
importance	importancia	preference	préférence
influence	influencia	importance	importance
preference	preferencia	influence	influence
the difference	la diferencia	the difference	la différence
a difference	una diferencia	a difference	une différence
What difference?	¿Qué diferencia?	What difference?	Quelle différence?
the preference	la preferencia	the preference	la préférence
a preference	una preferencia	a preference	une préférence
Key ending: words ending in '-tion' in English end in '-ción' in Spanish.		Words in English ending in '-ion' come from French. They have the same spelling and the same meaning.	
position	posición	position	position
condition	condición	condition	condition
reservation	reservación*	the condition	la condition
the reservation	la reservación	a condition	une condition
a reservation	una reservación	What condition?	Quelle condition?
		opinion	opinion
Key ending: words ending in '-ation' in English end in '-ación' in Spanish.			
What reservation?	¿Qué reservación?		

Key ending: nouns ending in '-ion' in English are the same in Spanish (-ión). There are nearly 1,200 of them. Exceptions are 'translation' and 'explanation'.		There are approximately 1,200 nouns in English and in French ending in '-ion'. Out of 1,200 there are only three exceptions: 'translation', 'explanation', 'vacation'.	
translation explanation	traducción explicación	translation explanation vacation	traduction explication vacances
Key ending: words in English ending in '-ic' and '-ical' end in '-ico' in Spanish.		Words in English ending in '-ical' end in '-ique' in French.	
political economic philosophical	político económico filosófico	political economic philosophical	politique économique philosophique
*Michel Thomas uses the word 'reservación' which means 'reservation' in Mexican Spanish and the Spanish spoken in the USA. In the rest of the Spanish-speaking world 'reservation' is translated by 'reserva'.			

TEACH ONLY ONE NEW SKILL AT A TIME

The second sequencing guideline is to ensure that one, and only one, new skill is taught at a time. A failure to do so may mean that the main point being taught is left ambiguous. This may sound straightforward but it is more difficult to achieve than might be imagined. It is generally thought that this is a realistic goal in a subject like mathematics where there is a logical progression from one skill to the next, but it is almost impossible in non-scientific subjects such as reading or learning a foreign language where such progressions are by no means as obvious or readily recognised. The order in which Michel Thomas teaches concepts and vocabulary is planned meticulously so that at any one time only one new concept is taught.

The difficulty in identifying, isolating and teaching only one thing at a time is illustrated in the following example from a government document demonstrating good practice in teaching phonics. Children were asked to stand in front of the class and hold a card on which single letters were written. Government advice stated:

> Further phonic work in the same 15-minute session focused on spelling. Selected pupils stood at the front of the class, standing in the correct order to spell the required word. This was reinforced by more changes of phonemes, for example, 'bent', 'pent', 'pelt', 'melt', 'met', 'net', 'nest'. Each change was accompanied by pupils quickly segmenting the sounds to spell the given word and blending to read it.[3]

As pupils display their letters the rest of the children state the sound represented by each letter followed by the word that they make when combined. Remember the aim of the activity was to teach spelling. The question is whether this task was really teaching spelling or reading.

Spelling actually requires pupils to hear a word, for example 'bent' and then work out which graphemes (letters) represent the phonemes (sounds in the word 'bent'). In the case of 'bent' there are four phonemes (/b/e/n/t/) which are represented by four letters, one for each phoneme. In Chapter 5 this process of breaking a word into its component sounds was described as 'segmentation'. However, the above task does not involve pupils in segmenting a word into sounds. Instead they are reading the letters on the card, one by one, and stating the word that emerges when the sounds are said together. This process is known as 'synthesis' and is at the heart of competent reading. If government inspectors in a document illustrating good practice do not know the difference between reading and spelling how are teachers expected to do so? The only certainty is that pupils are likely to be left confused. The problem arises because a fairly simple straightforward task has been turned into a game in order to make the activity more enjoyable. No doubt the pupils will have enjoyed coming to the front of the class and holding a card, but it is not actually improving their spelling.

In this example, like so many others, the nature of the task is constantly being changed every time the teacher adds something to make it more interesting or fun. Michel believed that learning was intrinsically exciting but not at the expense of altering what was being taught so that its purpose became obscure.

MICHEL THOMAS'S APPLICATION OF THE GUIDELINE TO TEACH ONLY ONE NEW SKILL AT A TIME

Michel Thomas's teaching methods are designed to teach one thing at a time and to make it absolutely clear to students what is to be taught. Table 9.3 shows the order in which skills are introduced in the first recording in the Spanish course. As stated earlier in the chapter Michel starts by saying that words ending in *-ible* and *-able* are pronounced differently from English but have the same meaning. Such words work in the same way and so can be taught simultaneously as they are treated identically.

• The first step is to teach students how to pronounce *possible* and *probable*.

- The second step is to teach the Spanish for 'it is' which is *es*.
- The third step is that *posible* and *probable* combined with *es* give the sentence *es posible* or *es probable*. During the third step Michel also gives four examples of the way that the rule works with other words ending in *-ible* and *-able*, for example, *es terrible* and *es acceptable*.
- In the fourth step students are taught 'for me' and 'for you' which are *para mí* and *para usted*.
- In the fifth step students combine what was learned previously in steps 2 and 4 to say 'it is for me' (*es para mí*).
- In step 6 students are shown how to make a negative sentence and start with 'it is not possible' (*no es posible*).
- Steps 7, 8, 9 and 10 do not present anything new but combine previous steps:
- Step 7 combines step 6, 'it is not' and step 4, 'for you' (*no es para usted*).
- Step 8 combines step 7, 'it is not for you' and step 5, 'it is for me' (*no es para usted; es para mí*).
- Step 9 is slightly different and requires students to generalise their existing knowledge, derived from step 6, 'it is not', step 1, 'possible' and step 4, 'for me' ('it is not possible for me' – *no es posible para mí*).
- Finally, step 10 combines step 3, 'it is possible' and step 4 'for you' (*es posible para usted*).

Table 9.3 The order for introducing skills in Spanish

Key endings: Words ending in *-ible* and *-able* are pronounced differently from English but often have the same meaning.		
Step 1	possible probable	*posible* *probable*
Step 2	it is	*es*
Step 3	It is possible. It is probable. It is terrible. It is acceptable.	*Es posible.* *Es probable.* *Es terrible.* *Es aceptable.*
Step 4	for me for you	*para mí* *para usted*
Step 5	It is for me.	*Es para mí.*
Step 6	**Use *no* to make negative sentences.** It is not.	 *No es.*
Step 7	It is not for you.	*No es para usted.*
Step 8	It is not for you; it is for me.	*No es para usted; es para mí.*
Step 9	It is not possible for me.	*No es posible para mí.*
Step 10	It is possible for you. It is acceptable for me.	*Es posible para usted.* *Es aceptable para mí.*

TEACH EASIER SKILLS BEFORE MORE DIFFICULT SKILLS

The third sequencing guideline is to teach easier skills before more difficult ones. This seems an obvious and logical thing to do. As already noted, this is easier to achieve in subjects where there is a clear progression in skill acquisition but not so in the area of foreign languages where it is less apparent which skills are easy and which ones are more difficult. The principle is perhaps therefore best illustrated, initially, through looking at how to teach children to add numbers to ten.

Typically in maths teaching children are taught several things at any one time. Many programmes teach children to rote count, count two groups, construct sets, name and write numerals and read equations simultaneously. While this may work for some children, there will be many for whom it does not and so a gradual, step-by-step approach, where easier skills are taught before more difficult ones and where only one new concept is presented at a time is preferable. Sequences derived from instructional psychology for teaching maths follow a logical progression. Each step in the sequence teaches only one skill at a time so children are taught to count by rote first before progressing to counting objects and constructing a set. More difficult skills such as skip counting (i.e. counting in twos, threes, fours, etc.), counting backwards or balancing equations come later but only after all the necessary pre-requisite skills have been taught.

MICHEL THOMAS'S APPLICATION OF THE GUIDELINE TO TEACH EASIER BEFORE MORE DIFFICULT SKILLS

This section illustrates Michel Thomas's analysis of teaching students to use verbs in Spanish which reflects a consistency of approach with other languages. The aim is to teach one skill at a time, and to sequence knowledge in such a way that learning occurs almost incidentally without any obvious effort on the part of the student. Teaching proceeds through a series of small steps of increasing difficulty to a point where ultimately, through the focus on generalisable skills, students have learned very much more than might have been expected in the time available. The steps in teaching students about how to use verbs in Spanish now follow. Note that the order in which items are presented within each step reflects the order in the Foundation Spanish Course.

Step 1: Introduces the general rule that a verb ending in *-o* expresses 'I'.

Step 1	*-o* verb ending expresses 'I', so there is no need to use the Spanish for 'I' (*yo*). If you do use *yo*, then it makes it more emphatic: '*I* am sorry'.

Step 2: Gives four examples of verbs in the 'I' form including negatives and pronouns, 'I'm sorry' (*lo siento*), 'I have' (*tengo*), 'I want' (*quiero*) and 'I need' (*necesito*).

Step 2	**I**'m sorry. (I feel it.) **I** have **I** don't have **I** have it. **I** don't have it. **I** want **I** want it. **I** need **I** need it. **I** don't need it.	Lo sient**o**. teng**o** no teng**o** Lo teng**o**. No lo teng**o**. quier**o** Lo quier**o**. necesit**o** Lo necesit**o**. No lo necesit**o**.

Step 3: Introduces the 'you' form of 'have' (*tiene*) with questions and pronouns.

Step 3	**you** have What? What do **you** have? **You** have it. Do **you** have it? **You** don't have it. Don't **you** have it?	tien**e**, **usted** tiene ¿Qué? ¿Qué tien**e**? Lo tien**e**. ¿Lo tien**e**? No lo tiene. ¿No lo tien**e**?

Step 4: Combines, through interleaved learning, the 'I' and 'you' forms, 'I want' (*quiero*) and 'you want' (*quiere*) with questions and pronouns.

Step 4	**I** want **I** don't want it. **you** want What do **you** want? **You** want it. Do **you** want it?	quier**o** No lo quier**o**. quier**e** ¿Qué quier**e**? Lo quier**e**. ¿Lo quier**e**?

Step 5: Gives examples of constructing a sentence where there are two consecutive verbs, 'I want' and 'to know' (*quiero saber*).

Step 5	to know I **want to know.** I don't **want to know.**	*saber* **Quiero saber.** *No* **quiero saber.**

Step 6: Gives examples of sentences with two consecutive verbs with pronouns, a negative and a question.

Step 6	to see to see **it** I want to see **it.** I **don't** want to see **it.** **Do you** want to see **it?** I can you can I can**not** see **it.**	*ver* *ver***lo** *Quiero ver***lo.** **No** *quiero ver***lo.** *¿Quiere ver***lo?** *puedo* *puede* **No** *puedo ver***lo.**

Step 7: It is only after students have practised constructing sentences with two consecutive verbs that Michel provides the rule governing their use.

Step 7	If there are two or more consecutive verbs in a sentence, the second and subsequent verbs will be in the full form (the 'to' form in English, i.e. the infinitive).	
	Can you see? You can see. What can you see?	*¿Puede* **ver***?* *Puede* **ver***.* *¿Qué puede* **ver***?*

Step 8: Michel explains to students how to form verbs from nouns that are similar in English and Spanish.

Step 8	Verbs that are derived from nouns that are similar in English and Spanish will also be similar. To make the verb in Spanish, you just add *-ar* to the English.	
	formation to form to conform to confirm	*formación* *form***ar** *conform***ar** *confirm***ar**

Step 9: Students will have covered a lot of ground by the time they reach Step 9, which is approximately 2.5 hours into the 8-hour course. Here they are introduced to the three verb endings for the infinitive which are -ar (*hablar*), -er (*comer*) and -ir (*venir*). This knowledge is an essential building block in speaking and listening in Spanish. It provides the basis for learning other forms of the verb such as the third person and plural pronouns ('we', 'you' and 'they') together with past and future tenses. By step 9 students have been taught the 'you' form of a limited number of verbs (have, want, be able).

Step 9	The whole form of a verb, the infinitive, is expressed with 'to' in English (for example, 'to eat'). In Spanish, it is expressed in an ending. There are three types of verbs: -ar (*hablar*), -er (*comer*), -ir (*venir*).	
	to speak	*hablar*
	to eat	*comer*
	to come	*venir*
	to leave	*salir*
	to speak	*hablar*
	to understand	*comprender*
	to say / to tell	*decir*
	All Spanish verbs have an -r at the end, so the stress is on the last syllable.	

Step 10: Introduces different pronouns and shows students where they are placed in sentences with one verb (infinitive) and two consecutive verbs.

Step 10	to see	*ver*
	I want to see **it**.	*Quiero ver**lo**.*
	to see **it**	*ver**lo***
	to see **you**	*ver**le***
	to see **them**	*ver**los***
	to see **them** (feminine)	*ver**las***
	I want to see **them**.	*Quiero ver**los**.*
	I want to see **them**. (all women)	*Quiero ver**las**.*
	I want to see **you**.	*Quiero ver**le**.*
	to see **me**	*ver**me***

Step 11: Teaches that the form for 'he/she/it' is the same as for 'you'. This is illustrated with the verb 'to go'. Step 11 begins by introducing and illustrating 'I go' in sentences with two consecutive verbs and pronouns.

Step 11	**I am going** to **I am going** to **I am going** to eat. **I am going** to buy it.	**voy** *a* **voy** *a* **Voy** *a comer.* **Voy** *a comprarlo.*
	For all verbs, the form for 'you' is the same as for 'he/she/it'. For example, 'you are going to' (*va a*) also means 'he/she/it is going to'.	
	You are going to do it. **He is going to** do it. **She is going to** do it.	**Va a** *hacerlo.* **Va a** *hacerlo.* **Va a** *hacerlo.*

Step 12: Develops what was introduced in step 9 and goes a little further in explaining the significance of the different verb endings. Verbs are divided into two categories or 'tracks', 'the -*ar* track' (*hablar* – 'to speak') and 'the -*er*/-*ir* track' (*comer* – 'to eat') (i.e. verbs ending in -*ar* are treated in one way which is different from verbs ending in -*er* or -*ir* which are treated in the same way). All verbs, whether they are on the -*ar* or -*er*/-*ir* tracks end in *o* for the 'I' form (*hablo, como*). 'You'/'he'/'she'/'it' on the -*ar* track ends in *a* (*habla*) but on the -*er*/-*ir* track 'you'/'he'/'she'/'it' ends in *e* (*come*).

Step 12	There are three types of verbs: -*ar*, -*er* and -*ir*. They are divided into two categories or 'tracks': the -*ar* track (*hablar, comprar, preparar*) and the -*er*/-*ir* track (*comprender, escribir, hacer, salir*).	
	On both tracks for 'I', after you push down you will surface on -**o**.	
	I speak **I** am preparing **I** am accepting it.	*habl**o*** *prepar**o*** *Lo acept**o***.
	On the -*ar* track for 'you/he/she/it', after you push down you will surface on -***a***.	
	you speak / **he** speaks / **she** speaks / **it** speaks	*habl**a***
	On the -*er*/-*ir* track for 'you/he/she/it', after you push down you will surface on -**e**.	
	you are leaving **you** are doing	*sal**e*** *hac**e***

Step 13: Teaches that for 'they' and the plural 'you' on both tracks, you add an *n* (*hablan*, *comen*) and that you also add an *n* for 'you all'.

Step 13	For 'they', you just add an *n* after *a* or *e* depending on which track you are on.	
	they speak **they** understand	*habl**an*** *comprend**en***
	The same *n* you use for 'they' also goes for 'you all' (you plural).	
	Why don't **you** sell it? Why don't **you** sell it? (talking to several people)	*¿Por qué no lo vend**e**?* *¿Por qué no lo vend**en**?*

Step 14: Teaches that both tracks are the same for 'we' where the *r* is dropped (*hablar*, *comer* and *salir*) and replaced with *mos* (*hablamos*, *comemos* and *salimos*).

Step 14	For 'we' the verb ending is *-mos*. Whenever you want to use 'we', go to the whole verb, drop the *r* and add *-mos*.	
	we speak **we** eat **we** are leaving	*habla**mos*** *come**mos*** *sali**mos***

Step 15: Presents the familiar form of 'you' (to be used with family members and close friends), where *s* is added to either the *a* or *e* in the less familiar form of 'you' depending on the track that you are on (*hablas*, *comes*).

Step 15	In Spanish, you have two words for 'you'. With family members and friends, you may switch from the use of *usted* to *tú*. For *tú* you hook an *s* to *a* or *e* at the end of the verb.	
Less familiar Familiar	Do **you** speak English? Do **you** speak English? (to Roberto or Roberta)	*¿Habl**a** inglés?* *¿Habl**as** inglés?*
Less familiar Familiar	Do **you** eat? Do **you** eat? (to Roberto or Roberta)	*¿Com**e**?* *¿Com**es**?*

Step 16: Introduces some exceptions to the general rules for expressing the 'I' form (see steps 1, 2 and 12) that are discussed in more detail in Chapter 10 on teaching concepts.

Step 16	There are only a few exceptions in the entire Spanish language where you do not have a clear *o* for the 'I' form. There are four exceptions where you have *oy* instead of *o*.	
	I am going **I** am (from *estar*) **I** am (from *ser*) **I** give	v**oy** est**oy** s**oy** d**oy**
	One exception where there is no *o* at all for the 'I' form is the verb 'to know'.	
	I know	s**é**
	The go-go verbs: some verbs add a *g* before the *o* in the 'I' form (see step 18).	
	I come **I**'m leaving **I** put **I** suppose	ven**go** sal**go** pon**go** supon**go**
	'to do' and 'to say' are short go-go verbs.	
	to do to say / to tell **I** do **I** tell	*hacer* *decir* ha**go** di**go**

Step 17: Shows how knowledge of 'you' singular endings on both tracks is used to form the 'imperative' or the 'command' form (replace *a* with *e* on the -*ar* track and the *e* with *a* on the -*er*/-*ir* track).

Step 17	If you switch tracks in the present tense (from *a* to *e* or *e* to *a*), that gives you the imperative (the command).	
	Speak Spanish with me! Buy the book!	¡Habl**e** español conmigo! ¡Compr**e** el libro!

Steps 9 to 17 explain how the majority of verbs are used in the present tense. There are of course a small number of exceptions but Michel only discusses these after the standard form has been introduced, usually through the principle of minimal differences (which is explained in Chapter 10). However, before considering Michel's use of this principle it should be noted that students are told very early in the Spanish course that a verb ending in *o* expresses 'I'. They learn that there is no need to insert the Spanish for 'I' (*yo*) when saying for example 'I have' (*yo hablo*) as the verb ending denotes 'I'. *Yo* is generally reserved for emphasis, for example as in 'I am sorry'. They are not given a broader explanation of the various verb tracks, *-ar / -er / -ir*, and their significance until much later in the course.

Step 18: Two verbs that students learn in the 'I' form at an early stage are *tengo* ('I have') and *puedo* ('I can'). Step 18 teaches more about the verb 'to have' (*tener*). Michel explains that the 'I' form, *tengo* reflects a pattern seen with several other verbs (see step 16 and the 'go-go' verbs). Strictly speaking, given the general rule explained above in steps 1, 2 and 12, 'I have' should be *teno*. However, it is not and instead the letter *g* has been inserted before the *o* to give *tengo*. The verbs introduced in step 16 (for example, *venir* (to come), *salir* (to leave) and *poner* (to put)) follow the same pattern. In each case the 'I' form should have been *veno, salo* and *pono* instead of which they are actually, *vengo, salgo,* and *pongo*. Michel calls these the 'go-go' verbs to help students to remember that the 'I' form ends with *go* instead of the usual *o*.

Step 18	I have	ten**go**
	'go-go' verbs: some verbs add a *g* before the *o* in the 'I' form.	
	I come I'm leaving I put I suppose	ven**go** sal**go** pon**go** supon**go**

Step 19: There is another unusual feature of *tener* which runs counter to our expectations given the general rules that are taught. The singular 'you' form should be *tene* but instead it is *tiene*. Those who have listened to any of the courses will be aware of Michel's focus on correct pronunciation; vital meaning is conveyed through how words

are pronounced and whether or not syllables are stressed. In Spanish, in the majority of instances the only permissible stress occurs on the penultimate syllable. There are exceptions which Michel covers (and are discussed in Chapter 12 in connection with the use of analogies to correct errors) but by and large the stress occurs on the penultimate syllable. So the stress should have occurred on the initial *e*, in *tene*. Michel explains how the *e* becomes *ie* (*tiene*) through creating the image of the *e* 'caving in' or 'splitting' when stressed and becoming *ie* under pressure.

Step 19	e in the second syllable before last (*tener*) becomes *ie* (*tiene*) when you push down in the present tense, except in the 'I' form (*tengo*).	
	to have	*tener*
	we have	*tenemos*
	you have	**tie**ne
	they have	**tie**nen
	you have (Roberto)	**tie**nes
	I have	*tengo*

Step 20: Explains how a similar process occurs with the following verbs: *venir* (to come), *querer* (to want) and *poder* (to be able). The 'I' form of *poder* should have been *pode*. However, Michel again uses the image of a letter 'caving in' when stressed to explain how *o* in the syllable before last in *poder* becomes *puedo*. In this case the *o* caves in to become *ue*. The same also happens with *puede* (you can) which should have been *pode* had the *o* not 'caved in'. Step 20 also explains that the *e* in *comprender* is locked between *r* and *n* and supports the *e* so it does not 'cave in'.

Step 20	**to** come **we** are coming **he** is coming **they** are coming **you** are coming (Roberto) **I** am coming	*venir* *venimos* *viene* *vienen* *vienes* *vengo*
	If you see *ie* in the present tense, you can deduce that the 'to' form is formed with e.	
	I want **you** want / **he** wants **they** want **you** want (Roberto / Roberta) **you** all want **to** want **we** want	*quiero* *quiere* *quieren* *quieres* *quieren* *querer* *queremos*
	o in the syllable before last becomes *ue* when you push down in the present tense.	
	I can **you** can / **he** can **they** can / **you** all can **you** can (Roberto / Roberta) **to** be able (can) **we** can **to** understand	*puedo* *puede* *pueden* *puedes* *poder* *podemos* *comprender*
	In *comprender*, the e is locked between r and n. This supports the e and it does not cave in (*comprende*, not *compriende*)	

SEPARATE SIMILAR SKILLS

The fourth sequencing guideline relates to ways in which similar items are best presented to minimise confusion should they look or sound the same. Michel Thomas skillfully negotiates this area and reflects many of the criteria specified by Engelmann and Carnine in *Theory of Instruction* for teaching skills and concepts. One of the most important principles is to separate items that are in some ways similar. This rarely happens in practice. For example, as mentioned earlier in the chapter, the majority of children are introduced to letters in an alphabetic sequence when they are taught to associate sounds with letters. However, this means that a number of letters that are frequently confused appear together e.g. b / d, m / n, e / i, u / v / w.

As a result, Carnine and his colleagues in *Direct Instruction Reading* proposed an alternative frequency-based sequence for introducing letter sounds (see the sequence on p 128). This order also reflects a desire to separate the items that are most readily confused: b / d are separated by eight letters, m / n by 14 letters, e / i also by 14 letters and u / v / w by five and three respectively.

Throughout his courses Michel Thomas adheres to this principle and separates items that are most likely to be confused. Some of the most obvious examples are presented in the next chapter on 'Teaching concepts'. In general, Michel presents examples that are consistent with a rule before introducing exceptions. Earlier in this chapter the steps involved in teaching Spanish verbs in the present tense were summarised. Step 12 explains that irrespective of whether a verb is on the *-ar* or *-er / -ir* track, the 'I' form ends in *o*. It is not until much later (and only after the rule has been practised and completely mastered) that the small number of exceptions are introduced.

The same happens with the 'you' form of verbs that are on the two tracks. Verbs on the *-ar* track end in *a* and verbs on the *-er / -ir* track end in *e*. This is introduced in step 12 but it is not until step 17 that Michel explains that if these endings are switched (i.e. ending a verb on the *-ar* track with *e* in the 'you' form or a verb on the *-er / -ir* track ending in *a*) a listener would infer that the imperative is being used and that a command is being given. In the French course students are taught that the 'you' form (singular) of a verb always sounds like the 'I' form although the spellings are a little different. After this has been well established students are then presented with exceptions.

It needs to be remembered when looking at the way skills are sequenced that Michel Thomas was trying to answer the question, 'What is the most effective way to teach foreign languages?' This means that what is taught has to first of all help the students learn more quickly than if left to their own devices, and secondly it has to make the teaching process as explicit as possible. Students are not left in the dark and were they to ask 'why are you teaching this?', there would be a clear rationale and explanation. Whenever students confuse things that they are learning it is usually the direct result of teaching them together. Michel found a way of addressing this problem through separating potentially confusing items.

SUMMARY

This chapter has discussed how best to structure instructional sequences. Four guidelines were introduced and examples presented of how Michel Thomas used them to develop his teaching courses. They are (i) teach what is most useful, (ii) teach only one thing at a time, (iii) teach easier items before more difficult ones and (iv) separate similar skills that are likely to be confused.

CHAPTER 10

TEACHING CONCEPTS

OVERVIEW

Chapter 9 highlighted how Michel Thomas decided what to teach. A critical feature of the instructional sequences used is the focus on teaching core concepts to students that enable them to generalise from specific instances to any number of similar examples. This chapter describes how Michel Thomas goes about teaching concepts.

Doug Carnine and Wes Becker published a seminal article in 1982 in the journal *Educational Psychology* entitled 'Theory of Instruction: Generalisation issues.' They were interested in providing a logical analysis for teaching students how to generalise based on the 'sameness' and 'difference' of certain examples. The ideas presented in the article are drawn from the *Theory of Instruction*, by Engelmann and Carnine, the most comprehensive analysis of concept teaching and the instructional process written to date. It is highly unlikely that Michel Thomas consulted either of these two publications and yet his teaching approaches embody the crucial instructional principles described by Engelmann, Carnine and Becker.

Children's conceptual learning commences before they start school, and the rate at which new knowledge is acquired is staggering. We are aware of the occasional errors such as the over-generalisations of the young child who calls all men 'daddy', all women 'mummy' or all four-legged animals 'dog'. However, these are quickly self-corrected with gentle guidance from parents and carers. Learning of this type occurs naturally and does not require any direct, formal input. Michel, and all teachers, have a very different task. What they are teaching would not be learned naturally and is dependent on expert intervention so that new concepts are mastered quickly and are not confused with other, similar concepts.

Engelmann and his colleagues, just like Michel Thomas, were striving for errorless learning so that mastery of new concepts was almost guaranteed when teaching programmes were structured and sequenced in the appropriate way. For example, tables come in all shapes and sizes. However, when we go into a furniture store we have no difficulty in giving them all the same label. We rarely confuse tables with other similar objects with four legs such as chairs or stools. The task faced by the teacher wanting to teach the concept of a table is to identify those elements of different tables which are the same and devise a teaching programme that makes these features absolutely clear to the learner. A key aspect of this approach is not only demonstrating what a table is but also showing students what a table is *not*. Thus, the use of positive and negative examples is crucial in concept teaching, and is equally a notable, and very powerful, feature of Michel's teaching programmes.

TEACHING CONCEPTS THROUGH POSITIVE AND NEGATIVE EXAMPLES

Before looking at how the use of positive and negative examples were utilised by Michel Thomas in teaching foreign languages, let's imagine that you want to teach a young child the concept 'over'. The goal is to devise a way of teaching 'over' so that it is consistent with one, and only one, interpretation and gives the child all the information that he needs in order for him to generalise his learning to other contexts. Figure 10.1 gives one possible sequence of steps for introducing the concept 'over'. It shows five examples of where a ball was displayed in relation to a table. Each time the teacher said, 'this is an example of "over"'.

Figure 10.1 Teaching the concept 'over': positive examples

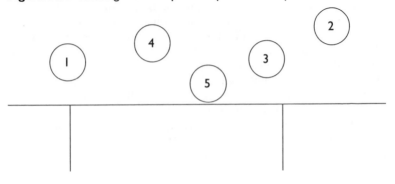

The next sequence of examples has to illustrate 'not over' so that the positive examples shown in figure 10.1 can be contrasted with negative ones. The question is where should the teacher place the ball (example 6) to illustrate that it is 'not over' in a maximally efficient way? Figure 10.2 shows a number of potential options. In these examples care has been taken to ensure that there is no ambiguity and that the ball is definitely 'not over' the table by placing it either well to the left or to the right or under the table. Which position or positions would be optimal?

Figure 10.2 Teaching the concept 'over': negative examples

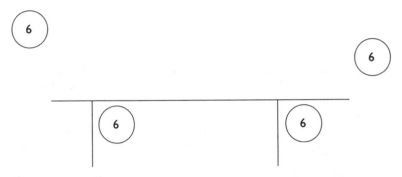

In fact none of these options is ideal. Figure 10.3 displays four alternative, and potentially optimal positions to place the ball. Each illustration reflects the juxtaposition of examples 5 and 6 and demonstrates the principle of minimal difference. Example 5 is 'over' and example 6 is 'not over' and the difference in each instance between 5 and 6 is as small as it possibly can be. The two central examples illustrate 5 as 'over' but in these instances the minimal difference has positioned 6 as 'not over' when the example is either 'on' the table or alternatively 'under' the table. (The teacher would continue to refer to example 6 as 'not over' until both 'on' and 'under' have been taught.) The examples to the left and right of the table show two further instances of over and not over which demonstrate a minimal difference.

Figure 10.3 Teaching 'over' and 'not over' through the principle of minimal differences

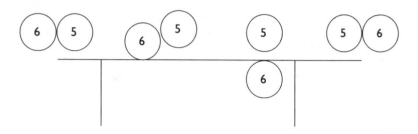

Figure 10.4 opposite shows that when presenting further examples (7–16) of 'over' (where example 7 is 'over' and minimally different from example 6 which is 'not over' in Figure 10.3) the teacher presents as wide a range of positive instances as possible where the ball is over the table. Sometimes the ball will be well above the table (e.g. 8, 9), other times it will be as low as possible, but without being 'on' the table (e.g. 7, 12, 15) and yet in other examples it will be either well to the left (e.g. 10, 12) or to the right (e.g. 9, 15). The student is effectively being shown the parameters of being 'over' the table. It does not matter how high or low the ball is or whether it is to the left or right of the table, the ball can still be categorised as 'over'.

Figure 10.4 Exaggerate the similarities

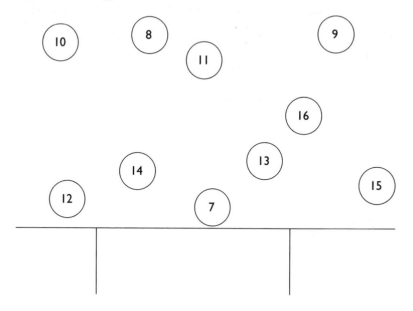

Figure 10.5 shows a further illustration of the concept of a minimal difference when switching from an example of 'over' (17) to 'not over' (18).

Figure 10.5 Switching from 'over' to 'not over'

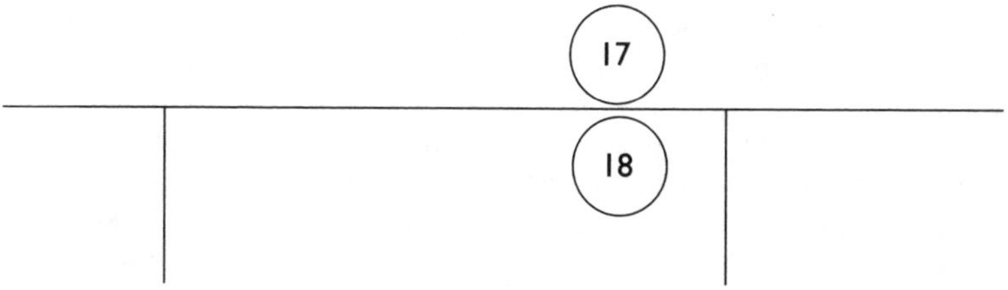

Figure 10.6 shows the parameters of 'not over' (examples 18–26) which illustrate that the position of the ball is immaterial as long as it is 'not over'. For example, it could be below the table (e.g. 18, 20, 23, 24, 25) or to the left (e.g. 19, 22) or right (e.g. 21, 26) of the table. What is important is that the ball is placed in a wide variety of positions which can all be categorised as 'not over'.

Figure 10.6 Exaggerate the differences

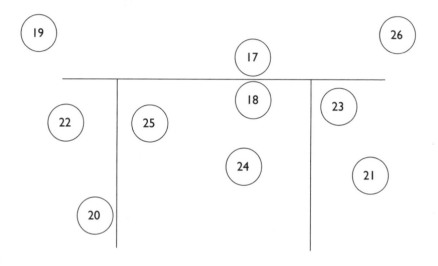

Showing a range of positive examples, using the principle of minimal differences to switch from a positive to a negative example (and vice versa) and showing a wide range of negative positions that are not instances of the concept being taught, all contribute to the presentation being consistent with only one interpretation. This increases the likelihood of the concept being taught successfully. Learning is also made much easier when the same object is used in all the examples. If the concept of 'over' was illustrated with different objects it would be much harder for students to identify the significant part of the presentation and work out what was being taught. Typically, teachers provide positive examples of concepts being taught but invariably neglect to show negative examples that do not illustrate the concept. When they do, it is *not* through the principle of minimal difference and so the boundaries of any concept are not made sufficiently explicit for generalisation to be guaranteed.

TEACHING CONCEPTS THROUGH MINIMAL DIFFERENCES

A major problem for students learning any subject is how to deal with information that appears very similar but is in fact different. Typically, items that are most likely to be mixed up are presented together which increases, rather than decreases, the likelihood of them being confused. This chapter has introduced the theoretical basis for teaching concepts through the principle of minimal differences which involves showing a wide range of positive and negative examples and minimising the difference when switching between the two.

Chapter 9 introduced an order for teaching letter sounds based on their frequency of occurrence in written English (a, m, t, s, i, f, d, r, o, g, l, h, u, c, b, n, k, v, e, p, w, j, y, x, q, z). This order also separates those items that are potentially confusing because they look (b, d, g, h, q, p) or sound (m, n) the same. The most effective way of teaching these letters and the sounds that they represent is through the concept of minimal differences. Many young children confuse 'b' and 'd' when reading and writing. Using the above sequence children would know 14 letter sounds (a, m, t, s, i, f, d, r, o, g, l, h, u, c) by the time they are taught 'b'. The concept of minimal differences would then be used to teach 'b' alongside the letter sounds with which it is invariably confused, 'd', 'g', and 'h'. The following presentations would gradually make the difference between 'b' and the letters it was presented alongside increasingly similar.

Presentation 1: The letter 'b' is presented frequently and initially alongside those letters which are not similar: b, m, b, s, b, f, o, b, b.

Presentation 2: Introduces letters which are more similar to 'b', namely 'h' and 'g'. The sequence might be: b, b, h, g, b, g, b, h, b, b, g, b.

Presentation 3: Introduces 'p' and 'd' which are probably most similar, and therefore minimally different from 'b'. The sequence might well be: b, b, d, p, b, p, b, d, b, b, p, b.

MICHEL THOMAS'S USE OF POSITIVE AND NEGATIVE EXAMPLES TO TEACH VERBS

Within instructional psychology concepts are taught through showing positive and negative examples. We can see how Michel

Thomas does the same and exploits the principle of minimal differences to clarify and contrast the two forms of the verb 'to be' in Spanish. In some instances the verb used is *estar* and on other occasions *ser*. 'I am' is first introduced in Recording 2, Track 8 as *estoy* which is derived from *estar*. It is not until Recording 3, Track 5 that *soy* is introduced which is the alternative form of 'I am' derived from *ser*. Michel Thomas explains that *estar* expresses temporary states such as how you might be feeling at any moment in time, for example, 'I am happy, tired', etc. It does not express permanent characteristics which is achieved through *ser*, as in 'I am a doctor'. In general, Michel separates teaching two or more concepts that are similar. In course guides for GCSE students, as will be discussed in Part 4, they are invariably presented together. Steps 1–7 give a range of instances and examples of how to teach the verb *estar*.

Step 1: Introduces 'I am' (*estoy*) and 'I am not' (*no estoy*). Note the adjective ending changes for males (*-o*) and females (*-a*).

Step 1	I am	estoy
	occupied / busy	ocupado
	I am busy. (masculine)	Estoy ocupad**o**.
	I am busy. (feminine)	Estoy ocupad**a**.
	tired	cansad**o** / cansad**a**
	I am tired. (masculine)	Estoy cansad**o**.
	I am tired. (feminine)	Estoy cansad**a**.
	I am not very busy today. (feminine)	No estoy muy ocupad**a** hoy.
	I am not very busy today. (masculine)	No estoy muy ocupad**o** hoy.

Step 2: Introduces 'you are' (*está*), the question 'are you?' (*¿está?*) and the verb 'to be' (*estar*).

Step 2	you are	está
	You are busy.	Está ocupad**o**.
	Are you busy now? (feminine)	¿Está ocupad**a** ahora?
	Are you busy now? (masculine)	¿Está ocupad**o** ahora?
	to be	estar

Step 3: Introduces how to use 'where' with *estar* to ask a question.

Step 3	Where are you now? How? How are you?	¿Dónde está ahora? ¿Cómo? ¿Cómo está?

Step 4: Revisits step 2 to give students another opportunity to practise asking questions.

Step 4	Are you tired? (masculine) Are you tired? (feminine)	¿Está cansad**o**? ¿Está cansad**a**?

Step 5: Develops step 2, this time asking questions with a pronoun (he / she).

Step 5	Where are you? Where is he? Where is she?	¿Dónde está usted? ¿Dónde está él? ¿Dónde está ella?

Step 6: Shows how to construct a sentence in the future tense with *estar* ('to be').

Step 6	He is going to be here soon. She is going to be here soon.	(Él) va a estar aquí pronto. (Ella) va a estar aquí pronto.

Step 7: Revisits and revises previous steps to give students further practice in the use of *estar*.

Step 7	ready I am ready. I am ready. (feminine) Are you ready? (feminine) Are you ready? (masculine) He is ready. She is ready. Everything is ready.	listo Estoy list**o**. Estoy list**a**. ¿Está list**a**? ¿Está list**o**? Él está list**o**. Ella está list**a**. Todo está list**o**.

MICHEL THOMAS'S USE OF THE PRINCIPLE OF MINIMAL DIFFERENCES TO TEACH ESTAR AND SER (IN SPANISH)

Table 10.1 introduces the alternative verb for 'I am', *ser*. Examples 1–3 compare *estar* and *ser* through the principle of minimal differences. The only difference between the two sentences given in each example is that the verb is either *está* to express a temporary characteristic or *es* which expresses a permanent state. Example 4 gives further instances of how to use *ser*.

Table 10.1 Teaching *estar* and *ser* through the concept of minimal differences

	Estar		Ser	
Definition	*estar* expresses 'to be' as a state of being: how one is, where one is, not permanent characteristics.		*ser* expresses permanent characteristics: who one is or what one is.	
Example 1	He (Pablo) is sick today.	*Pablo está enfermo hoy.*	He (Pablo) is a sick person.	*Pablo es enfermo.*
Example 2	Pablo is drunk.	*Pablo está borracho.*	Pablo is a drunk.	*Pablo es borracho.*
Example 3	He (Pablo) is well dressed today.	*Pablo está bien vestido hoy.*	Pablo is always well dressed.	*Pablo es bien vestido.*
Example 4			I am a professor. I am clever. He is clever. She is clever.	*Soy profesor. Soy listo. Él es listo. Ella es lista.*

The use of positive and negative examples and the principle of minimal differences is widely used throughout the courses but to particularly good effect when teaching students about verbs. Initially students are taught to express the 'I' and 'you' forms of a relatively small number of verbs (positive examples) but crucially they are *not* taught the infinitive of these verbs. Equally, students are not made aware of the general rule governing verb endings in the 'I' form until they are over four hours into the course. Students are then taught that in Spanish verbs have one of three endings, *-ar*, *-er* and *-ir* which are split into two tracks, the *-ar* track and the *-er / -ir* track. They are then taught that in both tracks the 'I' form ends with an *o*. However, there are a number of exceptions to this general rule (i.e. negative examples) which can be placed in one of three categories, which

Michel teaches through the principle of minimal differences.

- The first category has four exceptions which end in *oy* instead of *o*. 'I am going' (*voy*), 'I am' (*estoy*), 'I am' (from *ser – soy*) and 'I give' (*doy*).
- The second category is where the 'I' form is not derived directly from the infinitive (i.e. drop the *ar*, *ir* or *er* and add *o*), verbs that Michel refers to as the 'go-go' verbs. A *g* is inserted before the *o* in the 'I' form, for example *vengo* (I come), *salgo* (I leave), *pongo* (I put), *hago* (I do), *digo* (I tell) and *tengo* (I have).
- The third category has just one exception where there is no *o* at all in the 'I' form. This is the verb 'to know' (*saber*), where 'I know' is *sé*.

The first two categories represent a minimal difference between the usual way of forming the first person singular and the exceptions. The third category does not represent a minimal difference and is in fact introduced early in the Spanish course before the exceptions from the first two categories and before the students are given the general rule about expressing the 'I' form of any verb.

TEACHING PRONOUNS THROUGH MINIMAL DIFFERENCES

Another effective illustration of the use of minimal differences is in the teaching of pronouns. Very early in the course (after approximately 15 minutes) students are introduced to the Spanish for 'I have' (*tengo*) and 'it' (*lo*). Table 10.2 overleaf shows the way in which Michel Thomas teaches pronouns.

In sentences with a single verb in the present tense pronouns always precede the verb.

Steps 1–3: Give examples of the use of 'it' (*lo*) with three different verbs *tengo* (I have), *quiero* (I want), *necesito* (I need).

Step 4: Shows how the pronoun 'it' is used in a single sentence with two verbs. Step 4 combines what was taught in step 2, 'I want it' (*lo quiero*) and step 3 'I don't need it' (*no lo necesito*). The minimal difference involves connecting the two previously introduced phrases with 'but' (*pero*) which was taught earlier, and adding 'now' (*ahora*) at the end of the sentence.

Step 5: Indicates that the relationship between pronoun and verb is the same when a question is asked. The first example in step 5 takes

Table 10.2 Steps through which pronouns are taught in Spanish

Step 1	Students already know 'I have' (tengo) and 'I don't have' (no tengo). They are shown the position of the pronoun in each phrase.	
	I have	*tengo*
	I don't have	*no tengo*
	I have **it**.	**Lo** *tengo.*
	I don't have **it**.	*No* **lo** *tengo.*
Step 2	Demonstrates the same principle as step 1 with another verb.	
	I want	*quiero*
	I want **it**.	**Lo** *quiero.*
	I don't want **it**.	*No* **lo** *quiero.*
Step 3	Demonstrates the same principles as steps 1 and 2 with another verb.	
	I need	*necesito*
	I need **it**.	**Lo** *necesito.*
	I don't need **it**.	*No* **lo** *necesito.*
Step 4	Introduces 'now' and shows how the pronoun 'it' is used in a single sentence with two verbs.	
	now	*ahora*
	I want **it** but I don't need **it** now.	**Lo** *quiero pero no* **lo** *necesito ahora.*
Step 5	Shows that the position of pronoun is the same in the 'you' form, and for questions.	
	You have **it**.	**Lo** *tiene.*
	Do you have **it**?	*¿***Lo** *tiene?*
	You don't have **it**.	*No* **lo** *tiene.*
	Don't you have **it**?	*¿No* **lo** *tiene?*
	Don't you have **it** for me now?	*¿No* **lo** *tiene para mí ahora?*
Step 6	Position of pronoun shown with a verb in 'to' form. The position of pronoun changes and is 'hooked' on to the infinitive.	
	to see	*ver*
	to see **it**	*ver***lo**
	I want to see **it**.	*Quiero ver***lo.**
	I don't want to see **it**.	*No quiero ver***lo.**
Step 7	A further example of the position of a pronoun shown with two consecutive verbs.	
	I can	*puedo*
	you can	*puede*
	You cannot see **it**.	*No puede ver***lo.**
Step 8	A further example demonstrating use of a pronoun with two consecutive verbs.	
	to do / to make	*hacer*
	to do **it**	*hacer***lo**
	I don't want to do **it**.	*No quiero hacer***lo.**

previously taught information 'you have' (*tiene*) and inserts a pronoun 'you have it' (*lo tiene*). The next example turns 'you have it', through a minimal difference, into a question, 'Do you have it?' (*¿Lo tiene?*). Step 5 continues with further examples illustrating the 'you' form and 'negative'.

Steps 6–8: Demonstrate how a pronoun is used in a phrase with a single verb in the infinitive (to see – *ver*) or in a sentence when there are two consecutive verbs and where the second verb is the infinitive. In each case the pronoun is 'hooked' on to the infinitive. This sequence of steps illustrates how a concept is introduced through examples and is then followed by further examples which differ minimally from the previous one. In step 6 the first verb is the 'I' form and in step 7 it is the 'you' form. Step 8 repeats step 6 with a different verb. Only one thing changes from one step to the next.

TEACHING ADJECTIVES THROUGH MINIMAL DIFFERENCES

A final illustration of Michel Thomas's use of the concept of minimal differences is how he teaches students learning French that the ending of adjectives is determined by the gender of the noun. However, the starting point for teaching this is the general rule that the consonant at the end of a word in French is not pronounced unless it is followed by an *e*. Students are then given a number of examples which follow this rule, *restaurant, trop* (too), and *tard* (late). The next examples illustrate a minimal difference and teach *grand–grande* (big) and *petit–petite* (small) before giving an example of a word ending in *e* where the final consonant *is* pronounced, *vite* (fast).

Overall the key to Michel Thomas's use of positive and negative examples and the principle of minimal differences lies in the way that he teaches one concept first, until it has been mastered, before introducing exceptions and making the difference as small as possible. Everyone teaching foreign languages teaches the same things as Michel, the critical difference is in the way that concepts and examples are sequenced.

PERSONALITY THEORY AND THE ROLE OF OPPOSITES

There is another instance of a psychologist building a theory around opposites and positive and negative examples. However, it is not to be found in the literature on teaching reading, maths, foreign languages or any other subjects. Instead it was one of the defining features of George Kelly's 'Theory of personal constructs'. It is relevant to an understanding of the way Michel Thomas taught foreign languages because of the insights it offers into the way that we use language. The views of a number of Michel Thomas's critics are discussed at various points during this book. Kelly's 'Theory of personal constructs' helps to clarify whether the criticisms are saying anything about Michel's philosophy or teaching methodology or actually revealing more about the views and beliefs of those voicing their concerns. Part 4 of this book discusses currently accepted methods for teaching foreign languages. The way views are expressed reveal as much about their proponents' attitudes and beliefs as they do about students, the nature of teaching and learning, and how to teach languages.

Kelly was interested in how we make sense of the world and generate hypotheses and predictions about the behaviour of others. He offered a conceptual framework through which our perceptions could be understood and suggested that we view the world through what he called 'constructs'. These are the templates through which we observe life and can be thought of as a series of continua which incorporate and reflect our most important attitudes and values. The constructs are expressed through statements which reflect opposite ends of a continuum.

For example, think of how you might describe your best friends. You might say they are attractive, intelligent, happy, sensitive, humorous or thoughtful. For Kelly, descriptions such as these were not entirely complete. He felt they were only half the story and that it was only possible to fully understand the meaning of someone else's constructs through also knowing the opposite of these descriptors. For one individual the opposite of 'attractive' might be 'unattractive'. For someone else it might be 'poorly dressed'. Similarly, the opposite of 'intelligent' for some might be 'unintelligent' but for others it could be 'lazy'. Thus, the way we describe others and our lives can be more fully appreciated through these bi-polar statements.

There is one further point to make about Kelly's 'Theory of personal constructs' and its relevance to this book. In Chapter 1 reference was made to family history and the extent to which we might feel accepting or challenged by Michel Thomas's approach to teaching. Kelly's theory complements this idea through suggesting that our use of language reflects our constructs which in turn reflect our attitudes, values and beliefs. For example, the teacher who describes students as 'slow' or 'lacking in ability' or 'able' or 'intelligent' may or may not be telling us something about those students. However, what is unmistakable is that the teacher is telling us something about himself. The teacher is revealing attitudes and beliefs that would make it more difficult for him to be comfortable with Michel Thomas's philosophy. Michel would have seen such descriptors as saying more about how successful or unsuccessful students had been with this particular teacher. Michel would have reinterpreted a teacher's claims that students had failed due to *their* low ability as the teacher admitting that they had failed to teach due to *their* chosen methods being unsuccessful. The way Michel Thomas talked about teaching and the importance of education revealed not just his view on these topics but something much more fundamental about his core beliefs and attitudes.

SUMMARY

This chapter has explained how Michel Thomas teaches concepts through the use of positive and negative examples and the principle of minimal differences. This has been illustrated in relation to verbs, pronouns and adjectives. The chapter concluded with a summary of George Kelly's 'Theory of personal constructs', which also involves the use of positive and negative descriptors to help readers to analyse the language used by Michel Thomas's critics and to appreciate their differing starting points and beliefs about students, teaching, learning and assessment.

CHAPTER 11

DECIDING HOW TO TEACH

OVERVIEW

Chapter 4 summarised the research into how teachers teach. A dichotomy emerged between two styles of teaching. One is where teachers convey knowledge to students directly and explicitly. The other is where teachers take a less direct role and act as facilitators so that students develop their own understandings. Michel Thomas's methodology in fact embraces both approaches depending on what students need to learn next. This chapter relates decisions about how to teach to an instructional hierarchy that indicates that different teaching methods are used at different stages in the teaching and learning process. This is the second stage within the assessment-through-teaching framework described in the introduction to Part 3.

There is a tendency for educationalists to romanticise about the nature of learning and to value certain types of teaching more than others. This was illustrated in Zoë Heller's novel *Notes on a Scandal*. The narrator wrote as follows about teachers, which reflects the traditional and progressive teaching styles described in Chapter 4 and in so doing highlights the enduring tensions between what are perceived to be conflicting educational philosophies:

> Many of the younger teachers harbour secret hope of 'making a difference'. They have all seen the American films in which lovely young women tame inner-city thugs with recitations of Dylan Thomas. They, too, want to conquer their little charges' hearts with poetry and compassion. When I was at teacher training college there was none of this sort of thing. My fellow students and I never thought of raising self-esteem or making dreams come true. Our expectations did

> not go beyond guiding our prospective pupils through the three Rs and providing them with some pointers on personal hygiene. But then it strikes me as not coincidental that in the same period that pedagogical ambitions have become so inflated and grandiose, the standards of basic literacy and numeracy have radically declined. We might not have fretted much about our children's souls in the old days, but we did send them out knowing how to do long division.[1]

In the late 1970s and early 1980s the rhetoric behind child-centred education was always more appealing and persuasive than the dour and systematic vocabulary associated with the structured forms of teaching favoured by Zoë Heller's narrator. Similarly, the way teaching and learning are described by Michel Thomas did not resonate with the educational establishment when academics were approached with a view to researching his methods. For example, in the past, structured approaches to teaching have been described as 'rigid' and 'mean spirited' whereas the more progressive approaches talk about giving students 'choices' and 'responsibility', concepts that are much more warmly welcomed. We admire great works of art, are moved sometimes to tears by certain pieces of music and watch top sports people perform with grace and elegance. We appreciate their natural talents but rarely recognise the hours of relentless practice required to master core artistic, musical or sporting skills to enable them to reach creative heights. We all want learning to be purposeful, stimulating and rewarding. However, there are significant and inevitable periods when these goals are facilitated by something more mundane and routine, but nevertheless essential, and students just have to practise what they have been taught until it is remembered.

The theory underpinning Michel Thomas's philosophy rejects the notion that these educational philosophies are mutually exclusive, instead it embraces the two within the theoretical framework of the 'instructional hierarchy'. The hierarchy provides a template for structuring teaching and learning and emphasises the role of practice and the mastery of core skills and concepts in enabling students to generalise and become creative in how they apply what they have been taught. The mistake is to see practice and creativity as different, representing contrasting beliefs and ideals rather than complementary stages within the same overall process. Students have to be helped to recognise this and it is often down to the teacher to give the less appealing, but absolutely fundamental aspects of teaching an appropriate context and purpose.

THE INSTRUCTIONAL HIERARCHY

The hierarchy was initially proposed in 1978 by two American psychologists, Norris Haring and Marie Eaton.[2] They suggested that there are a series of stages to follow when teaching new skills, knowledge and concepts so that students experience a smooth transition from initially becoming familiar with and acquiring new information, to being able to generalise and apply that information to new and novel contexts. The five stages in the hierarchy are: acquisition, fluency, maintenance, generalisation and application, and they provide a coherent way of describing a teaching process that can be applied to learning any new skill whether it be foreign languages, playing a sport, cooking a new recipe or playing a musical instrument.

For example, a musician must first of all become familiar with, and fluent in playing a new piece of music before being in a position to interpret and improvise. Similarly, new techniques learned when playing any sport have to be mastered and performed automatically, without thinking, before they can be incorporated into a larger repertoire of skills and used spontaneously and to good effect during the course of a game. The instructional hierarchy goes further than describing the transition that the (naïve) learner negotiates to achieve competence; it also identifies the different teaching approaches that accompany and facilitate each stage.

Stage one, 'acquisition', describes the stage how unfamiliar information is first presented where the goal is to become accurate. The second stage, fluency, emphasises the need to perform skills with fluency as well as accuracy. The assumption is that accuracy alone is not sufficient to secure long term retention. A major problem experienced by low-achieving students who are seen to experience difficulties is that even if they become accurate in learning new skills, they are moved on to new tasks before they have had the opportunity to consolidate their knowledge and become fluent.

The fluency building stage, within the terms of reference of the hierarchy, is equivalent to the hours of practice of the musician or sportsman before a big concert or match. It is often the stage of teaching that is omitted as teachers hurry to cover all the topics they have to teach to prepare students for examinations. However, within instructional psychology, fluency is a measure of learning and so we can only really be confident that students will retain what they have learned when they perform skills to high levels of fluency as well as accuracy.

It could certainly be said of Michel Thomas, that as a teacher he was a perfectionist. During the recordings he was unwilling to move on from one task to another or start teaching new skills until both students were ready and he was absolutely sure that they had learned what had gone before. He gave considerable opportunities to practise new skills to reach high fluency levels and so reduce the likelihood of them forgetting.

The third stage in the hierarchy, 'maintenance,' describes the phase in learning when a skill can still be performed in the absence of any further teaching. It is the point where fluency levels are maintained without any additional direct help. It is equivalent to the state reached when you never forget how to swim or ride a bicycle. It is only after maintenance has been reached that students can progress to generalising and applying their newly acquired skills.

Michel Thomas provides structured opportunities for generalisation, stage 4, which occur when newly learned skills are practised alongside previously taught ones. It is characterised by a significant level of teacher support, guidance and feedback on progress as students discriminate between new and previously acquired skills and knowledge within familiar contexts. Generalisation is perhaps best thought of as equivalent to practising sporting skills during a training session under the watchful eye of a coach who can intervene at any time and give feedback.

'Application' describes the final and fifth stage where students use skills spontaneously in less familiar contexts with less direct support from their teacher. It is like playing a competitive match in a sport where the student is very much on their own and the goal is to apply all that has been practised to a new context. The difference between generalisation and application can be seen as comparable to the difference between the concert pianist rehearsing with a conductor and orchestra (generalisation) and the performance itself (application).

Much of Michel Thomas's teaching is based on a teaching strategy that is linked to the instructional hierarchy, and is widely used within instructional psychology, known as 'model-lead-test' but which is often rephrased as 'my turn', 'together', and 'your turn'. In other words, the teacher provides a model ('my turn'), teachers and students have a go together ('together') before students finally have a go on their own ('your turn'). During the acquisition and generalisation stages of the instructional hierarchy the focus tends to be on all three steps in the sequence, 'my turn', 'together' and 'your turn', whereas fluency building and application are exclusively concerned with 'your turn'. Michel makes full use of this teaching approach without ever labelling it as such. He invariably models how to pronounce and use a new grammatical structure or vocabulary before giving students opportunities to practise with him (i.e. when longer sentences are broken down into smaller components). He then lets them have a go on their own and always leaves students with an accurate model after they have attempted a translation.

MICHEL THOMAS'S APPLICATION OF THE INSTRUCTIONAL HIERARCHY

Acquisition

Michel uses a general strategy (see also the section on generalisation) to teach skills to accuracy, which was illustrated in Chapters 9 and 10. There are six steps in the sequence: (i) teach students to use a skill without any explanation; (ii) provide an explanation, rationale or rule for the use of the skill; (iii) teach the skill further with more examples; (iv) introduce exceptions to the rule; (v) teach exceptions through the principle of minimal differences and (vi) show more negative examples. Once skills have been taught to accuracy Michel Thomas provides additional practice through the process of interleaved learning (see Chapter 8), ensuring that what has been taught is revised on a regular basis, which contributes to fluency building and helps to maintain accuracy levels.

Building fluency: Practice makes perfect

The role of practice in the creative process was tellingly revealed by Gary Player, a well known golfer in the 1960s, 70s and 80s, who was a contemporary of Arnold Palmer and Jack Nicklaus and was renowned for his hours of dedicated practice. On one occasion, after a particularly good round of golf when everything seemed to go well he commented in response to a question about the reasons for his success, 'the more I practise the luckier I get'. The same could be said of various other sports people regularly in the public eye. David Beckham, the footballer, and renowned free kick specialist has frequently talked about the endless hours of practice involved in learning to position and bend a football with such skill and artistry. Similarly, the rugby union player Jonny Wilkinson sensationally kicked the winning drop goal in the dying seconds of the 2003 Rugby Union World Cup. It was a supreme moment of sporting drama. It happened in a split second and looked effortless. However, the simplicity of the kick and its elegant execution belied the hundreds of hours that Wilkinson spent practising. His training sessions are legendary. After his team mates had long since gone home he would stay behind to practise his kicking. He would not leave until he had kicked ten successive goals, and frequently stayed late into the night until he had achieved his target. It was this dedication and drive that enabled him to make it all look so easy and natural. These sporting examples reflect the thoughts of a primary headteacher who used to remind his staff when they complained that certain children struggled to remember anything that 'constant repetition will penetrate even the "dullest" mind'.

Repetition rather than variety

Various explanations were offered during the 'Language Master' to explain why Michel Thomas's live courses were so successful. Some suggested that it was down to his personality, more specifically his charisma, or as some of the students involved in the programme suggested, his ability 'to read minds' and know exactly what they were thinking. Others attributed the success of the courses to their intensive nature. When this was put to him by the head of French at the school where the documentary was filmed, Michel immediately rejected the suggestion and said instead that it was down to the method. His calm voice, broad smile and confident demeanour implied that this option was rarely contemplated by those speculating on the reasons for their impact.

The head of French in citing the courses' intensive nature as the reason for their success was not totally wide of the mark but not for the reasons she thought. The students were taught intensively over a period of five days, their usual timetable being suspended so that they could devote the entire week to learning French. However, a more significant factor was the opportunities that students had to recall information that they had already learned. When asked about what helps students to learn, teachers invariably refer to whether the teaching methods are interesting, motivating, building on what students already know, or actively engage students in the learning process and offer variety. They rarely if ever mention the number of opportunities that students have to recall what they are learning. Yet psychological research indicates that it is the simple act of frequent recall that is one of the most powerful factors in facilitating students' progress. This is why Michel was so confident that students did not need to do homework or rote learn word lists. He knew that he had given them sufficient practice for the skills, knowledge and concepts that he had taught to be remembered long-term.

One reason why 'interleaving' learning and contextual diversity are so powerful is that they demand that taught information is recalled frequently. They effectively require that what is to be learned is revisited over increasingly long intervals in a variety of contexts. This is a key feature of Michel Thomas's courses where vocabulary and sentence structures introduced at the beginning of the courses keep reappearing. The discussion in Chapter 7 on rational analysis presented evidence that showed that repetition helps us to recognise the importance of what we are learning and that it is worth memorising due to the regularity with which it is recalled.

Teaching students to generalise

Students are taught to generalise in three ways. The first is through the process of interleaved learning (described and illustrated in Chapter 8 on instructional principles), which emphasises the importance of teaching newly acquired skills, knowledge and concepts alongside previously learned information. The second is through applying the instructional principle, 'contextual diversity' (also described and illustrated in Chapter 8) where students are shown how to use what they have learned in different contexts. The third way students are taught to generalise is through the teaching strategies adopted.

Teaching strategies are methods which remain largely the same for teaching different concepts, skills or knowledge. For example, within Direct Instruction the same generalisable strategy is used in maths for teaching students to balance any equation irrespective of whether it involves addition, subtraction, multiplication or division, or whether it is presented horizontally or vertically. Typically, students find multiplication and division equations more difficult than addition or subtraction equations and although they draw on slightly different mathematical knowledge, the overall strategy through which they are taught remains the same within the instructional hierarchy. The strategy is underpinned by the idea that what pupils are being taught is how to balance an equation rather than 'doing sums' or 'finding the answer.' It involves three key steps: (i) knowing the 'equality principle' which states that whatever you have on one side of the equals sign you must end with on the other, (ii) balancing an equation through a series of common steps that apply to any equation, (iii) checking that the equation balances.

Michel Thomas has used a similar approach in his language courses and devised strategies that are equally applicable to teaching Spanish,

French, German and Italian or any language. The strategies are not labelled in this way by Michel but are evident, powerful and frequently offer a stark contrast to conventional language teaching. Michel often teaches students grammatical structures or verb forms to a high degree of fluency before providing a general rule governing their use. Students therefore can often use aspects of a language before they understand how it works.

Previous chapters have already described different generalisable strategies. For example, Chapter 9 described a strategy for teaching verbs and Chapter 10 described strategies for teaching pronouns and adjectives. Table 11.1 shows the strategy for teaching pronouns in Spanish and French. The steps illustrating the strategy are the same for both languages, the only difference being that in Spanish, examples are not given for 'to understand him', 'to understand her' and 'to understand us'. However, through what is covered elsewhere in the Spanish course it is anticipated that students would be able to apply their knowledge of pronouns to translate these phrases. The strategy shown in Table 11.1 for teaching pronouns in Spanish is similar to the one presented in Table 10.2. The difference is that Table 10.2 demonstrates the use of the same pronoun ('it') with five different verbs. Table 11.1 in contrast shows the use of different pronouns with one verb. These two examples of teaching pronouns in Spanish further illustrate the principle of contextual diversity through showing that pronouns are in the same position in sentences with a single verb irrespective of the context.

Table 11.1 Michel Thomas's strategy for teaching pronouns in Spanish and French

English	Spanish	French
to understand	comprender	comprendre
to understand **it**	comprender**lo**	**le** comprendre
to understand **him**		**le** comprendre
to understand **her**		**la** comprendre
to understand **them**	comprender**los**	**les** comprendre
to understand **them** (females)	comprender**las**	
to understand **you**	comprender**le**	**vous** comprendre
I cannot understand **you**.	No puedo comprender**le**.	Je ne peux pas **vous** comprendre.
to understand **us**		**nous** comprendre
to understand **me**	comprender**me**	**me** comprendre
Can you understand **me**?	¿Puede comprender**me**?	Pouvez-vous **me** comprendre?

Chapter 9 showed a sequence through which verbs are taught in Spanish. The following example applies Michel Thomas's strategy to teaching verbs in French. The steps are the same but presented in a slightly different order to take account of the differences between French and Spanish.

Step 1: Illustrates the use of 'it is' (*c'est*) in simple sentences.

Step 1	**It is** possible.	**C'est** *possible.*
	It is comfortable.	**C'est** *confortable.*
	good	*bon*
	It is good.	**C'est** *bon.*
	very	*très*
	It is very good.	**C'est** *très bon.*
	It is very comfortable.	**C'est** *très confortable.*

Step 2: Explains that the 'to' form of a verb is usually expressed in an ending with *-r*. 90% of French verbs end in *-er*.

Step 2	to speak	*parl**er***
	to stay	*rest**er***
	to go	*all**er***
	to come	*ven**ir***
	to leave	*part**ir***
	to know	*sav**oir***
	to have	*av**oir***
	to sell	*vendre*
	to understand	*comprendre*
	to take	*prendre*

Step 3: Explains how to form the first person of a verb. With all *-er* verbs you cut off the *-r* from the infinitive and sound the consonant.

Step 3	**I** am staying.	*Je rest**e**.*
	I'm sorry.	*Je regrett**e**.*
	I am eating.	*Je mang**e**.*
	I am starting.	*Je commenc**e**.*

Step 4: Illustrates that asking questions in French is by inversion.

Step 4	Do you speak? / Are you speaking?	*Parlez-vous?*
	Do you go? / Are you going?	*Allez-vous?*
	Are you waiting?	*Attendez-vous?*

Step 5: Explains how to form the first person of verbs that do not end in *-er* and that you do not sound the consonant. For non *-er* verbs in the first person you have an *-s* ending.

Step 5	to understand	*comprendre*
	I understand	*je comprends*
	I would like	*je voudrais*
	to do	*faire*
	I do / I'm doing	*je fais*

Step 6: Shows that for all verbs, the form for 'he', 'she' and 'it' has the same sound as the 'I' form, but that it has a *t* at the end. For example, for 'he can' think of 'I can'.

Step 6	I can	*je peux* (also see step 8)
	he can	*il peut*
	it can	*ça peut*
	I am doing	*je fais*
	he is doing	*il fait*

Step 7: Explains that the ending for *vous* is *-ez*.

Step 7	you speak	*vous parlez*
	you leave / you are leaving	*vous partez*
	you are staying	*vous restez*

Step 8: Explains that there are only two verbs for which the ending for the first person is *x* not *s*: *pouvoir* and *vouloir*.

Step 8	I can	*je peux*
	I want	*je veux*
	I want it.	*Je le veux.*
	I don't want it.	*Je ne le veux pas.*

Step 9: Explains that the ending for *nous* is *-ons*.

Step 9	we are leaving	*nous partons*
	we are waiting	*nous attendons*
	we speak	*nous parlons*
	we are starting	*nous commençons*

Step 10: Introduces the three exceptions to the rule formerly presented in step 6, that the verb forms for 'he', 'she' and 'it' follow the sound of the 'I' form (although the spelling is different).

Step 10	To make the verb forms for 'he', 'she' and 'it', you follow the sound of 'I' with three exceptions: I am / he is, I have / he has, I'm going / he is going.

Step 11: Presents the rule for verb usage in sentences with two or more consecutive verbs.

Step 11	Whenever you have two or three consecutive verbs, you do not conjugate the second or third verbs. They are always in the infinitive.	
	He must be here soon.	*Il doit être ici bientôt.*

Step 12: Introduces the three one-syllable exceptions to the rule presented in step 7, that the ending for *vous* is *-ez*.

Step 12	The ending for 'you' is always *-ez* with three one-syllable exceptions: *vous êtes* (you are), *vous faites* (you do / make), *vous dites* (you say).	
	you are	*vous êtes*

Step 13: Explains the ending for *ils* is *-ent*.

Step 13	*-ent* at the end of a verb is silent and means 'they'.	
	they are staying	*ils restent*
	they are leaving	*ils partent*
	they are selling	*ils vendent*
	they are waiting	*ils attendent*

Applying what you know

There are a number of ways in which students who have followed one of Michel Thomas's courses can apply and reinforce their knowledge. These involve finding different contexts to use and experience languages through speaking, listening and reading. Although opportunities to speak may not be readily available, all kinds of opportunities exist for listening and reading. Most high street newsagents carry newspapers from European countries and foreign language novels are increasingly available from book stores and over the internet. Satellite television offers European channels and the prospect of hearing foreign language programmes. Films create further chances to translate languages into English with the potential advantage of feedback through subtitles. It should also be acknowledged that there are many other commercial language courses that could be helpful in checking whether what has been learned can be applied. For example, a variety of courses aim to teach those aspects of a foreign language, particularly vocabulary that might be of use to a traveller. It may well be that these are far more useful as follow-up courses once the content of one of Michel's courses has been learned. They do not give the same in depth knowledge of language usage as Michel, but can provide additional vocabulary which could be helpful.

THE ROLE OF QUESTIONS

Questions can be used as a teaching strategy to help to develop students' understanding. Questions that probe and stimulate and which are open-ended and do not imply a correct answer can lead students to think in different ways and evaluate their current knowledge. However, think back to school days and how often you were asked questions where the teacher already knew the answers. Being in the classroom is often like being on the panel of a quiz show where teachers ask all the questions but also know all the answers.

Pupils may or may not know the answers and if the purpose of the questions is to find out what students know, that is fine. However, if the goal is to inform students of something they do not already know then questioning as a methodology is often highly flawed.

There are at least two possible outcomes when teachers ask questions: the worst case scenario is that no one knows the answer resulting in the teacher having to tell the students anyway; the second scenario is that one of the students has a stab at the answer, and although bits of it are close, overall the response is unclear and leaves the children none the wiser. Again, the teacher is left to pick up the pieces and try to provide a coherent answer, as well as clear up any confusion arising from the students' initial attempts.

Michel Thomas illustrated the problem with this approach when asking students to define 'nouns', 'adjectives' and 'verbs'. He knew that the students involved in the recordings would not provide the answer he was looking for. Nouns are not 'a name, place or thing,' (as commonly taught) but any word in front of which you can place the article 'the' (the happiness, the pride, the situation, the condition). Any word in front of which you can place 'am' or 'is' is an adjective (happy, proud) and verbs are not 'actions' but any word in front of which you can place the word 'to' (i.e. to be, to have, to go). Michel did ask the students on the Spanish recordings if they could define nouns, adjectives and verbs but on the French recordings gave the students this information himself. Using questions is not a very effective way of teaching new skills, knowledge or concepts. It is interesting that in all the research on how best to use questions effectively, the focus is always on the questions that teachers ask pupils. To my knowledge there is little research on the questions that students should be encouraged to ask their teacher so that they can feel sure that they have fully understood what is being taught.

MNEMONICS

Mnemonics are words, phrases and rules that help to improve memory through giving learners a quick way of remembering information. For example, young children when learning the colours of the rainbow are taught 'Richard of York gave battle in vain' (red, orange, yellow, green, blue, indigo, violet). When learning to spell, most of us remember the rule 'i' before 'e' except after 'c'. Michel Thomas frequently introduces mnemonics to help students learn useful vocabulary and rules. For example, in the French course Michel introduces the mnemonic CAREFUL to highlight whether consonants at the end of a word are pronounced. The rule is that 'a consonant at the end of a word which is not followed by an *e* is not pronounced with exception of the CAREFUL consonants which are C, R, F and L'. So when words end in *c* (*avec* – 'with') the *c* is pronounced (with the exception of when *c* is preceded by *n* for example, *blanc* – 'white'). Similarly, in words ending in R, F and L the final consonant is pronounced.

A comparable mnemonic is used in Spanish. In general, words that end in a vowel are stressed on the penultimate syllable whereas words that end in a consonant are stressed on the last syllable. However, there are two exceptions to the rule about consonants. Where words end in *n* or *s* the stress appears on the penultimate syllable just like words ending in vowels. Michel Thomas helps students to remember the exceptions through the NOSE rule which draws attention to the consonants *n* and *s*. There are also some exceptions to the NOSE rule that are highlighted (when reading) by an accent over the syllable that is to be stressed (*reservación, condición, posición*).

SUMMARY

This chapter has introduced Haring and Eaton's instructional hierarchy which provides a framework for determining how to teach, as well as demonstrating how different levels of learning are required to enable students to generalise and apply what they learn from one context to another. The chapter also summarised the limitations of using questions as a teaching method whilst acknowledging their role in assessing students' learning. The chapter concluded by referring to Michel Thomas's use of mnemonics as an additional teaching method.

CHAPTER 12

ENGAGING AND ASSESSING STUDENTS' LEARNING

OVERVIEW

This chapter discusses how Michel Thomas engages and motivates students. This is then related to his use of praise and the way students' learning is assessed. This is the third stage in the process of assessment-through-teaching described in the introduction to Part 3.

ENGAGING STUDENTS IN THE TEACHING AND LEARNING PROCESS

In general, most approaches to teaching foreign languages try to find some connection between the students, the languages that are being taught and the countries where they are spoken. School-based language courses for students up to the age of 16 focus on a country's history, culture, people and various themes and topics (e.g. introducing yourself, school subjects and timetables, restaurant language and the weather, directions and places, hotel accommodation and arriving at a campsite, etc.); evening classes often stress conversational skills, and courses for overseas travellers concentrate on the language and scenarios most likely to be needed to survive and get by within a new country. Understandably, it is felt that students will be more motivated when the learning is purposeful and relevant, and it is difficult to argue with this starting point. However, in addition to these established strategies there are numerous other ways of making learning motivating and exciting. Ultimately the difference between Michel Thomas's approach and others is the question he sought to address, 'what is the most effective way to teach?' which opened up alternative ways of thinking about how to make learning relevant and worthwhile.

Christopher Robbins in Michel's biography, *The Test of Courage*, recounts how Michel engaged a group of disaffected eighth-grade students (14 years of age) in the US. The Principal of the school had indicated to Michel that he was interested to know whether he could take a subject that was irrelevant to the pupils, French, and make it relevant. Michel identified three groups within the class that he labelled 'shy', 'indifferent' and 'belligerent'. He focused on the first two groups but largely ignored the third. His strategy was to give students an early sense of achievement by emphasising that they already had a substantial French vocabulary, possibly of over a thousand words, through words that are the same or similar in English and French. Michel's overall approach and emphasis on his role as the teacher and its implications were described by Christopher Robbins:

> No one was ever questioned directly, or allowed to raise his hand. Students were never called on by name but were encouraged through eye contact. If anyone apologised for making a mistake, Michel asked 'Why are you apologising? Why are you concerned? Eliminating mistakes is my problem. Why are you worrying? You are not supposed to know the language yet.' His gentle, continued insistence that he alone was responsible for each student's progress, and his acceptance of blame for all mistakes, led to an immediate reduction in anxiety and tension. He had removed what he describes as 'the terrible burden of expectation'.[1]

Throughout the early stages of teaching, Michel ignored the belligerent group. However, he was aware that he had won over just about everyone else. At the end of the first day he addressed the whole class to make arrangements for the following day absolutely clear:

> I came here to teach. To show you that you can learn. That you can learn anything. If you want me to come back tomorrow I want to know I can teach without disturbances. There are some here because they want to learn. I also notice that some of you are not interested in learning. I feel it is unfair that those who want to learn should be disturbed and interfered with by those who do not. So I am going to separate the class and only teach those who want to learn. Will those who do not want to learn French please raise their hands. Not one hand went up.[1]

During the following days and weeks Michel gradually secured the confidence of the remaining sceptics and built a trusting relationship with all the students. They started to talk about the things that interested them and what they might want to study after leaving school. Students experiencing difficulties in learning to read requested extra sessions, incidences of disruption were non-existent and perhaps most significantly of all, truancy rates showed a dramatic reduction. The teacher evaluating Michel's success with the class of hitherto reluctant, disruptive students wrote:

> He uses no aversive controls, never scolds, never raises his voice, never acts as if he were disappointed in a student's performance, never frowns … The reports I've had from other students convince me that the excitement and satisfaction which I experienced were in no way unusual, but something experienced by virtually all of Mr Thomas's students, whether poorly educated youngsters from the black ghetto or presumably better educated persons with graduate degrees.[1]

This may appear to be an account of an extraordinary teacher with great personal charm engaging a group of largely disaffected and unwilling learners. However, such an explanation fails to acknowledge the core principles of effective behaviour management which underpin Michel Thomas's methods. I have written in *Classroom Management: From Principles to Practice* with my colleague Shirley Bull of the ways in which the behaviour of children can be managed which draw heavily on behavioural psychology, which was introduced in Chapter 7. In summary this involves focusing on students' positive behaviour and the instances where they are ready to learn. All the attention goes to these students. The other, more reluctant learners invariably fall into line, one by one as Michel found, and are encouraged and involved in the lessons. In the end students find that it involves more effort to resist being taught than it is to participate, especially if they can see that their peers are having fun and learning. Michel Thomas had the confidence to hold his nerve when faced with a potentially disruptive element within the class but knew that those students who participated would learn, experience success and find the sessions enjoyable. It is a difficult combination to resist.

Michel Thomas sought to involve students by making learning explicit, successful and enjoyable. Margaret Thompson, the head of French in the school where 'The Language Master' was filmed, commented:

> I think the real lesson is that the sheer interest in learning
> is enough for the students. Knowledge keeps them
> interested. He's really on to something here, something
> very important.[2]

Michel Thomas was able to articulate not only what he was teaching
but *why* he was teaching it so that students would begin to develop
their understanding of the teaching and learning process.

Perhaps the most fundamental and powerful component of Michel
Thomas's approach was the success that students achieved, which in
itself is highly reinforcing and reassuring. Experiencing success has
ramifications that go far beyond the confines of learning a new
language. Chapter 2 referred to the weekly articles in the *Times
Educational Supplement* called 'My Best Teacher' where figures in the
public eye describe the significance of individual teachers in their
careers and lives. Similarly the pupils in 'The Language Master' talked
glowingly and animatedly about what it was like to learn with
Michel. They enthused about how he put them at their ease, how he
never criticised them, how he appeared to 'read their minds', and of
course, how they experienced success. The added appeal of Michel's
approach is that the promise of success was to be achieved without
homework or rote learning which so often characterise teaching and
make it onerous and unappealing.

Michel was reluctant to talk about his method and its origins and
was extremely protective of his work. It is unclear therefore, how he
might have responded to questions about how he chose to engage
students in the teaching and learning process. Nevertheless, it is
evident from the BBC documentary ('The Language Master'), his
biography and published interviews that he sought to involve
students through offering a very different approach to learning to
anything that they were likely to have encountered in the past. The
assumptions he made, his determination to take responsibility for
learning and his analyses of different languages meant that many
potential students were intrigued by his approach and doubts were
generally dispelled once they started the courses.

ASSESSING STUDENTS' LEARNING

Assessing students' learning is the final piece in the instructional
jigsaw. Michel Thomas was able to engage students and keep them
motivated because they experienced immediate success. This could
only be accomplished because he continuously assessed *his* teaching
to check whether students had learned what he intended to teach.

Many students fail to become motivated and enthused by learning as a direct result of how their progress is assessed, particularly where they develop a growing sense that they are not improving. The more formal ways of assessing progress through public examinations were introduced in Chapter 2. However, there are less formal approaches which are critical to Michel's way of teaching. There are effectively three ways in which any student's learning can be interpreted.

The first is to compare students with each other, very much in the manner of a race, and see who is doing best and comes first and also who is doing less well and comes in towards the back of the field or last. The second type of assessment does not involve comparisons with others but seeks to find out what a student can or cannot do. To continue the athletics analogy, this form of assessment attempts to establish whether an athlete can run a given distance within a specified time. For example, can the athlete complete a marathon in under two and a half hours, can the golfer complete a round of golf in under par, can the tennis player serve at over 70 miles an hour, etc. The third form of assessment compares a student's current performance with how they performed in the past, answering the question, 'is the student improving?' However, the mark of improvement is not how they are doing compared to their peers but whether they are improving on their own previous performances. It is the equivalent of seeking a 'personal best time' in athletics or the lowest score for a round of golf, or serving faster than ever before in a tennis match. The first form of assessment is referred to as 'normative', the second as 'criterion-referenced' and the third as 'ipsative'.

Michel Thomas's courses combine criterion-referenced and ipsative assessments. He assesses progress, particularly pronunciation, against generally accepted standards. For example, on the Spanish recordings he gives the two students frequent feedback on the importance of how verbs are pronounced. The rule is, 'There is only one stressed syllable per word in Spanish. When a word ends in a vowel, the stress will usually be on the penultimate syllable, so *importante*. There is a clear criterion and Michel is assessing whether the students can pronounce the words correctly or not, and by 'correctly' he implies that the pronunciation is sufficiently clear to be understood by a Spanish listener. This form of assessment is criterion-referenced. Similarly in French, Michel takes great care and patience to ensure that the students' pronunciation is accurate, particularly when teaching them to use the definite article (*le* or *la*) and indefinite article (*un* and *une*) with nouns.

Michel also uses ipsative assessment in the way that he identifies the appropriate feedback for each student. There are occasions when students make more than one error and what Michel corrects is largely dependent on his perception of their past performance. He corrects what will be most helpful to the student and what he or she needs to improve first. Michel's success as a teacher is in no small part due to his understanding of the teaching and learning process and in-depth knowledge of the languages he is teaching. As a result, when he assesses student responses he knows exactly what the teaching implication is and which aspect of what has been taught needs to be repeated or corrected.

Teachers need to have feedback on whether students are heading in the right direction and the forms of assessment used by Michel provide him with that information. This approach to assessment provides the link between teaching, learning and assessment. They are inextricably related and so in one sense, as far as instructional psychology is concerned, there is no teaching without learning. In other words (as discussed in Chapter 4), teaching is defined, not in terms of what teachers do or how hard they work or how committed they are to their jobs, but only whether students learn as a result of a teacher's input. Within instructional psychology assessment-through-teaching (ATT) is also sometimes known as curriculum-based assessment and both are very similar to the educational approach to assessment known as 'assessment-for-learning'.

What makes Michel Thomas's courses unique is that they try to create for the listeners a sense of what it would be like if they had been taught directly by Michel. The recordings genuinely involved students who had limited knowledge of the languages that they were learning. The only thing about the recordings that was unrealistic was that they took place over a period of a couple of days rather than weeks or months and so do not recreate the kind of time scale available to those actively involved in the courses. The short period over which the recordings were made meant that the rate at which new information was presented was rapid and possibly did not always allow quite sufficient time for appropriate consolidation. The vocabulary introduced in the latter few hours of the recordings will be retained less well by students than that at the beginning of the course, simply because it will have been heard and recalled less frequently.

Many of the mistakes that the two students on each recording made were typical of those that would be made by most students embarking on a new language. Vocabulary and grammar were forgotten, confused and mispronounced, errors familiar to anyone learning a new language. They offer the listener considerable insights into learning languages that are not available through more carefully managed courses where the listener is only ever exposed to 'the correct answers'.

When learning foreign languages through recorded and television courses the complete beginner is usually expected to make progress purely through listening to fluent speakers conversing on a range of topics. It is like asking someone about to learn the piano to listen to a concert pianist and then work out a strategy so that they too could play at a comparable level. Expert performers in any field can inspire and give us a model to which we can aspire but seeing and hearing them perform will not alone be sufficient to help those just starting out.

Michel Thomas's courses give students a front row seat to observe and participate in the teaching and learning process. The student who pauses the recordings, as advised by Michel Thomas, and responds to the prompts will possibly find themselves making the same errors as the participating students. Hearing how errors are corrected is as much a part of the learning process as getting everything right. It has been said at various points during the book that Michel did not take a negative view of errors and mistakes. Far from it, his position was that they can tell you more about the effectiveness of teaching than achieving 100% success. This view was reflected in a message pinned to a school notice board that said 'a mistake is not an error until you refuse to correct it'.

PRAISE AND SUCCESS

A heartening feature of 'The Language Master' was hearing the students talk with such enthusiasm about being taught by Michel Thomas. They had all experienced repeated failure in learning a foreign language but here they were, after only a couple of days providing interim feedback and they could barely contain their excitement. It is personal testimonies such as these that appeared in the documentary, and have accompanied articles about Michel, that give rise to the myth that he is a worker of miracles or that he succeeds through the allure of his personality alone. However, as Michel was always quick to say, his success as a teacher was attributable, purely and simply to the method through which he taught.

Michel's understanding of the role of errors in learning, his focus on his teaching and his in-depth knowledge of languages gave his feedback a highly positive edge. His insistence that he is responsible for students' learning is reassuring and motivating, and it gives students the confidence to 'have a go' without fear of embarrassment or criticism if they make a mistake. Michel's focus on praise and encouragement is planned and targeted and a particular strength of his teaching. Like everything else it did not happen by chance. During the courses Michel constantly provides feedback and says 'right' to students to let them know their response was either correct or good enough.

The use of praise, although widely acknowledged as important, is not always the regular feature of classroom life that might be predicted. Kevin Wheldall from Macquarie University in Sydney, Australia and Frank Merritt from the University of Birmingham in England have conducted numerous studies into teachers' use of praise which they have reported in *Positive Teaching in Secondary Schools (Effective Classroom Behaviour Management)*. They found that when monitored systematically over time in the classroom, teachers used far less praise than they had thought. There was a tendency for teachers to use more praise when students completed work satisfactorily than when they behaved appropriately. Teachers had clear expectations about how students should behave but rarely praised them for doing so. However, as soon as students misbehaved they were reprimanded almost immediately, which often had the unintended effect of giving them attention, which they desired, for doing the wrong rather than right thing. Teachers' unwillingness to use praise is reflected in the comments of Alan Ball, a member of England's World Cup winning team of 1966. He said of his father's response to successes and failures, 'I did not need telling when I had not played as well as I'd have liked: but he told me all the same. I also did not need him to tell me when I'd played well: and he never did.'[3]

It is quite possible that for some readers a lack of success in learning a foreign language in the past correlates highly with low levels of praise, just as it did for the students in 'The Language Master' documentary. As a result, Michel's use of praise and his desire to develop a positive learning environment will not have been everyone's experience of school life. This may lead some to misinterpret Michel's encouragement and feedback and relate any success they may have in following his courses to his personality, patience and encouraging nature, rather than his well-designed and presented teaching strategies.

MICHEL THOMAS'S VIEW OF ERRORS

There are two ways of looking at errors. The one that instinctively comes to mind is that they reflect on a student's capacity to learn. Within this scenario errors indicate that the student was not able to learn what had been presented and are associated with teachers' familiar cries of frustration from the classroom such as, 'Why don't you listen?', or 'How many times do I have to tell you?' A teacher may feel that the student needs more time to practise but ultimately errors are interpreted in terms of what they say about how students are learning. The alternative is to see errors in relation to how effectively teachers are teaching.

The real significance of Michel Thomas's acceptance of student learning being *his* responsibility is that failure leads straight back to an analysis of the way students have been taught, rather than the suggestion that a student has a difficulty in learning. The next step in the 'students has failed' narrative is to try to find a cause of the difficulty rather than critically evaluating the teaching methodology with a view to identifying any flaws and making appropriate adjustments. Michel interpreted every student error as *his* error, every mispronunciation as *his* mispronunciation and every failure as *his* failure. Rather than thinking such students were not very talented linguists, or feeling depressed at any lack of success, he recognised they offered him the opportunity to improve the quality of his teaching so that mistakes were minimised and potentially eliminated. Skinner, whose theories were introduced in Chapter 7, in drawing on Francis Bacon's statement that 'to obey the environment is to command it', effectively states that the 'child is always right!' In other words students learn when the teaching is appropriate and only fail when teachers get it wrong.

The logical conclusion of Michel's way of looking at errors is for teachers to turn round to their students at the end of a less than successful lesson and apologise that they had not learned as intended. Teachers would tell their students to go home, relax and forget about the lesson. Teachers would promise to analyse where they had gone wrong and try to find a more effective way of teaching next time. Teachers would make it absolutely clear that it was *their* job to get things right and that it was *their* problem if students failed to learn. Of course the upside of this interpretation of events is that when students succeed and do well, teachers can take credit for their success.

CORRECTING MISTAKES

Michel Thomas acknowledged that students learn at different rates and that some would find learning easier than others. Nevertheless, he believed that all students could be taught effectively and when they made mistakes it was his job to recognise the source of the error and make the necessary amendments in the teaching approach. During the courses he often uses a tennis analogy to try to create an image for students and put them in the shoes of the listener. He frequently refers to the 'let ball' (i.e. the time in tennis when the ball is served, hits the net and hovers on the net cord before falling back on the side of the server or teetering over into the court of the receiver) to suggest that in the split second before the ball drops on one side of the net or the other, the listener is trying to work out whether what was said could be understood, whether as Michel Thomas said, the server 'got the ball over the net'. At other times, when errors occur Michel quietly and patiently corrects them, usually by breaking a sentence into smaller components and going through it step by step until the error has been self-corrected.

Every time errors occur Michel Thomas assesses their cause and corrects them through three main strategies. With the first strategy he provides the correct word or mispronunciation. With the second strategy he uses an analogy. For example, in the Spanish recording students were given the following sentence to translate, 'I want to know at what time it is going to be ready because I need it and I want to have it today if it is possible.' In the middle of the sentence is the phrase 'I need it'. The correct translation is *lo necesito* but the student made an error and said *necesito lo*. Michel corrected the student by taking him back to first principles and asking him to translate 'I want it' (*lo quiero*) and 'I have it' (*lo tengo*). This was done accurately so Michel returned to the original sentence which was then translated correctly. The student had been shown, through analogy, that 'I need it' is translated in just the same way as 'I want it' and 'I have it'.

The third strategy Michel Thomas uses for correcting errors is through what is known as 'shaping'. This is when a student makes an error, usually a mispronunciation, and Michel accepts successive approximations to finally arrive at a totally correct response. Michel realises that it might be too much for the student to go from making an error to being 100% accurate so he accepts the next response which might be 75% correct. The next time he accepts a response which is 85% correct until the student gradually works their way towards 100% accuracy.

Summary

This chapter has discussed how Michel Thomas seeks to engage students in the teaching and learning process and contrasts this with more conventional approaches which will be examined further in Part 4. Michel focused on two main forms of assessment which are largely informal and gave him regular feedback on students' learning. This in turn guided future decision making about what and how to teach.

PART 4

The implications of Michel Thomas's approach to teaching foreign languages

Part 4 has three main objectives. The first is to relate Michel Thomas's philosophy, instructional principles and methodology to the way foreign languages are conventionally taught. The second is to consider how teachers of foreign languages, particularly those working within primary and secondary schools, can implement Michel's methodology in their own teaching. The third is to explore the wider implications of Michel's methodology to bring about a radical rethink and change to the way students are taught more generally, not just in the area of foreign languages.

Chapter 13 considers recent trends, principles and tensions in teaching foreign languages and discusses the decline in the number of students learning foreign languages over the last five years. Chapter 14 focuses on how foreign languages are typically taught and assessed and relates current practice to Michel Thomas's methods. Chapter 15 considers what foreign language teaching might look line if it drew on Michel Thomas's philosophy, instructional principles and methodology. It provides a template for implementing his approach and considers the implications for teachers, the whole school, students and parents. Part 4 concludes with Chapter 16 which outlines a framework for working towards a 'learning revolution' which Michel fervently hoped would be the ultimate outcome of his life's work.

CHAPTER 13

TEACHING FOREIGN LANGUAGES: TRENDS, PRINCIPLES AND TENSIONS

OVERVIEW

This chapter reviews developments in the teaching of foreign languages. In many respects they parallel the debates about different teaching styles discussed in Chapter 4 where teachers have oscillated between formal and student-centred methodologies. The chapter also highlights a number of core principles that conventionally underpin language teaching and which create tensions with Michel Thomas's teaching methods.

This book was completed during one of the wettest Wimbledon Tennis Championships in living memory. Instead of non-stop tennis there was torrential rain and every commentator became an instant expert at forecasting the weather and interpreting cloud formations. Amid all the reruns of past matches there was a steady stream of interviews with players past and present. Very few of the leading singles tennis players came from English-speaking countries. However, without exception all interviews were conducted in English and the majority of interviewees responded in almost perfect English. It is difficult to imagine the reverse scenario with British sportsmen and women being equally fluent in any European language. Such a prospect is becoming increasingly unlikely, not only because there is a dearth of top-ranked British tennis players, but because the teaching of foreign languages is in a state of decline. Fewer students are taking public examinations in foreign languages than ever before and English children spend far less time learning a foreign language than their European counterparts. In the future the most likely route to learning a foreign language for the vast majority of the population, if current trends continue, will not be at school but through language courses such as Michel Thomas's.

FOREIGN LANGUAGE TEACHING IN ENGLAND

In the UK, children can give up learning a foreign language after only a couple of years in secondary school. This is at a time when Britain is forging closer business ties with the European Community and travel to Europe has never been more accessible or cheaper. The Centre for Information on Language Teaching (CILT), which looks at trends in examination entries for English secondary schools, has recently reported on the growing appeal of Spanish. Whereas numbers taking French and German have declined rapidly over the last five years, there has been a steady increase in those studying Spanish over a similar period. Spanish is now the official language of 20 countries and is spoken by approximately 5% of the world's population. It is on track to overtake English (spoken by 7%) as the most spoken tongue after Mandarin Chinese.

Until September 2004 language learning was compulsory up to the age of 16 in English schools. Thereafter learning a foreign language ceased to be mandatory in the final two years of compulsory schooling. The percentage of children taking a GCSE in a foreign language at the age of 16 has fallen from 80% in 2000 to 51% in 2006. This figure declined even further in 2007 with only 48% of 16 year olds taking French, German or Spanish in their GCSE examinations. As far as GCSE results are concerned, although there has been a national trend for GCSE results to improve annually, the percentage of pupils being awarded A*–C in English, maths, science and a foreign language was only 29.5% in 2001 and went down to 25.7% in 2006, a decrease of 3.8% in five years. British schools are now the only ones in Europe where children can drop languages at the age of 14.

In September 2004 language learning was introduced to primary schools (children aged between 5 and 11) with the aim that all primary aged pupils would be learning a foreign language by 2010. A review of foreign language teaching in England (The Dearing Review named after its chair, Sir Ron Dearing) reported in March 2007 that this had been achieved in approximately 70% of primary schools. It indicated that languages are enjoyed by children across the ability range and suggested that there is no lack of enthusiasm, interest or keenness to learn. However, it was not clear how much time was being devoted to languages per week or what the content of the majority of lessons entailed. So although the overall picture appeared encouraging there was probably considerable variation with some schools doing no more than teaching a few nursery rhymes and basic vocabulary, while others might have been more ambitious and introduced a wide range of conversational and written skills.

The Dearing Review looked at ways of widening participation in foreign language learning and offered a number of innovative and imaginative strategies to engage students. It recommended that languages become part of the statutory curriculum for Key Stage 2 (children aged between 7 and 11) in primary schools when the National Curriculum is next reviewed. This reiterated the recommendation in a consultation document, *Language Learning*, published in the UK in February 2002, where the government stated that all children had an entitlement to learn a language at primary level by 2012 (but stopped short of making languages compulsory owing to the shortage of trained teachers). The Dearing Review noted the success of introducing languages to the primary sector and asked whether it should be extended to younger children aged between 5 and 7. The question was raised because of the trend in mainland Europe to start teaching foreign languages at an increasingly young age.

In December 2006, three months before the publication of the Dearing Review, 50 leading academics wrote to the *Observer* newspaper to express their concerns about the slump in the number of pupils taking GCSEs in foreign languages. A study by CILT found that nearly a third of schools had less than 25% of pupils studying a foreign language after the age of 14. The poorest teenagers were least likely to be learning languages. The fall in numbers taking languages at age 16 is closely related to social class, and to overall performance in national tests at 14 and 16; the proportion of pupils entitled to free school meals gaining a language qualification at 16 (the end of Key Stage 4) is only half that of pupils from more advantaged backgrounds. The proportion of pupils taking languages who obtained five A*–C passes (the expected minimum number of passes) is about twice that of the less successful pupils. Thus, while the policy of languages for all appears to be working across the whole range of social class and ability in primary schools it was never fully achieved at secondary level, even before languages ceased to be compulsory. A study by the European Commission reported that the UK had a better record than only one out of 25 European Union countries in the proportion of citizens able to have a conversation in a second language. Only 30% of people could converse in a foreign tongue in the UK compared to 99% in Luxembourg, 91% in Holland, 88% in Denmark, 45% in France and a European average of 44%.

The National Institute of Adult Continuing Education (NIACE) published a survey *Figures of Speech* in May 2007 which looked at adult language learning in the UK. It estimated that half a million fewer adults are learning a foreign language today than ten years ago. The two most popular languages studied are French and Spanish. Women are more likely than men to sign up for classes or have a friend teach them, whereas men tend to study independently through books, CDs or DVDs. However, it appears that there is an arrest in the decline. The number of people studying languages outside school is now increasing, perhaps fuelled by the boom in buying houses abroad.

The current picture indicates that we are unlikely to produce an adequate supply of foreign language teachers in the very near future. Fewer students than ever are studying a foreign language after the age of 14 and although many primary schools have started teaching languages, there is no sense at the moment that this is going to substantially change things long term. In part this is because the content of what is covered in primary schools is superficial and the extent to which foreign languages are being taught by actual specialist *language* teachers is unknown. So although government policy advocates teaching foreign languages for all young students, the decline in learning foreign languages amongst older students has been marked.

DO YOU NEED AN APTITUDE TO LEARN FOREIGN LANGUAGES?

The more successfully students have learned in the past, particularly in relation to a foreign language, the greater the likelihood that they will attribute their progress to a special ability, aptitude or inspirational teacher rather than the structure of the curriculum or quality of the teaching methods (which is Michel Thomas's claim). It is undeniable that some of us find it easier to learn than others, and Michel Thomas did not attempt to contradict this common sense view of the world. However, he reframed the concept of ability from an instructional perspective and in so doing helped to clarify its general and more accessible meaning.

Previous chapters have addressed the difficulty in spotting either sporting or academic talent, although we tend to recognise linguistic ability when children are older than the other fields where talent spotting takes place. Thus, teachers and parents will already have begun to form impressions of students and their abilities well before they start to learn a new language. They are more likely to assume that those who excel generally will do so when they learn a foreign language.

Within traditional ways of teaching foreign languages the notion of 'aptitude' is bound up with how much students have learned. The British sometimes looks towards Europe, particularly Scandinavia and Holland with a sense of envy arising from how fluently they can speak not only English but other foreign languages as well. It can feel strange visiting cities such as Amsterdam where everyone, no matter what the context, appears to be fluent in English. Is this because the Dutch have an aptitude for learning languages or because they start at a young age, see it as a priority and so spend far longer learning English than the equivalent pupils in England spend learning any foreign language? Norbert Pachler and Kit Field in *Learning to Teach Modern Foreign Languages in the Secondary School* lament the time typically allocated in the secondary school curriculum to teaching foreign languages which is often no more than twice a week. It is far less likely that students will become engaged with, and develop an enthusiasm for, any subject that is studied so infrequently.

From an instructional point of view, it is inevitable that some students will learn more than others and some will learn more quickly than others. Problems arise in assuming that such differences are the consequence of variations in ability rather than variations in a whole range of learning experiences and opportunities, not only those solely related to foreign languages. At best, the notion of 'aptitude' is just one hypothesis, albeit the one that is generally advanced and accepted to explain discrepancies in progress, to account for why some students know more and learn more quickly than their peers. However, there are other hypotheses, even if they are rarely acknowledged or are deemed less plausible. These focus on the quality and appropriateness of how students have been taught which in turn lead to different explanations to account for variations in students' learning.

For example, Oliver James in *They F*** You Up: How to Survive Family Life* looks at the family background of what he terms 'exceptional achievers'. He writes as follows about the practice regimes of talented musicians:

> Although it is often assumed that musical ability is inherited, there is abundant evidence that this is not the

> case. It seems that all of us are born with perfect pitch, the capacity to match notes perfectly. Highly musical children were sung to more as infants (and in the womb), and were encouraged more to join in singing games as toddlers, than less musical ones…Studies of classical musicians prove that the best ones, the soloists, practised considerably more from childhood onwards than ordinary orchestral players; this is because their parents urged them to put in the hours from a very young age.[1]

The clear message, although counter-intuitive and very different from the conventional wisdom, is that the environment is critical in determining what students learn and the exceptional talents that they display. James also links outstanding achievement to unfulfilled parental ambitions which he notes are:

> …most common in childhoods of exceptional achievers. In general, we are more likely to pursue a similar profession to one of our parents and, if we are prodigiously good at a subject from a young age, it is almost always because this was one in which our parents were either accomplished or wished that they had been.[1]

There are clearly individual differences in foreign language learning but these say as much about differences in environmental and instructional factors as the psychological differences between individual students. The notion that Michel Thomas wanted to dispel is the assumption that those who are perceived to be of lower aptitude would have a difficulty in learning a foreign language and fail to meet generally agreed standards in speaking, reading and writing. Michel Thomas's philosophy encourages a distinction between an observed aptitude (i.e. how much a student has learned to date and their rate of learning) and future learning opportunities (i.e. the extent to which it is considered appropriate for them to continue learning a foreign language). Those of higher ability are assumed to be capable of excellent progress whereas those of lower ability are often discouraged from continuing to learn a foreign language. Michel would have argued that a perceived lower aptitude just meant that instead of withdrawing students from language learning, they need to be given more appropriate teaching and opportunities to learn.

For Michel Thomas the notion of aptitude was not particularly relevant or of interest because he believed that he could teach anyone, no matter what their background, previous experience or supposed ability. This was illustrated in 'The Language Master' and motivated both his work in schools and his desire to teach languages in the first instance. If Michel Thomas had ever been the head of languages in a school he would have predicted that every student would achieve the desired target for their age, which in England and Wales would culminate in 100% of pupils achieving A*–C at age 16 in the GCSE examinations. This was not to be awkward or obtuse but because he had complete conviction in his method of teaching. It would be the same in any other country, whatever the expectation for students' learning at a particular age, Michel would anticipate that this could be achieved by every student taught by his methods. The litmus test of whether an education system is reducing inequalities and achieving the aspirations of John Rawls described in Part 2, is the extent to which that system focuses on the learner and identifying those with special needs and the gifted and talented, rather than concentrating on the teacher. The greater the tendency to attribute progress to the learner rather than the teacher, the longer potential imbalances in achievement will exist between those from more advantaged and less advantaged backgrounds. Equally, when the emphasis is on the learner, students from certain ethnic, social and financial backgrounds are usually under and over represented amongst those perceived to have difficulties or exceptional talents.[2]

Michel Thomas believed that everyone had an entitlement to learn regardless of perceptions of students' abilities or aptitudes. We all have our own expectations for how people will learn and make predictions for our children and others. It is a process that takes place continuously and we have all benefited or lost out to its effects to varying degrees. It is second nature to the way we conventionally think about human learning. Ultimately, within Michel Thomas's frames of reference, the only true way of ascertaining and establishing aptitudes and abilities in any area of human endeavour is when everyone has received the same, high quality teaching and learning experiences which could not be improved. Only then could we rank everyone in terms of their aptitude for learning languages. Until such a point is reached students perceived to be lacking ability are seen by Michel merely to have received inappropriate teaching and learning opportunities.

MAKING FOREIGN LANGUAGES RELEVANT

Various government documents, statutory frameworks and examination specifications underpin modern foreign language (MFL) teaching. A major change in emphasis in recent years has been from a curriculum that focused on formal grammar, translation, reading and writing to one emphasising communication skills that goes by the name of 'communicative language teaching' (CLT). CLT concentrates on everyday personal, 'functional' (what would be useful when visiting a foreign country. For example, transport, finding and booking accommodation, coping with illness, etc.) and classroom language, and what is frequently termed 'authenticity', which refers to finding real contexts for students to use a foreign language, whether it be in relation to speaking, listening, reading or writing. Courses have concentrated on areas such as those shown in Table 13.1 opposite, which lists the topics covered in traditional Spanish language course books. Topics reflect the kind of conversations and interactions that students are thought to be most likely to have in a European country and portray a less formal style of teaching. CLT was introduced in an attempt to make foreign languages more appealing and accessible to a wider range of students. Although CLT tends to focus on speaking and listening skills, students are still required to read and write. The difference is that these skills are no longer based around formal activities such as translating pages from a foreign language into English or vice versa.

Instead, students read texts which are of genuine interest to them; the 'authenticity of texts and tasks has become increasingly important, as has using the target language in real contexts for communicative purposes'.[3] Clearly, translating from English into a foreign language or vice versa is an integral part of all language teaching but the revised emphasis on translation is more concerned with being able to respond orally to what is said and heard. These areas, particularly the increased attention given to speaking and listening activities, can now be seen to be at the heart of the way many educationalists think about teaching and learning more generally, not only in relation to foreign languages. For example, it is central to the new primary framework for teaching literacy. Despite its positive influence in the field of language learning, CLT has however failed to give us a generation of talented and motivated linguists. It is clear that there is still a great amount of work to be done.

Table 13.1 Topics taught in GCSE Spanish taken from traditional language course books.

Topics	Areas Covered
Yourself	Introducing yourself Introducing other people Describing your house or flat Describing the place where you live Expressing opinions and making comparisons
School	Subjects and timetable Talking about your school Describing what you do every day Talking about free-time activities Talking about holiday plans
Holidays	Restaurant language and the weather Asking for tourist information Making plans based on weather and local activities Booking a table and ordering your meal Reading about holidays Describing what you did on holiday
Towns and travel	Directions and places in town Getting travel information Finding your way around the station and buying tickets Expressing opinions about travel Dealing with accidents and breakdowns Describing what happened
Health, hotels and problems	Health problems and advice Saying why you feel ill or how you've hurt yourself Booking hotel accommodation and arriving at a campsite Checking into a hotel or campsite Describing lost property Making complaints in a hotel
Work	Food meals and numbers Saying what you do to help at home and why Describing part-time jobs and how you spend your money Talking about work experience Describing your lifestyle and giving health advice Discussing TV programmes and films

Shopping	Shopping transactions Shopping in a department store Expressing opinions and preferences about shopping Buying food in the market Buying clothes and making comparisons Complaining about problems with purchases
Socialising	Arranging to go out Reading about what's on and buying tickets Making a date Reading and discussing newspapers, magazines and comics Saying what you thought of a film
Yourself	Personal descriptions Describing personality Describing problems at home and at school Discussing the dangers of drug dependency Talking about environmental issues
Careers	School subjects and jobs Discussing the options for further study Talking about career choices Making a job application Thinking about the future

IS THERE MORE THAN ONE WAY TO TEACH?

A recurring theme in language learning is the need to find a variety of ways of motivating students. It is suggested that students are becoming increasingly alienated, in part because they cannot see the value of learning a foreign language. Students are consequently demotivated and find it difficult, which results in them experiencing a lack of success. In European countries some of these difficulties are masked through English being seen as a world language that is central to the lives and culture of young people through films, television and music, a process which does not have a parallel in the English-speaking world.

The Dearing Review argued that after the age of 14 students need to be offered alternative routes to continuing to study a foreign language that are appropriate to their needs. The three routes of study are 'specialist', 'vocational' and 'personal', and it assumed that at least one will appeal to students and motivate them to continue studying a language. It is also assumed that there is not a 'correct' way of teaching and that one way to engage students is to vary the teaching methods according to their needs. Pachler and Field frequently suggest that different methods will meet the needs of pupils of differing linguistic abilities. They see foreign language teaching as an 'art' which involves 'choosing the most effective and appropriate methods to develop in pupils the relevant knowledge, skills and understanding about the target language and culture(s) to maximise their learning'. They also state that 'there is no single way of MFL teaching'[4], and that teachers therefore need to develop a personal approach to teaching.

The Dearing Review commented as follows on whether there is a 'right way' of teaching:

> The best way of teaching a language has been debated for decades and the debate continues. Teaching has become more demanding in terms of the need to win the engagement of the pupil than in previous generations, when greater reliance could be placed on a pupil's duty to listen and learn. This poses a particular challenge to teachers whose subject requires hard learning, and languages is one of these.[5]

The Review acknowledges that successful language learning takes place when (i) learners are exposed to rich input of the target language; (ii) they have many opportunities to interact through the language; (iii) they are motivated to learn. The Review then proceeds to stress the need to develop a curriculum that engages students, and emphasises that this can be achieved by schools in a variety of ways. While this is undoubtedly true, it generally misses the point that ultimately, no matter how students are engaged and motivated, they have still to learn the essential core vocabulary and grammar associated with any foreign language. The conventional view is that a variety of teaching approaches need to be tried to establish which ones engage and enthuse students. However, the debates take a different form from Michel Thomas's perspective.

As far as Michel was concerned there could be any number of ways to inspire students, but he believed that the excitement of learning and experience of success was the greatest motivator of all. A clear distinction needs to be made between ways of motivating and involving students in learning, which can be many and varied, and the methods through which students are then taught. For Michel Thomas, some methods were clearly more effective than others and

Chapter 5 explained why he believed that his own methods were the most effective. He saw that his methods were exciting and enabled students to experience tangible success. His courses had been developed and refined over a 50 year period and been trialled with some of the lowest attaining pupils in the USA.

Overall the debates about how best to teach foreign languages mirror the more general debates about how best to teach that were discussed in Chapter 4. The lack of experimental, classroom-based research into what works means that views on effective teaching methods are subject to the whims of fashion. While this continues to be the case, the evidence is that the students that Michel Thomas was most concerned to work with will continue to fail within the current system.

SUMMARY

This chapter has reviewed recent trends in foreign language learning. Three major issues were highlighted (the decline in numbers of students choosing to study a foreign language, the notion that students need an aptitude in order to experience success in learning a language and finally the difficulty teachers have in motivating and engaging learners of a foreign language) which remain areas of tension and potentially provide substantial barriers to trying to widen students' participation in learning a foreign language.

CHAPTER 14

FOREIGN LANGUAGES: TEACHING, LEARNING AND ASSESSMENT

OVERVIEW

This chapter reviews the way that teaching, learning and assessment are typically addressed within foreign language teaching and relates methodologies in these areas to Michel Thomas's way of teaching.

TEACHING AND LEARNING

One of the most significant differences between Michel Thomas's courses and conventional approaches to teaching foreign languages is the relationship between teaching and learning. Chapter 2 discussed how the two are conventionally seen to represent the separate activities of teachers and students. All aspects of the teacher's behaviour define the process of teaching and this occurs irrespective of its impact on students and whether or not they learn. Therefore teachers are regarded as having taught even if their students do not learn anything. Learning is the outcome of what students do and is defined by their behaviour and the steps that they take to master new things, rather than being directly related to, and dependent upon, the actions of teachers.

Pachler and Field write that the, 'National Curriculum is very much a framework for teaching rather than learning'[1]. They also recognise that teachers need to develop a personal approach to foreign language teaching based on 'the learning styles and individual differences and needs of pupils and their personal preferences concerning teaching styles'. This statement further underlines the dichotomy existing between teaching and learning within conventional practice and reinforces the belief that benefits will accrue from acknowledging pupils' learning styles. Pachler and Field identify four potential learning styles which describe the preferred ways in which students might learn a language. They are: (i) 'off-by-heart (OBH) language learning' where students learn by rote; (ii) 'learning to manipulate language for personal use (LMPU)' where the learner takes responsibility for their own learning and becomes motivated through realistic and successful communication; (iii) 'exposure, repetition and practice (ERP)' where learning occurs through total immersion with the target language and (iv) the 'structured grammar approach (SGA)' where it is argued that 'the explanation of grammatical concepts in a logical sequence and the structured application of this knowledge leads to a sound understanding of language structures'.[1] Similarly, Sue Field in *Presenting new Vocabulary and Structures* refers to the ways in which students' preferred learning styles will determine how they best remember new vocabulary. She suggests that some learners will associate new vocabulary with a visual image whereas others might make auditory connections.

The research on the controversial issue of learning styles in education was discussed in Chapter 5, where it was suggested that there is little evidence to support the idea that some ways of learning suit students better than others. The continued use of these learning styles in foreign language teaching further illustrates the distinction between teaching and learning and creates a notable obstacle to a wider acceptance of Michel Thomas's methods.

For Michel Thomas, as discussed in previous chapters, teaching and learning were inextricably linked. He considered that he had taught only when there was evidence that students had learned. For him there could be no teaching without learning. This is what he was referring to when he said that, 'the responsibility for your learning is with me, the teacher'. It is not the student's responsibility. Although there can be no teaching without learning, the converse is not the case – there can be learning in the absence of teaching; students learn many things which are not the direct result of their teachers' actions.

THE ROLE OF TEACHERS AND STUDENTS

The tensions surrounding different teaching styles and the role of cognitive and instructional psychology discussed in Chapter 4 resurface in the differences between conventional methods and Michel Thomas's approach to teaching foreign languages. The teaching methods used by Michel mirror the five stages in the instructional hierarchy. Michel was a perfectionist and his reasons for teaching foreign languages were so important that he did not leave anything to chance. His methods focus directly on the task, teach only one thing at a time so that they are consistent with only one interpretation and use a variation of the sequence 'my turn', 'together' and 'your turn' (which was introduced in Chapter 11). Any discussions about how to improve students' learning were immediately reframed to concentrate on teachers and what *they* could do by way of adapting and amending their teaching methodology.

More traditional approaches to teaching foreign languages take a different view. Pachler and Field note that as students are exposed to more language, 'pupils increasingly have to manage the process of learning for themselves. Each pupil is different, will favour different teaching and learning styles and will employ different strategies to manage their own MFL learning.' It is further claimed that, 'pupils need to assume responsibility for their own learning through active participation'. This active participation is usually expected to occur without prompting by teachers and implies that such pupils are more motivated than students who are less active participants. The teacher is 'no longer merely the source for information but an advisor, facilitator, consultant and fellow communicator'.[2] Thus, it is the students who take responsibility for what they learn and the teacher facilitates this process. This viewpoint reflects the different teaching styles that were discussed in Chapter 4, which contrasted teacher directed and student-centred approaches. The same potential tensions exist in foreign language teaching in the degree to which students' learning is the responsibility of the teachers or the students.

Michel Thomas's position on where the responsibility lay, not only for ensuring students learned but also their level of participation, is absolutely clear, unambiguous and in stark contrast to the views expressed by Pachler and Field. Just as Michel assumed responsibility for what students learned he also assumed responsibility for students' active participation in lessons. He would not construe a lack of participation as indicating a lack of motivation any more than he would assume that the pupils who frequently volunteer answers to questions are enthusiastic. He did not interpret students' behaviour in these terms at all. If Michel wanted students to respond he would ask them directly, irrespective of whether or not their hand was raised. This approach probably went a long way to keeping his students on their toes and engaged in the session as will be discussed in more detail in Chapter 15 and was evidenced in the BBC documentary, 'The Language Master'.

DECIDING HOW TO TEACH:
TEACH ONE THING AT A TIME

It is rare to find that what is taught is analysed and dissected to such an extent that only one thing is taught at a time. This was a defining feature of Michel Thomas's courses but is all too rare within conventional teaching methods. Indeed, for the most part, teaching *more* than one thing at a time is intentional, largely on the grounds that it is seen to be a good idea. It is common practice when teaching young children mathematical skills. For example, when children begin school and learn to count to ten, as they state each number (e.g. seven) they will (i) rote count to seven; (ii) get seven objects to represent the numeral; (iii) name the numeral seven and (iv) write the numeral seven. Teaching the tasks simultaneously makes them more demanding, given the instructional principles underpinning Michel Thomas's approach, which suggest that children would find it easier to understand the concepts being taught if they were presented separately.

The previous chapter discussed recent trends in teaching foreign languages and the emphasis placed on listening, speaking, reading and writing within 'communicative language teaching'. Pachler and Field comment that:

> ...although the skills of listening, speaking, reading and writing can be developed independently of each other, this is not advisable, as pupils must understand the need to integrate skills in order to be able to communicate effectively.

For Pachler and Field, failing to integrate the four creates the risk of producing 'a "walking phrase book" (where students are) incapable of using language spontaneously and of generating their own language in response to stimuli'.[3]

However, a feature of Michel Thomas's language courses, and a core instructional principle is that students are only taught one thing at a time, so from an instructional perspective teaching speaking, listening, reading and writing skills simultaneously is problematic. Michel actually teaches them sequentially within his courses. Students start with speaking and listening, which are taught to high levels of fluency. During the courses they are given details of how words are spelt, which will initially help with reading and then ultimately with writing. Michel therefore follows a progression from easier skills (listening) through to more difficult ones (writing).

MAKE TEACHING EXPLICIT AND OPEN TO ONLY ONE INTERPRETATION

Pachler and Field and the articles edited by Pachler and Redondo in *A Practical Guide to Teaching Modern Foreign Languages in the Secondary School* contain many descriptions of games and activities for teaching foreign languages. The problem with such teaching methods is that the exact purpose of what is being taught is not always made explicit to the student and so the games can be interpreted in a variety of ways. As a result, students may learn what was intended by the teacher but it is equally possible that they will learn something entirely different. Table 14.1 overleaf describes an activity from Pachler and Field for teaching present tense verb endings in German. The interesting point about this activity is that it can be completed without any knowledge of German at all. What is required is knowledge of how verbs are usually taught and a degree of familiarity with tasks of this type so that it can be concluded that:

- *ich* is 'I'
- *du* is 'you'
- *er / sie / es* are 'he', 'she' and 'it'
- *wir* is 'we'
- *ihr* is 'you'
- *sie* is 'they'.

With this knowledge it can be seen that example 1 is 'she', so the ending is *t*, making the verb *spielt*. Example 2 is 'he', so the ending is *t*, making the verb *schwimmt*. Example 3 is 'we' so the ending is *en*, making the verb *tanzen*, and example 4 is 'I', so the ending is *e*, making the verb *gehe*. Finally, example 5 is 'she', so the verb ending is *t*, making the verb *schreibt*.

Table 14.1 An activity to practise present tense verb endings in German

Die Regel					
ich spiel **e**			wir spiel **en**		
du spiel **st**			ihr spiel **t**		
er/sie/es spiel **t**			sie spiel **en**		
Teil 1					
Schreibe den richtigen Satz.					
1	Meine Schwester spiel	e t en		gern Fußball.	
2	Mein Freund schwimm	st t e		im Hallenbad.	
3	Mein Bruder und ich tanz	e t en		in der Disko.	
4	Ich geh	st en e		oft in die Stadt.	
5	Sie schreib	e st t		viele Briefe.	

INTERLEAVED LEARNING AND MEMORISING NEW VOCABULARY

One of the least appealing aspects of studying languages is the amount of vocabulary that has to be learned. Most traditional language course books cover certain areas, as listed for example in Table 13.1. Vocabulary that needs to be mastered is listed at the end of each section. There are two obvious problems with this approach from Michel Thomas's perspective. The first is that asking students to memorise huge chunks of vocabulary in this way is hardly motivating. It is usually presented by teachers as a necessary evil that just has to be done but, nevertheless, even if this is fully understood and appreciated by students it will still take considerable effort and motivation to sit for the necessary time so that everything is learned to sufficiently high levels of accuracy and fluency. Secondly, and more worrying, is that even if students work diligently and master their first vocabulary list, it is extremely likely that it will have been forgotten by the time they have moved on to the next block of vocabulary. This will only add to students' sense of frustration and lack of competence. It will then become even harder to keep students motivated when they realise that even if they put in the hours to learn the necessary vocabulary it will be forgotten quickly.

Learning vocabulary is comparable to the way in which children are traditionally given their weekly spellings. You may recall from Chapter 8 that they frequently have to learn these independently at home. Here the usual problems of forgetting occur, including 'catastrophic interference' (which was discussed in Chapter 8 and is evident when new information effectively wipes out and erases previous learning). However, they can be overcome through the strategy of 'interleaved learning', which effectively means mixing the new with the old. Applying the principle of interleaved learning to foreign languages requires that when students learn new vocabulary it is mixed with what is already known. Only when this has been mastered would students be presented with the next lot of new vocabulary. Even though such an approach could be relatively successful, it would not completely overcome issues of motivation and engagement that are likely to arise when students have to learn on their own. It is always going to be difficult, and something of an uphill battle, for students to find the energy to learn vocabulary, even where it is interleaved, after a long day at school. Michel Thomas's approach teaches vocabulary in a way that does not require the rote learning of lists of vocabulary in isolation from the contexts in which it is used. His introduction to the courses stresses that there is no memorising of vocabulary. Vocabulary is always introduced gradually and systematically and practised through a dialogue between teachers and students.

Pachler and Field state in relation to learning grammar that, 'opportunities for practice must be introduced on a regular basis and the revisiting of grammatical features needs to be well planned'.[4] This is in complete concordance with Michel Thomas where the extent to which anything is practised is made transparent. The general principle is that when material is first introduced it is repeated frequently and then less so over time. As a result, vocabulary and grammar introduced at the beginning of the recordings is still encountered towards the end. Everything that students learn is achieved without recourse to any form of rote learning. However, a potential concern for students following Michel's recordings is that the material introduced at the end of the courses will be less well mastered, primarily because it will have been practised less often. It is therefore advisable to return to later sections in the recording more often than to earlier ones.

Overall, two points need to be remembered when contrasting the way Michel Thomas addresses memorising with more familiar methods. The first is that discussions about how students remember are framed with reference to Haring and Eaton's instructional hierarchy (which was described in Chapter 10). It provides a framework for conceptualising how new information is fully mastered and incorporated into students' overall understanding. Students need to become accurate and fluent, although fluency alone will not help to develop flawless memories of recently acquired material. It has to be reinforced and practised alongside previously learned material where students have to discriminate the new from the old. The second is that all new vocabulary and grammar introduced in the courses is used immediately and practised within the context of full sentences. It is never learned in isolated word lists (which not only limit how much will be remembered for the reasons already discussed but also limit how well students can use what they have been learning in appropriate contexts). This means that the introduction of new items is carefully regulated and 'interleaved' so that familiar and less familiar items are practised alongside each other. This in effect removes the effort from memorising and is why interleaved learning is such a compelling teaching method.

ASSESSMENT

For Michel Thomas, assessment is a fundamental part of the teaching and learning process. Just as there is no teaching without learning, the only means of judging whether learning has occurred is through a process of continuous assessment. This is highly compatible with the principles, purposes and processes of teacher assessment described by Pachler and Field where the focus of assessment is to give students specific feedback on whether they are progressing, on what they have done well and on what is coming up next. Acronyms such as 'WWW' ('What Went Well?') and 'EBI' ('Even Better If') refer to the kind of feedback that students are given, and most lessons end with a plenary where students and teachers reflect on set objectives and the extent to which they have been met and what happens next.

The differences between contemporary practice and Michel's approach arise with the role of pupil self-assessment. The aim is to give students an opportunity to reflect on what they feel that they have learned and to engage in a dialogue which it is to be hoped will be motivating and meaningful. There are a number of reasons why this would not be seen as particularly relevant or helpful, given the nature of teacher assessment. It is usually difficult for learners to monitor their progress especially in speaking, listening and reading. There is nothing for them to see as evidence of improvement, other than a teacher's feedback and so their own and / or peer assessments are likely to be heavily influenced by their teacher's perceptions.

Teacher assessment in Michel's courses is focused and extremely positive, providing students with immediate and concrete feedback on their progress. During the recordings Michel lets students know whether their translations were accurate and he rarely, if ever, uses any form of negative feedback. The structure and progressions used for teaching each language mean that tangible evidence of progress is constant, even though this is usually quite difficult to achieve with speaking and listening activities. Within an hour of starting the Spanish course students progress from translating 'it is' (*es posible*) to:

- 'I want to know why you can't do it that way.' (*Quiero saber por qué no puede hacerlo así.*);
- 'For what restaurant do you have a preference tonight?' (*¿Para qué restaurante tiene una preferencia esta noche?*)
- 'Do you have a reservation for me for tonight?' (*¿Tiene una reservación para mí para esta noche?*)

This represents a considerable achievement and the sense of progress it conveys is extremely convincing. Sometimes on the recordings there are audible gasps of astonishment when students are asked to translate what appear to be extremely complex sentences that, on first hearing, appear to be way beyond their level of linguistic competence. However, Michel breaks the translations down into smaller more manageable segments so that students can appreciate that they have in fact mastered the necessary skills to translate the sentences successfully. This is a very powerful teaching device and its impact cannot be underestimated. Knowing that the time spent being taught is productive, enabling students to learn new skills and knowledge, creates both expectations for students and a growing sense of what they might be able to achieve with appropriate guidance from their teachers. Michel found that even the most reluctant, potentially disruptive students he encountered could not resist this opportunity.

One final point to be made on assessment is that on the recordings students always end up with 'the right answer' no matter how many mistakes are made or corrections required en route from their first to final responses. Michel also concludes by giving the correct translations himself so that other students, whether they are listeners to the courses or peers in the same room, always get to hear the correct version twice. This form of immediate feedback is compelling and means students are never left wondering whether they have got the correct answer, which in itself is tremendously reassuring.

SUMMARY

This chapter has focused on teaching, learning and assessment to explain the differences between current practice in teaching foreign languages and Michel Thomas's approach. The discussion addressed the role and responsibilities of the teacher, the need to teach one thing at a time to avoid ambiguity and the importance of interleaving tasks to maximise student retention. The tensions surrounding whether the responsibility for students' progress lies with the teacher or the student were summarised in relation to assessing students' learning and the role of pupil self-assessment.

CHAPTER 15

THE WIDER APPLICATIONS OF TEACHING FOREIGN LANGUAGES THROUGH MICHEL THOMAS'S APPROACH

OVERVIEW

Parts 2 and 3 of this book have described the instructional principles that underpin Michel Thomas's approach to teaching and demonstrated how they are applied to teaching foreign languages. Currently the courses do not explicitly demonstrate how to apply the principles or develop the content for use in schools or colleges or in preparing students for public examinations. This chapter looks at the implications for teaching foreign languages in schools or colleges and considers how a school or individual teacher might go about incorporating elements of Michel's methodology and the psychological principles introduced in this book into their everyday teaching.

It is difficult to know how language specialists would see Michel Thomas's approach fitting into existing ways of teaching. The recordings certainly cover some of the ground which comprises current GCSE course content. It is possible that the recordings will be received as offering little that is new and that they essentially focus on teaching grammar. Such a perception fundamentally fails to appreciate what Michel's methodology offers in contrast to previous occasions when grammar was taught. Within the courses there is very little direct discussion of grammar or very little attempt to present an exhaustive account of the different grammatical components that are presented in the recordings. Students are shown how to use the languages covered largely through listening, speaking and translating.

The only direct reference to grammar is in connection with Michel's definitions of nouns, verbs and adjectives, which appealed so greatly to the students participating in 'The Language Master' because they were so much clearer than the definitions they were familiar with. For example, Michel defined a verb as any word in front of which you can place 'to' (i.e. to be, to have, to go, to see). This contrasts with the notion of a verb being a 'doing word', which is mentioned by Pachler and Field where they state, 'the use of terminology like "doing words" and "describing words" has a place in the learning process and pupils should not necessarily be discouraged from using their own terms'.[1] Despite this difference there are many areas of commonality between Michel's approach and current foreign language teaching methods and both relate in similar ways to a number of issues. For example, both recognise the need for frequent teaching sessions and regular opportunities to practise. There are no reasons why the key aspects of Michel's methodology could not be incorporated into core language teaching. What might this look like in practice?

ASSUMPTIONS AND PRINCIPLES

The assumptions and principles that underpin Michel Thomas's approach have been discussed in each part of the book and clearly represent a different starting point from conventional ways of teaching foreign languages. The contrasting beginnings are reflected in numerous ways, for example, interpretations of the concept of ability, responsibility for learning, the links between teaching, learning and assessment, whether there is a 'correct' way of teaching, teaching more than one thing at a time, etc. Research reviewed in previous chapters has repeatedly endorsed the need to retain high expectations for students' learning and the discussions have reflected Michel Thomas's perspective on this, and other key issues that shape teachers' attitudes, beliefs and expectations. Attitudes and beliefs either enable or create barriers to students' learning and they are as much a part of implementing Michel Thomas's methods as any other feature of the teaching and learning environment.

DECIDING WHAT TO TEACH

The course content for schools is laid out by the examination boards and Table 13.1 (see Chapter 13) illustrates the kind of topics that are covered. Whether such topics are genuinely motivating for pupils is questionable and will vary from student to student. Applying Michel Thomas's approach in schools means that students will be equipped first and foremost with all the vocabulary, grammar and structures they need; the vocabulary necessary for public examinations can be easily added later. As Michel Thomas said – he is the architect of the house (the language), it is up to the student to furnish it (by adding the vocabulary).

Chapter 6 described Pareto's Law and how it is reflected in Michel Thomas's courses. The courses teach a relatively small amount of information but cover what is most useful and generalisable, hence the focus on structures and verb usage which Michel believed were the backbone of any language. Michel frequently said that 'if you know how to handle the verbs, you know how to handle the whole language'. He encouraged students to 'guess' when they were unsure of vocabulary, often reminding them, particularly in relation to French, that a significant number of English words are the same or similar to those in the language they are learning. However, he did not permit such freedoms over verb usage and sentence construction which he made sure were mastered by students. Thus, Michel identified the critical linguistic structures and, where possible, ensured that they were the same for each language. Similarly, if you understand the instructional principles underpinning Michel Thomas's approach, you will know how to teach because they too are the backbone of the teaching and learning process. They can be applied to teaching anything not just foreign languages, and will enable any teacher to be more effective.

Chapter 8 introduced the instructional principle 'contextual diversity' and discussed its role in enabling students to generalise what they learned from one context to another. A small amount of critical information is applied in many different contexts, which over time helps students to achieve to a higher level than they would have done without the opportunity to use what they know in a wide variety of settings. The great bonus of such an approach is that students can listen, speak, read and write about whatever they want because the small number of skills that they have been taught will be widely applicable and will be useful in discussing any topic or theme.

Given the concerns about student engagement and motivation, applications of Michel Thomas's approach to schools would retain the structure, content, and progressions of the current courses and then enable students to apply their knowledge to topics and themes of their own choosing. Some of these may well be embraced by those identified within the traditional courses but will also include topics that are more pertinent to the students' lives and interests. The verb, grammar and language structures taught would mirror Michel's courses, with additional vocabulary taught later. So, instead of speaking, listening, reading and writing about yourself, schools or holidays, the focus might be *Neighbours*, current affairs or MySpace.

SPEAKING, LISTENING, READING AND WRITING

Michel Thomas's courses focus on speaking and listening and require students to translate from English into one of the languages taught. Initially, therefore, in a more formal school setting all the teaching would focus largely on speaking and listening. The aim would be to enable students to speak with fluency and achieve a good level of understanding before requiring them to read and write. Students who can read and write fluently in English will be able to read and write in a foreign language with relative ease through Michel's approach, once suitable levels of oral competence have been reached.

Being able to write is dependent on being able to spell accurately and there is a tendency to think of spelling as being a purely written activity. Most school spelling tests involve writing but this is largely for pragmatic reasons so that the spelling of a whole class can be assessed at the same time. However, spellings can be checked orally as well. The key task in spelling is being able to translate phonemes (i.e. sounds) into print and through using letter names we are able to indicate that we know the letters that represent different sounds. For example, if you are asked to tell someone over the telephone how to spell your name you can obviously do this without having to write your name as well. In the current recordings Michel provides the spellings to a significant proportion of the vocabulary that is taught and interleaves those spellings (see Chapter 8 for a description of interleaved learning) through introducing them one at a time. He gives students the necessary pre-requisite skills to read and write without actually requiring them to read or write anything.

OPTIMAL TEACHING AND READING, WRITING AND TRANSLATING

Michel Thomas taught what was most useful and generalisable. As a result there are certain features of conventional foreign language teaching that do not feature prominently in Michel's courses, for example reading and writing. However, Michel expected that students would be able to generalise and apply their knowledge to these and other tasks without having to receive the same direct teaching that is provided in speaking. One example just discussed is that of spelling. Michel anticipated that students would be able to generalise from the knowledge that he gave them to enable them to write correctly. He also believed that this would be the case with reading. He encouraged students to read newspapers, magazines and books in their chosen language as a way of reinforcing what they already knew. All the translations are from English into the target language, which is in fact more difficult than translating from a foreign language into English. Michel anticipated that, with practice, students would again be able to generalise from the knowledge gained through the courses to being able to read, write and translate into English. Michel believed that students were taught what they needed to know to develop these other skills through the solid foundations that he provided. The implication for implementing Michel's methods more widely is that the focus is on speaking and translating from English into the desired foreign language; reading, writing and translating into English will almost take care of themselves, with appropriate teaching, when students are shown how to generalise their existing knowledge.

DECIDING HOW TO TEACH

Underpinning any application of Michel Thomas's teaching methodology is the instructional hierarchy which indicates that different ways of teaching are required for each stage in the hierarchy. So everything taught, irrespective of the topic covered, starts with the methods involved in securing accuracy and fluency, followed by those that promote generalisation and application.

IMMERSION COURSES

A major decision has to be made about when to schedule teaching sessions and there are two options. Michel Thomas's recordings represent what is frequently referred to as an 'immersion course'. This is where students are taught one subject throughout the day for a relatively limited period, perhaps a week, which was the time scale for the BBC documentary. The Foundation and Advanced language courses, when combined, would form the basis of such a course, probably lasting up to six to seven days. The idea is to study intensively for relatively short periods and teach the necessary core skills to give students a thorough grounding and introduction to their chosen language.

The Dearing Review noted that languages do not need to be taught in 'lockstep, weekly doses', and saw four purposes in more intensive, immersion courses: (i) to improve the knowledge of pupils transferring from primary to secondary schooling. This was identified as a key step in maximising the impact of the policy of introducing languages to primary schools; (ii) to help students at the end of their third year in secondary school, the final year of compulsory language teaching, to catch up with their peers where they have fallen behind; (iii) for those pupils who are planning to start a new language in their fourth year of secondary education and (iv) to offer a more stimulating and relevant course for students studying languages in the fourth and fifth years of secondary schooling, particularly for those taking combined courses, specialised diplomas or planning to work abroad. To this list could be added starting languages in the primary school. All primary schools are expected to have introduced foreign language teaching by 2010 and it would be relatively easy to devote an entire week to language learning in this way. An immersion course would lend itself to a highly creative framework for foreign language teaching where the content of Michel Thomas's courses could readily sit alongside learning about a country's culture, history and people in ways similar to those encouraged within CLT (Communicative Language Teaching) that were discussed in Chapter 13.

Michel Thomas's courses make perfect immersion courses, widely applicable to a huge variety of situations. Immersion courses have clear advantages and can engage students in languages through giving them a good working knowledge quickly and the impetus to develop their skills. However, when developing Michel Thomas's courses in schools there is a limit to the amount of time that can be exclusively devoted to studying a single topic. Immersion courses can cover the main content of the programmes but need to be supplemented with regular practice to promote fluency, long-term retention and create opportunities for students to apply their skills in different contexts to different topics and areas of interest. There is always the slight danger with immersion courses that they will not fulfil their purpose unless they are followed up and complemented with further teaching sessions.

For the application of the principles underpinning the courses to have the greatest long-term impact, the ideal is for students to receive daily teaching of relatively short duration, perhaps around 30 minutes, in the languages that they are learning. This is an example of distributed practice, which is the second option for organising the teaching of foreign languages. This way teachers can review what has been taught previously and systematically introduce new information through the process of interleaved learning.

However, there has been a growing trend in secondary schools to increase lesson length to minimise movement round a school, which is when disruptive incidents are most likely to occur. It often means that students have no more than two or possibly three one-hour lessons a week. As a result there are more days each week when students are not being taught a foreign language than when they are. If students only have two lessons of an hour a week, it means that there are five days (including weekends) when there is no language teaching. This is often why students are given homework (see below), which is intended to bridge the gap between lessons.

There are reasons other than preventing disruption for longer lessons which are often to do with students having time to get involved in a subject or to complete experiments in science, work in art or participate in sporting activities which would be difficult within shorter periods. Nevertheless, longer lessons present major disadvantages to teaching languages, particularly when applying the principles underpinning Michel Thomas's courses.

Shorter lessons would be more effective for a range of subjects. In secondary schools, teachers rather than students would move between classrooms, except where specialist facilities were required. It is more important to have daily teaching with Michel's approach than with other methodologies because of the central role of the teacher throughout the teaching and learning process. Students would undertake independent work only after high levels of fluency had been achieved and maintained in the core skills that are taught.

TEACHING METHOD: WHOLE-CLASS TEACHING

A potential problem with Michel Thomas's interactive style of teaching might be seen to be the size of the teaching group. It could be argued that the approach would only work on a small group or one-to-one basis with a teacher. In fact the size of the teaching group is largely immaterial and the approach works equally well with any number of students, irrespective of their language knowledge. Michel's descriptions of using his courses with mainstream, teenage students in Los Angeles involved large class sizes. The key to whole-class teaching of this type lies in the way that Michel questions students. After giving students something to translate, he waits before seeking a response. This is conventionally known as 'thinking time' and because the students have not been told who will answer at this point, the expectation is that they will all try and work out the appropriate response. After giving a suitable amount of thinking time Michel Thomas then asks a student to translate.

A common problem with the questioning techniques of many teachers is that they start with the name of the pupil who is to respond and then ask the question. This effectively gives all but the nominated student the chance to switch off and have a rest. A further problem with the usual questioning techniques is that after posing a question and giving thinking time, teachers wait for students to put up their hands to see who knows the answer and then ask a pupil with their hand up to provide the response. What students learn here is that as long as they are quiet and keep their hands down they are very unlikely to be asked a question. They might be asked every so often but the worst case scenario is that they will be told to listen more carefully or on parents' evenings their parents will be told that they do not participate enough in class. Michel's strategy, which was evident in 'The Language Master', is to select students irrespective of whether their hands are up. This strategy maximises participation and keeps all the students involved. Students conclude that they have to stay alert and concentrate just in case they are asked a question.

Michel Thomas's questioning strategy also works when there are students with different levels of knowledge in the class. Teaching such students is usually a reason for setting and placing students in groups according to perceived levels of ability. Setting is the subject of recurring debates in education. It is assumed that teaching pupils of similar ability levels is easier than mixed groupings where there is a broader range of attainments. The rationale for this strategy is the same as that for teaching lower-achieving pupils in small groups or on a one-to-one basis. Although this is a strategy that is pursued almost without exception by schools and government, it is potentially flawed for two reasons. The first is that if the curriculum content is not sufficiently well designed and structured to start with, it will make little difference to the learner whether it is presented to them within a whole class or individually. The second is that the progress of students in small group teaching or ability groups is rarely compared to that of students in whole-class teaching so that there is no evidence that the policy actually works. Effective differentiation refers to the process whereby students with different attainments are all taught according to their needs, despite being within a whole class.

Laura Shapiro, from the University of Aston, has compared the impact of effective, differentiated, whole-class teaching with small-group or one-to-one teaching in relation to teaching children to read. Students in both groups, those receiving whole-class teaching and those in receipt of small group or one-to-one teaching were placed in rank order. The higher achievers (top 25%) and lower achievers (bottom 25%) in each group were identified. The research had two very interesting outcomes, which are counter-intuitive. The first is that the 25% of lower achievers taught on a whole-class basis made better progress than the 25% of lower achievers, taught individually or in small groups. The second finding was that not only did effective whole-class teaching have a significant impact on the lowest achievers; it also had a marked impact on the higher achievers as well. Contrary to the conventional wisdom which states that if teaching raises the attainments of the lowest achieving pupils the remaining students will somehow be held back, Shapiro's research indicates that there are benefits in whole-class teaching for all pupils, higher and lower achievers.

One possible explanation for these unexpected findings runs along the following lines. Imagine learning to play tennis but never having the opportunity of watching top-class tennis on television or in the park in the aftermath of any one of the four major tennis tournaments. Let's imagine that an initial assessment of your skills places you in the bottom group of beginners with fellow players who also have limited skills. Your only models would be other players of comparable low quality. It would be hard to get an accurate picture of what good tennis playing actually looks like. However, if instead, you are given the opportunity of seeing professional tennis and the finest players in the world, knowing how the game should be played could have a very positive effect on even the poorest players. Mixed attainment grouping gives the lowest achievers the chance to see what reading or maths or speaking a foreign language should be like. When all students are kept together but taught according to their specific needs, there is usually someone just one step ahead so you can see where you are heading. In the case of the highest achievers, it appears that they are not disadvantaged by the absence of others who are one step ahead of them. Knowing that they are progressing well, with differentiated teaching that meets their needs, is sufficient to keep them motivated and learning.

THE CLASSROOM ENVIRONMENT

The first thing that Michel Thomas did in the BBC documentary 'The Language Master' was to change the layout of the classroom. He believed that the traditional arrangement of tables and chairs was not conducive to effective teaching. He therefore replaced them with comfortable sofas and brought in soft lighting and plants to create a very different atmosphere. Vast sums of money are currently being devoted to building new schools and refurbishing old buildings. It is not too fanciful to think that this includes designing an environment that promotes learning through its furniture, lighting, wall displays and equipment. For example, the majority of classrooms are equipped with computer systems so students could listen to music as they entered the classroom, which would set a mood conducive for learning which could well continue into the lessons.

HOMEWORK

Government and parents are both supportive of the notion that homework is a necessary ingredient in educational achievement with the result that it is increasingly being given to primary-aged children. It appears to be logical that the more work students do, the better their results. However, reviews on the effects of homework have reported somewhat contradictory findings. A major difficulty in trying to evaluate the role of homework is trying to separate its impact on students' attainments from their social background and other factors that influence their learning. A recent report from the Institute of Education at the University of London confirmed that there was little evidence to justify its widespread use.[2]

This topic has specific relevance to Michel Thomas's language courses because he was vehemently opposed to the notion of 'homework'. He believed that students could make excellent progress without doing additional activities at home as long as their work in class was suitably structured and organised. For Michel it was all about working 'smarter' rather than 'harder'. He took the view that devoting extra time to practising the wrong thing was potentially more damaging than spending less time on the right things. Effective teaching and regular reviews of what has been learned militate against the need for homework.

Pachler and Field claim that homework plays a critical role in acquiring linguistic skills. One reason for their claim is that if students are only being taught a couple of times a week, independent study at home becomes essential so that the necessary course work can be covered. A second reason, which again reinforces the different views of teaching and learning with Michel Thomas's approach and traditional teaching, is that although the language teacher has a vital role to play in the learning process, they 'cannot do the learning' for their pupils. This implies that to a degree students' learning is independent of what the teacher does and rests largely on students carrying out a certain amount of study at home. This is one of the reasons why students from more disadvantaged backgrounds give up learning a foreign language at the earliest opportunity. They are less likely, for a variety of reasons, to work at home than peers from more advantaged backgrounds. From Michel Thomas's point of view, a further drawback of homework is that students complete activities that do not involve direct interaction with their teachers, so they would not get immediate feedback on how they had done and could spend half an hour practising and reinforcing the same error.

MOTIVATION AND LOWER ACHIEVING PUPILS

A major concern in the teaching of modern languages has been how best to engage pupils, particularly when the focus was on secondary-age students from a wide range of backgrounds and with perceived differing levels of ability. Communicative Language Teaching (CLT), a curriculum that focuses on everyday, accessible and useful language as opposed to the former emphasis which was on formal grammar, translation, reading and writing, highlights the communicative aspects of learning a foreign language and the role of speaking and listening. It was introduced in part through the belief that this might be a more successful way of engaging lower-attaining students whilst recognising that learning a foreign language is an entitlement for all.

For those students who have particular difficulty in reading and writing English, using a predominantly oral approach to learning a foreign language (such as CLT) could be hugely beneficial. They would be able to participate in language lessons and their lack of literacy skills in English would not present any sort of barrier to achieving oral competence in a foreign language. The problem that arises, however, is that we judge students' ability on their reading and writing skills. The conclusion would be that if a student had not mastered either of these skills they would be seen to have a learning difficulty and therefore it would not be deemed appropriate to teach them a foreign language.

Bizarrely, students who may not yet have reached fluency in reading and writing English may find it relatively easy to read and write in certain foreign languages. British children are currently taught to read through a largely phonic approach and are given books to read which although phonically regular, convey little real meaning. Where the foreign language being taught is largely phonically regular, such as with Spanish or German, students who are seen to experience difficulties reading may, paradoxically, find it easier to read in a language where there is greater consistency between sounds and print. This would work where students are asked to read texts that they can understand (through speaking and listening) and where they can match phonemes to the letters that represent them. The distinct advantage is that whereas in English various letter combinations (e.g. 'ai', 'ea', 'ou') can represent up to six, seven or eight different sounds, in Spanish and German any letter only ever represents one sound. It would be predicted, from the perspective of instructional psychology, that teaching students to read phonically regular and meaningful texts in Spanish or German might be highly beneficial and give students a degree of confidence and sense of achievement in reading in another language. If successful, the implication would be that it is the nature of the English language that is providing the barrier to their learning rather than a difficulty in learning to read.

ASSESSING STUDENTS' LEARNING

The principles of assessment associated with Michel Thomas's approach (described in Chapter 12), would also be applied in developing his methods more widely. Daily teaching allows for daily assessments and reviews of students' progress. They are built into the course content through the process of interleaved learning where new material is always practised alongside more familiar material. This enables teachers to constantly revisit and extend students existing knowledge.

Assessments focus on whether students have mastered taught skills (criterion-referenced assessments) and whether they are improving on their previous performance (ipsative assessment). Assessing whether students know more today than they did yesterday creates a different focus and dynamic in the classroom. It means that all students are being assessed by the same criteria, irrespective of how much they knew initially. Teaching students with different attainments together can mean that the lower achievers become disheartened because they know less than their peers and cannot speak with the same ease and fluency. Higher achievers on the other hand become bored because they are not challenged sufficiently.

However, students rarely have difficulty acknowledging that some students are taller than others or that some can run faster than others. Within the framework for assessment being proposed, the task for every student is to master whatever they are currently being taught and to improve from one day to the next. Although some students will know much more than others, this becomes less relevant as the emphasis changes from absolute levels of knowledge (i.e. how much students have learned) to relative gains to ensure that everyone, irrespective of where they started, is improving and masters what they are currently learning.

DEVELOPING CONSISTENCY:
A WHOLE SCHOOL APPROACH

Chapter 3 stressed the importance of teachers feeling that they can make a difference to students' learning regardless of the general school ethos and leadership style. Nevertheless, it is likely that the implementation of Michel Thomas's approach to teaching foreign languages within an educational setting would have greater impact if it were part of an overall school philosophy where teachers shared Michel's values and beliefs and recognised the importance of developing theory and research-led practice. The rationale for what and how to teach foreign languages described in Part 3 applies to other curriculum areas, largely because what was described were generic principles of teaching and learning. For any subject the Theory of Optimal Instruction is valid and it is possible to identify core skills and knowledge that represent the most useful and generalisable information to teach. Equally, the instructional hierarchy which underpins the analysis of Michel Thomas's approach to teaching foreign languages is highly generalisable and applies to teaching most subjects.

Adopting the attitudes, beliefs, theories, principles and frameworks underpinning Michel Thomas's approach would have three immediate advantages. The first is that it would create a common language and way of thinking about teaching and learning. The second is that teachers would have a greater appreciation of how all subjects were being taught which would give greater clarity and coherence to the teaching and learning process. The third is the considerable implications for how lower achieving pupils are being taught. If every teacher is familiar with the instructional principles and teaching methods associated with raising the attainments of lower achieving pupils they can be consistently reinforced throughout the school day within every subject area. This in turn would have an impact on students' overall progress and is an effective example of contextual diversity (discussed in Chapter 8), where students are shown how to use the same skill in different contexts.

MAKING LEARNING FUN

A report published in 2003 (based on data collected in 2001) by the National Federation for Educational Research[3] looked at the standards of reading of ten year-olds in 35 different countries. England was ranked third in terms of reading achievement but was one of the countries with the widest span of ability levels, a characteristic usually associated with overall lower reading standards. Students in England had a poorer attitude towards reading, and read less often for enjoyment than similar students in other countries. The study was repeated in 2006 and the results, which were published in November 2007[4], were far less encouraging. This time English ten year-olds came 19th in reading accuracy and there was a noticeable decline in those who reported enjoying reading compared to 2001.

In his speech on World Book Day in 2005, David Bell, formerly Head of Ofsted, noted that inspectors rarely commented that children enjoyed reading:

> When my inspectors visit schools, they frequently ask pupils why they think that reading is important. The answers are illuminating. Most pupils, even those in primary schools, will give essentially pragmatic answers. They will say that reading helps you to get a job. They will say that it helps you to do well in tests. They will say that it helps you to do well in school by teaching you good words to use or helping your spelling. All of these things are true but it is disappointing how few mention the joy of reading.[5]

In March 2007 Unicef published the results of a study looking into the lives and well-being of children and adolescents in economically advanced nations. Overall the UK came bottom of a league table for child well-being across 21 countries. Children were measured on six separate dimensions and children from the UK were in the bottom third for five of these. In relation to education, the report drew on an OECD (Organisation for Economic Co-operation and Development) study that addressed three areas; school achievement at age 15, the percentage of children aged 15–19 staying in education and the transition to employment. The UK came 20th out of 24 countries in this study. The sixth dimension was where children rated themselves in a number of areas, which included the percentage of children who said that they liked school a lot. The UK came last on this dimension out of 20 countries and 16th in relation to those children who said that they liked school a lot with just over 20% responding positively to this enquiry.

Overall these studies and others drawn on throughout this book paint a worrying picture of school life for many students. A significant proportion of students do not achieve to the expected standards and do not appear to see learning as fun or rewarding. While there are many factors that contribute to this state of affairs, what and how students are being taught are certainly two of them. Michel Thomas wanted learning to be enjoyable but not at the expense of students failing to acquire critical skills and knowledge. He felt that by creating the right atmosphere in the classroom and developing a positive learning ethos, students would learn and this would bring its own rewards. They would feel more positive about themselves and begin to see learning as something that was both enjoyable and enriching. Students would end each day with a sense of achievement knowing that there were things that they could do which they had not been able to do when they go up that morning. More generally from an instructional perspective, the more varied the school day in terms of offering a wide, challenging and balanced range of activities (i.e. art, drama, humanities, maths, science, sport, English, languages, etc.), the greater the potential excitement and sense of success that would be experienced.

SUMMARY

This chapter has outlined how Michel Thomas's methodology could be adopted and applied in schools. The process starts with sharing Michel Thomas's beliefs and expectations about students learning and has implications for deciding what to teach, deciding how to teach and how to assess students' learning. Introducing students to foreign languages through an immersion course and following this up with daily teaching sessions would help to consolidate existing knowledge and to show students how to generalise and apply their knowledge and skills.

Hodder and Stoughton have now published Spanish (*¡Es Posible!*) and French (*C'est possible!*) versions of Michel Thomas's language courses for schools. These courses give students a practical and functional use of the spoken language, allowing for communication in a wide variety of situations, and are complemented by a series of worksheets and activities. An interactive CD-ROM is included to help students to review what has been taught – go to www.michelthomasforschools.co.uk for more information.

CHAPTER 16

WORKING TOWARDS A
LEARNING REVOLUTION

OVERVIEW

This chapter highlights the ways in which the assumptions, theory, instructional principles and teaching methodology associated with Michel Thomas's philosophy could lead to a learning revolution. Michel's background and early life left him with a profound desire to make a real difference to the world of education. He believed unequivocally that education was central to creating better life opportunities for all.

MICHEL THOMAS'S LEARNING REVOLUTION

The concluding section of this book highlights the key areas that pave the way for a different way of thinking about the teaching and learning process and provides a framework for creating a different kind of education system: Michel Thomas's 'learning revolution'.

VISION

Despite the turbulent and horrendous events of Michel Thomas's early life, he remained an optimist and had great conviction in the power of education to transform lives. He believed that any society had to be judged in terms of how the most advantaged behaved towards the least advantaged and how those with power treated those without power. At the heart of any democracy was a well educated population who were trusted to participate in the decision making processes that affected their futures.

Michel Thomas wanted to make a difference to the way that all subjects were taught, not just foreign languages. Languages were the vehicle through which he was able to demonstrate the power of teaching and the capacity for anyone to learn anything. His philosophy is radical in challenging many traditional barriers to what students can achieve. To argue, as Michel Thomas did, that notions of ability, family background, ethnic and social origins need not be limiting factors in determining what can be learned did not imply that efforts to reduce inequalities were not necessary – far from it. There are enormous political and social issues that need to be addressed by governments in the UK and throughout the world. The information on who succeeds and fails academically presented in Chapter 5 makes this absolutely clear. Despite the vast spending in recent years, the research into school effectiveness and improvement, the National Literacy and Numeracy Strategies and central control of what is taught, very little has changed for the lowest achieving pupils. If anything, things are getting worse.

According to the recent research report on the impact of the initiatives to teach reading commissioned for the Primary Review, we are still 'bedeviled by a long tail of underachievement'[1] despite the widespread use of one-to-one and small-group teaching which specifically target those who are failing. Clearly a political solution will take some time and this is the one commodity that students do not have. Michel Thomas believed that individual teachers could contribute to reducing educational inequalities through the way that they taught.

So what would a school look like that worked towards an instructional model that reflected Michel Thomas's vision? Three defining features of such a school are identified. The first is that teachers would be working towards a common goal and take total responsibility for what students learned. Too often, students deemed to have problems are seen to be the responsibility of a learning support team rather than the entire staff. The second is that teachers would have a broader understanding of how students were being taught in *all* subjects, not just their own, so could support and reinforce key learning points throughout the day. This would effectively be an example of 'contextual diversity', according to which students are more likely to learn when they practise their skills in a range of different contexts. Acquiring core literacy skills that could equally be applied to the teaching of foreign languages, history, geography, science, etc. would create opportunities that would potentially accelerate learning. The third defining feature relates to teachers' expectations which are addressed in the next section.

OPTIMISM

Michel Thomas was an optimist and his teaching methodology encourages students to feel optimistic about learning. Much has been written in the educational literature about the self-fulfilling prophecy (see Chapter 5), the notion that what students learn often reflects and is limited by teacher expectations. One of the exciting and distinctive features of Michel Thomas's philosophy is his willingness to take full responsibility for his students' learning. Although this may well appeal to students and some teachers, it is far from being accepted within the educational community whose practices are based on a very different assumption. The concept of a learning difficulty implies that a failure to learn is the direct result of students having the difficulty rather than not receiving appropriate teaching. This is perhaps the point at which Michel loses many potential admirers of his approach.

In all the years I have been conducting research on students' learning and demonstrating how even the hardest to teach students can learn effectively and bridge the curriculum gap with their peers, it is very rare indeed to find that teachers, administrators, academics or parents change their understanding of the cause of students' low achievement. Once students are labelled as having a difficulty they very rarely lose the tag.

Michel Thomas's starting point challenges conventional wisdoms and offers a different perspective on teaching and learning. It is perhaps a little too confrontational to suggest that instead of thinking about 'students with learning difficulties' we should be talking about 'teachers with teaching difficulties'. It would be more realistic to recognise that some students challenge teachers' teaching skills. Michel Thomas provides teachers with a series of optimistic options for how best to modify and adapt their teaching. Ultimately translating Michel Thomas's philosophy into schools is not about transferring blame for failure from pupils to teachers, but asking teachers to assume that students will learn when the teaching is right.

EQUAL OPPORTUNITIES

The evidence summarised in Part 2 paints a depressing picture of who succeeds and fails within the current education system. It is even more depressing to look at the vast sums of money that have been spent trying to redress the imbalance and improve the educational, and ultimately life opportunities of those students from low income families that are housed in some of the most socially disadvantaged areas of the country. In recent years we have had the implementation of strategies to teach literacy and numeracy, Educational Action Zones, Excellence in Cities and School Academies, yet students' performances in public examinations, including foreign languages, can still be predicted to a considerable degree on the basis of family income and background. As stated in the introduction to Part 2, John Rawls, the American political philosopher, has formulated the 'good society test' which states that a society should aim for a condition in which a preborn individual would be indifferent to which home and family he or she was born into because they would still be able to fulfil their potential. We are nowhere near achieving any kind of breakthrough in achieving this goal.

The situation is worse now than it was ten years ago. Fewer pupils from lower income families are reaching the acceptable standards for their age in public examinations at ages 11 and 16 and fewer students from lower income families learn a foreign language up to the age of 16 than their peers from more financially advantaged homes. Furthermore, fewer students from less advantaged areas go to the leading universities. Spending more and more money on new curricula and buildings does not appear to be the answer to ensuring that these pupils' needs are met.

It is important to remember that Michel Thomas wanted to impact on the lives of the most disadvantaged students, which is one of the reasons he chose to teach foreign languages in the poorest areas of LA. He felt that he demonstrated that irrespective of any other factors that might raise the attainments of the most socially and financially disadvantaged, a major component of their success relies on what is taught, the way knowledge is structured and the teaching methods used. If, as Michel believed, his methods could impact so dramatically on students' learning there are a number of implications for how other aspects of their education are organised to try to ensure that their broader educational opportunities are also improved.

THEORY

Very little of what is currently known about how best to teach, particularly in the area of foreign languages, is based on theory. Best practice emerges from observations of teachers seen to be effective or identifying successful and improving schools and trying, through questionnaires, interviews, classroom observation or case studies, to pin-point what leads to success. It is not often that theory drives practice, rather if anything it tends to be the other way round where attempts are made for practice to drive theory.

Michel Thomas based his teaching methods on psychological theory. However, what marked his perspective out as 'different' is that he was not interested in the psychology of children and their development, which is what most working in the field of education are attracted to, but the psychology of instruction. He wanted to draw on areas of psychological theory that would offer him a better understanding of how to teach and enable him to identify generalisable principles of teaching and learning that would apply to all students and would be equally effective for all teachers. These principles would enable students, irrespective of their individual differences, to learn more effectively and all teachers, irrespective of their individual differences, to teach more effectively.

A teaching methodology inspired by Michel Thomas would place theory at the heart of the teaching and learning process and would focus on the learning environment, instructional processes and factors within the sphere of influence of teachers and schools rather than adopt a developmental perspective and look at the individual differences between students. Only when all possible modifications, adaptations and amendments to the learning environment had been exhausted would it be legitimate to switch tack and study the 'within' student factors that might account for different learning outcomes. This leads to the *instructional paradox* which states that we can only establish which students genuinely have a difficulty in learning when all their teaching is based on the assumption that they *do not* have a difficulty. The moment we start thinking that students might have a problem we begin to behave differently and instead of finding more effective ways of teaching, the tendency is to find out 'what is wrong' and what problems are preventing students from learning. Discussions in education are often about individual differences between students. Michel was more interested in the differences between teachers. He developed an approach that was designed to minimise the impact of these differences on students' learning while at the same time helping all teachers to become more effective.

RESEARCH

Just as there is little theory informing the teaching and learning process, there is even less research that demonstrates, with a suitable degree of confidence, that certain methods are more effective than others. The favoured methodologies within the field of education, irrespective of their strengths in addressing certain questions, do not go as far as demonstrating that any one way of teaching is preferable to another. This can only be achieved by an experimental methodology which, despite its possible limitations, is nevertheless, the only way of showing what actually works in the classroom. Experimental methodology appealed to Michel Thomas as it represented a move away from rhetoric-driven to research-based teaching. Although Michel's methodology has not been researched and compared to other approaches to teaching foreign languages, the principles on which it is based have been shown to impact significantly on students' learning. Similarly, approaches to teaching literacy and maths that have adopted the same methodologies as Michel Thomas's language courses have been shown to be more effective than those methods to which they have been compared.

LEARNING HOW TO LEARN

The theoretical underpinnings to Michel Thomas's courses provide both teachers and students with a clear rationale and explanation of not only what to teach and how, but also why things are taught in the way that they are. The instructional principles derived from rational analysis, Direct Instruction and behavioural psychology give students a clear understanding of how learning occurs. Principles such as 'interleaved learning', 'distributed practice' and 'contextual diversity' offer students insights into how to organise their own future learning. They can begin to appreciate that distributed practice (a little but often) is preferable when the goal is long-term retention but when preparing for examinations or activities requiring primarily short-term retention, massed practice (learning over longer but fewer blocks of time), might be an advantage.

There are further hugely significant implications of applying the core instructional principles underpinning Michel Thomas's courses more widely to other areas of teaching and education. It would lead to greater consistency in the way that students are taught and enable teachers from different subjects to share a common language with each other.

UNDERSTANDING

As well as helping students to learn how to learn, Michel Thomas's approach also gives them a better understanding of the stages in teaching and learning. One consequence of understanding is having insights into, and an understanding of, the teaching and learning process. The instructional hierarchy, for example, not only provides a framework for working out how to teach through linking each stage in the hierarchy with specific teaching methods, it also addresses key areas of learning that make increasingly greater demands on students. By the time they are being shown how to apply their knowledge, students will have an appreciation of what was being taught and the stages that they went through (from being shown something for the first time and developing accuracy to finally generalising and applying their knowledge). The hierarchy avoids the tendency to see different ways of teaching as representing different philosophies and polarising opinion. Instead, the hierarchy embraces different teaching approaches and areas of learning and construes them as complementary rather than mutually exclusive. Alerting teachers to the differing but essential elements of contrasting teaching methodologies and aspects of learning potentially creates a different dialogue for teachers and students.

INCLUSION

Much is written about schools being 'inclusive' without it being clear what this actually means in practice. For some, 'inclusive education' is closely associated with 'special education' where the goal is to include students with a range of disabilities. Other interpretations focus more on students with a range of abilities and consider how students with vastly differing levels of achievement can be taught together. Michel Thomas was not interested in the labels that are traditionally used to classify students whether they related to ability, personality, ethnicity, etc. He saw little value in labelling students according to how they differed, largely because at best it was irrelevant and at worst because it might lead to a self-fulfilling prophecy and limit what students achieve. Michel Thomas was able to meet the diverse learning needs of individual students because he matched what he taught to what they already knew. Teaching was pitched at the right level and individual responses were monitored so that everyone received the appropriate feedback. Michel was able to meet students' varying needs and so addresses the only difference that matters: what they had already learned and what needed to be taught next.

OPTIMAL TEACHING SYSTEM

Michel Thomas's courses represent an optimal teaching system and reflect the Theory of Optimal Instruction which was described in Chapter 7; what students learn will be determined by their learning environment in its broadest sense, much of which is under a teacher's direct sphere of influence. There are three features of optimal teaching. The first is to teach what is most useful (where what we think of as being useful is a reflection of what will be used most often). The second is to focus on areas where teachers can have optimal impact. Figure 1 in the introduction to Part 2 illustrates the various aspects of the environment that could influence what students learn and have been the subject of much research in recent years. Michel was only interested in one small, but potentially most significant area in raising the attainments of the most disadvantaged students. Through focusing on what is taught and how, teachers are effectively selecting the areas of optimal influence that will do most to enhance students' learning. Reassuringly, they do not require radical changes in the school or substantial additional funding. The third feature of optimal teaching is to organise the learning environment to optimise the impact of teaching. This involves the use of differentiated, whole-class teaching where students with varying attainments are taught together but have their individual needs met through the way teachers structure the content of each lesson. Such a strategy demands that teachers are in total command of subject knowledge and how this can be broken down into small steps. Learning is organised so that students receive daily teaching in most subjects and the curriculum and teaching methods are structured so that students are taught only one new thing at a time to high levels of fluency before being taught to generalise and apply their skills and knowledge.

NO HOMEWORK OR DEPENDENCE ON HOME INVOLVEMENT

Reorganising the timetable would have one further major implication. This would be a dramatic reduction in the use of homework. For reasons already discussed, homework potentially discriminates against pupils who do not have a home environment that is conducive to undertaking the vast amounts of work that are currently expected to be completed at home. It is also questionable whether setting homework involves any teaching at all; it is more appropriate to think of it as self-teaching or self-learning. Being critical of homework does not mean that students would not be expected to undertake extended tasks or work independently at appropriate times, but this could be conducted within clearly defined time frames within an extended school day.

There would be three immediate consequences of restricting the amount of work students were expected to complete at home. The first is that teachers could be on hand to give students feedback and guidance if more work was undertaken in school. The second is that it would create clearer boundaries between school and home at a time when there is already much discussion about how to achieve an effective work / life balance. The third is that it would create a clearer distinction between schools, parents and students. Students are told that if they come to school, participate and complete set activities they will be given feedback, shown that they are learning and achieve examination success. Parents would be free to parent and share time with their children without feeling responsible for what their children learn in school. Parents could then relax and feel reassured that their children would do well because of how and what they were being taught at school, irrespective of what was happening at home; they would still be partners in their childrens' education and be involved and informed about that part of their education that takes place at school without having to duplicate the teacher's role at home.

SUMMARY

This final chapter has highlighted the key features of a learning revolution which, when linked with the discussion in Chapter 15 on implementing Michel Thomas's methods in schools, offers a new way of thinking about teaching and learning, creating opportunities for the widespread teaching of foreign languages and increasing the attainments of all. The key features of the learning revolution in summary are:

- Research
- Equal opportunities
- Vision
- Optimism
- Learning how to learn
- Understanding
- Theory
- Inclusion
- Optimal teaching system
- No homework or dependence on home involvement.

BIBLIOGRAPHY

Alexander, R. (2006) *Why No Pedagogy?* Cambridge: University of Cambridge.

Anderson, J. R. (1990) *The adaptive character of thought*. Hove: Lawrence Earlbaum Associates.

Anderson, J. R. and Schooler, L. J. (1991) Reflections of the Environment in Memory. *Psychological Science*, p2, pp396–408.

Bell, D. (2005) *A good read: Speech to mark World Book Day*. Retrieved from http://www.ofsted.gov.uk/assets/3848.pdf

Bennett, N. (1976) *Teaching Styles and Pupil Progress*. London: Open Books.

Bennett, N., Desforges, C., Cockburn, A. & Wilkinson, B. (1984) *The Quality of Pupil Learning Experiences*. London: Lawrence Earlbaum.

Berthoud, J. (1996) *Pecking Order: How your place in the family affects your personality*. London: Weidenfeld and Nicholson.

Bibb, S. (2005) *The Stone Age Company: Why the companies we work for are dying and how they can be saved*. London: Cyan.

Brown, G. D. A. (1998) The endpoint of skilled word recognition: The ROAR model. In J. L. Metsala and L. C. Ehri (Eds.), *Word recognition in beginning literacy*. Mahwah, NJ: LEA.

Bull, S. J. and Solity, J. E. (1989) *Classroom Management: Principles to practice*. London: Routledge.

Carnine, D. and Becker, W. (1982) Theory of Instruction: Generalisation Issues. *Educational Psychology*, p2, pp249–262.

Carnine, D. W., Silbert, J. & Kameenui, E. J. (1997) *Direct Instruction Reading*. New Jersey: Prentice Hall.

Cassen, R. and Kingdon, G. (2007) *Tackling Low Educational Achievement*. York: Joseph Rowntree Foundation.

Central Advisory Council for Education (1967). *Children and their primary schools* ('The Plowden Report'). London: HMSO.

Chapman, C. (2005) *Improving Schools Through External Intervention*. London: Continuum.

Collins, J. (2001) *Good to Great*. London, Random House.

Collins, J. (2005) *Good to Great and the Social Sectors*. Boulder, Colorado: Jim Collins, (www.jimcollins.com).

Croll, P. and Moses, D. (1985) *One in Five: Assessment and Incidence of Special Educational Needs*. London: Routledge.

Demos (2005) *About Learning: Report of the learning working group*. London: Demos.

Department of Education and Science (1978) *Special educational needs (The Warnock Report)*. London: HMSO.

DfEE (1998) *The National Literacy Strategy: Framework for teaching*. London: DfEE.

DfEE (1999) *The National Numeracy Strategy: Framework for teaching*. London: DfEE.

DfES (2007) *Languages Review (The Dearing Review)*. London: Department for Education and Skills.

Dutton, Y. and Meyer, S. (2007) *Figures of Speech: The NIACE survey on languages*. Leicester: NIACE.

Engelmann, S. and Carnine, D. (1982) *Theory of Instruction: Principles and application*. New York: Irvington.

Feinstein, L., Hearn, B., Renton, Z., Abrahams, C., & Macleod, Mary (2007) *Reducing Inequalities: Realising the talents of all.* London: National Children's Bureau.

Field, S. (2007) Presenting New Vocabulary and Structures. In N. Pachler, and A. Redondo (eds) *A Practical Guide to Teaching Foreign Languages in the Secondary School.* London: Routledge.

Galton, M. (1989) *Teaching in the Primary School.* London: David Fulton Publishers.

Glaser, R. (1962) *Training, Research and Education.* Pittsburg: University of Pittsburg Press.

Goffee, R. and Jones, G. (2006) *Why Should Anyone Be Led by You?* Massachusetts: Harvard Business School Press.

Gontijo, P. F. D., Gontijo, I., & Shillcock, R. (2003) Grapheme-phoneme probabilities in British English. *Behavior Research Methods, Instruments, & Computers*, p35, pp136–157.

Greenfield, S. (2007) Style Without Substance. *Times Educational Supplement Magazine*, 27 July, pp24–25.

Hallam, S. (2004) *Homework: The Evidence.* London: Institute of Education, University of London.

Hargreaves, D. (1994) *The Mosaic of Learning.* London: Demos.

Haring, N. G. and Eaton, M. D. (1978) Systematic instructional procedures: An instructional hierarchy. In N. G. Haring (ed) *The Fourth R – Research in the Classroom*, Ohio: Charles E. Merrill.

Harris, A., James, S., Gunraj, J., Clarke, P. & Harris, B. (2006) *Improving Schools in Exceptionally Challenging Circumstances.* London: Continuum.

Heller, Z. (2003) *Notes on a Scandal,* London: Penguin.

Hillage, J., Pearson, R., Anderson, A. & Tamkin, P (1998) *Excellence in Research on Schools.* Norwich: Department for Education & Employment (DfEE).

Hills, J. and Stewart, K. (eds) (2005) *A More Equal Society: New labour, poverty, inequality and exclusion.* Bristol: Policy Press.

Hughes, Martin (1986) *Children and Number: Difficulties in learning mathematics.* London: Blackwell.

Hulme, C., Hatcher, P. J., Nation, K., Brown, A., Adams, J. & Stuart, G. (2002) Phoneme awareness is a better predictor of early reading skill than onset-rime awareness. *Journal of Experimental and Child Psychology*, p82, pp2–28.

James, O. (2007) *They F*** You Up: How to survive family life.* London: Bloomsbury.

Koch, R. (1998) *The 80/20 Principle: The secret to success by achieving more with less.* New York: Doubleday.

Levitin, D. (2007) *This is Your Brain on Music: Understanding a human obsession.* London: Atlantic Books.

Luria, A. R. (1986) *The Mind of a Mnemonist.* Massachusetts: Harvard University Press.

Mansell, W. (2007) *Education By Numbers: The tyranny of testing.* London: Politico Publishing.

Mortimore, P., Sammons, P., Stoll, L., Lewis, D. & Ecob, E. (1987) *School Matters: The junior years.* London: Open Books.

Muijs, D. and Reynolds, D. (2005) *Effective Teaching: Evidence and practice.* London: Sage.

Ofsted (2001) *Teaching of Phonics: A paper by HMI.* London: Ofsted.

Ofsted (2003) *Teaching Phonics in the National Literacy* Strategy. Paper Presented to DfES Seminar, London: March 2003. Retrieved from http://www.standards.dfes.gov.uk/primary/publications/literacy/686807

Pachler, N. and Field, K. (2002) *Learning to Teach Modern Foreign Languages in the Secondary School.* London: Routledge.

Pachler, N. and Redondo, A. (eds) (2007) *A Practical Guide to Teaching Foreign Languages in the Secondary School.* London: Routledge.

Peters, T. (1994) *The Tom Peters Seminar: Crazy times call for crazy organizations.* London: Macmillan.

Powell, M. and Solity, J. E. (1998) *Teachers in Control.* London: Routledge.

Progress in International Reading Literacy Study (2003) *Reading All Over the World.* Slough: NFER.

Progress in International Reading Literacy Study (2007) *Readers and Reading*. Slough: NFER.

Reynolds, D. (1996) Turning Around Ineffective Schools: Some evidence and some speculations, in J. Gray, D. Reynolds, C. Fitz-Gibbon, C. & J. Jesson (eds) in *Merging Traditions: The future of school effectiveness and school improvement*. London: Cassell.

Rhine, W. R. (ed) (1981) *Making Schools More Effective: New directions from Follow Through*. New York: Academic Press.

Robbins, C. (2003) *The Test of Courage*. London: Hodder & Stoughton.

Shapiro, L. R. and Solity, J. E. (2008) Delivering Phonological and Phonics Training within Whole Class Teaching. *British Journal of Educational Psychology, in press*.

Simon, B. (1953) Intelligence Testing and the Comprehensive School, reprinted in B. Simon (1971) *Intelligence, Psychology and Education*. London: Lawrence and Wishart.

Simon, B. (1981) Why No Pedagogy in England?, in B. Simon & W. Taylor (eds) *Education in the Eighties*. London: Batsford Educational.

Skynner, R. and Cleese, J. (1984) *Families and How to Survive Them*. London: Methuen.

Skynner, R. and Cleese, J. (1993) *Life and How to Survive it*. London: Methuen.

Solity, J. E. (2003) *Teaching phonics in context: A critique of the National Literacy Strategy*. Paper Presented to DfES Seminar, London: March 2003. Retrieved from http://www.standards.dfes.gov.uk/primary/publications/literacy/686807

Solity, J. E. and Raybould, E. C. (1988) *A Teacher's Guide to Special Needs: A positive response to the 1981 Education Act*. Milton Keynes: Open University Press.

Stannard, J. and Huxford, L. (2007) *The Literacy Game: The story of the National Literacy Strategy*. London: Routledge.

Stanovich, K. E. (2000) *Progress in Understanding Reading: Scientific Foundations and New Frontiers*. London: The Guilford Press.

Stewart, I. (1996) *Nature's Numbers*. London: Phoenix.

Sulloway, F. (1996) *Born to Rebel: Birth order, family dynamics and creative lives*. London: Pantheon Books.

Thomas, B. and Dorling, D. (2007) *Identity in Britain: A cradle-to-grave atlas*. Bristol: Policy Press.

Tizard, B., Blatchford, D., Burke, J., Farquhar, C. & Plewis, I. (1988) *Young Children at School in the Inner City*. London: Lawrence Earlbaum.

TLRP (2007a) *Principles into Practice: A teacher's guide to research evidence on teaching and learning*. London: Teaching and Learning Research Programme.

TLRP (2007b) *Neuroscience and Education: Issues and opportunities*. London: Teaching and Learning Research Programme.

Tooley, J. and Darby, D. (1998) *Educational Research: A critique*. London: Office for Standards in Education (Ofsted).

Toynbee, P. and Walker, D. (2005) *Better or Worse: Has Labour delivered?* London: Bloomsbury.

Twist, L., Schagen, I. & Hodgson, C. (2007) *Readers and Reading: the National Report for England 2006* (PIRLS: Progress in International Reading Literacy Study).

Tymms, P. and Merrell, C. (2007) *Standards and Quality in English Primary Schools Over Time: the national evidence* (Primary Review Research Survey 4/1), Cambridge: University of Cambridge Faculty of Education.

Unicef (2007) *Child Poverty in Perspective: An overview of child well-being in rich countries*. Florence: UNICEF Innocenti Research Centre.

Vousden, J. I. (2007) Units of English spelling-to-sound mapping: A rational approach to reading instruction. *Applied Cognitive Psychology*, p21, pp1–26.

Webber, R. and Butler, T. (2006) *Classifying pupils by where they live: how well does this predict variations in their GCSE results?* CASA Working Paper No. 99, London: University College.

Wheldall, K. and Merrett, F. (1989) *Positive Teaching in the Secondary School: Effective Classroom Behaviour Management*. Paul Chapman Publishing: London.

Wragg, E. C., Wragg, C. M., Haynes, G. S. & Chamberlin, R. P. (1998) *Improving Literacy in the Primary School*. London: Routledge.

END NOTES

INTRODUCTION

1 *A Change in Mind: The autobiography of a non-person* Yorkshire Television Limited, 7 March 1978.

CHAPTER 1

1 *The Test of Courage* Robbins, Christopher, p6.
2 *The Test of Courage* Robbins, Christopher, p251.
3 *The Test of Courage* Robbins, Christopher, p251.
4 *Born to Rebel: Birth order, family dynamics and creative lives* Sulloway, Frank, p69.
5 *Life and How to Survive It* Skynner, Robin and Cleese, John, p69.
6 Jonathan Sacks interviewed by John Humphrys in the BBC Radio 4 series *Humphrys in Search of God*, 14 November 2006.
7 *The Test of Courage* Robbins, Christopher, p307.
8 *The Test of Courage* Robbins, Christopher, p311.

PART 2

1 *Class Still Rules in Our College Life* Hutton, Will *Observer*, 23 September 2007.

CHAPTER 2

1 Hargreaves, David, see *Mosaic of Learning*, p45.
2 Hillage, J., Pearson, R., Anderson, A. & Tamkin, P. (1998) *Excellence in Research on Schools.* Norwich: Department for Education and Employment (DfEE).
3 Tooley, J. and Darby, D. (1998) *Educational Research: A critique.* London: Office for Standards in Education (Ofsted).
4 Beard, R. (1999) *National Literacy Strategy: Review of Research and other Related Evidence.* Suffolk, DfEE.
5 Merrell, Christine and Tymms, Peter: see *Standards & Quality in English Primary Schools Over Time*, p20.

CHAPTER 3

1 Tough, S. and Brooks, R. *School Admissions: Fair choice for parents and pupils.* London: Institute for Public Policy Research, 2007.
2 Mansell, W. (2007) *Education By Numbers: The tyranny of testing.* London: Politico Publishing.

3   Chapman, C. (2005) *Improving Schools Through External Intervention*. London: Continuum.

4   *Improving Schools in Exceptionally Challenging Circumstances* Harris, Alma; James, Sue; Gunraj, Judith; Clarke, Paul and Harris, Belinda, p34.

5   Reynolds, D. (1996) Turning Around Ineffective Schools: Some evidence and some speculations, in J. Gray, D. Reynolds, C. Fitz-Gibbon, C. & J. Jesson (eds) in *Merging Traditions: The future of school effectiveness and school improvement*. London: Cassell.

6   Bibb, S. (2005) *The Stone Age Company: Why the companies we work for are dying and how they can be saved*. London: Cyan.

7   *Why Should Anyone be Led by You?: What it takes to be an authentic leader* Goffee, Rob and Jones, Gareth, pp9–10.

CHAPTER **4**

1   Muijs, D. and Reynolds, D. (2005) *Effective Teaching: Evidence and practice*. London: Sage.

2   http://www.standards.dfes.gov.uk/phonics/programmes/publishers/

3   Galton, M. (1989) *Teaching in the Primary School*. London: David Fulton Publishers.

4   *Improving Literacy in the Primary School* Wragg, Ted; Wragg, Caroline; Haynes, Gill & Chamberlin, Rosemary, p205.

5   *Principles into Practice: A teacher's guide to research evidence on teaching and learning* Teaching and Learning Research Programme 2007 (a).

6   Simon, B. (1953) Intelligence Testing and the Comprehensive School, reprinted in B. Simon (1971) *Intelligence, Psychology and Education*. London: Lawrence and Wishart.

7   *Why No Pedagogy in England?* Simon, Brian, p125.

CHAPTER **5**

1   Adams, M. J. (1990) *Beginning to read*. Massachusetts: MIT Press.

2   Bryant, P. and Bradley, L. (1985) *Children's Reading Problems*. Oxford: Blackwell.

3   NRP, National Reading Panel (2000a) *Teaching children to read: An evidence-based assessment of the scientific research literature on reading and its implications for reading instruction*. Washington, DC: National Institute of Child Health and Human Development (NICHD).

4   *About Learning: Report of the learning working group* Demos, p11.

5   *Neuroscience and Education: Issues and opportunities* Teaching and Learning Research Programme 2007 (b), p16, p15, p10.

6   *Style Without Substance* Greenfield, Susan, pp24–25.

7   *Special educational needs* Department of Education and Science.

8   *The 1981 Education Act: A Positive Response*. Solity, Jonathan and Raybould, Ted, Chapter 2, p10.

9   *Rusedki: British tennis must acquire a winning mentality – and steal all of Belgium's ideas* Ornstein, David *Guardian* 9 December 2006.

10 *Better or Worse: Has Labour delivered?* Toynbee, Polly and Walker, David.

11 *A More Equal Society? New Labour Poverty, Inequality and Exclusion* Hills, John and Stewart, Kitty.

12 *Classifying pupils by where they live: how well does this predict variations in their GCSE results?* Webber, Richard and Butler, Tim.

13 *Reducing Inequalities: Realising the talents of all* Feinstein, Leon; Hearn, Barbara & Renton, Zoe with Abrahams, Caroline and Macleod, Mary.
14 *Tackling Low Educational Achievement* Cassen, Robert and Kingdon, Geeta.

CHAPTER 6

1 *Children and Number: Difficulties in learning mathematics* Hughes, Martin.
2 Koch, R. (1998) *The 80/20 Principle: The secret to success by achieving more with less.*
3 *Grapheme-phoneme probabilities in British English* Gontijo, P., Gontijo, I. & Shillcock, R.

CHAPTER 7

1 *Could this 5-year-old be the future of tennis?* Robson, Douglas *USA Today* 30 July 2007.
2 *Does your child have what it takes to be the next Lewis Hamilton?* Ornstein, David *Guardian* 16 June 2007.
3 *Reflections of the Environment in Memory* Anderson, J. and Schooler, L. (1991).
4 *Units of English spelling-to-sound mapping: A rational approach to reading instruction* Vousden, Janet (2007).
5 *The endpoint of skilled word recognition* Brown, Gordon (1998).
6 *A Change in Mind: The autobiography of a non-person* Yorkshire Television Limited, 7 March 1978.
7 *Making Schools More Effective: New directions from Follow Through* Rhine, Ray.

CHAPTER 8

1 *Teaching Phonics in the National Literacy Strategy* Ofsted, p1.
2 *Teaching phonics in context: A critique of the National Literacy Strategy* Solity, Jonathan (2003).

CHAPTER 9

1 *Nature's Numbers* Stewart, Ian, p1.
2 *Phoneme awareness is a better predictor of early reading skill than onset-rime awareness* Hulme, Charles and colleagues (2002).
3 *Teaching of Phonics: A paper by HMI* Ofsted, p5.

CHAPTER 11

1 *Notes on a Scandal* Heller, Zoë, pp27–28.
2 *The Fourth R – Research in the Classroom* Haring, Norris and Eaton, Marie.

CHAPTER 12

1 *The Test of Courage* Robbins, Christopher, p282, p283 and p285.
2 *The Test of Courage* Robbins, Christopher, p310.
3 *Circle can never be squared as we mourn Ball and innocence lost* Wilson, Paul *Observer* 29 April 2007.

CHAPTER 13

1 *They F*** You Up: How to Survive Family Life* James, Oliver, p52 and p54.

2 *One in Five: Assessment and Incidence of Special Educational Needs* Croll, Paul and Moses, Diana (1985).
3 *Learning to Teach Modern Foreign Languages in the Secondary School* Pachler, Norbert and Field, Kit, p43.
4 *Learning to Teach Modern Foreign Languages in the Secondary School* Pachler, Norbert and Field, Kit, pxxii.
5 *Languages Review (The Dearing Review)* DfES, p29.

CHAPTER 14

1 *Learning to Teach Modern Foreign Languages in the Secondary School* Pachler, Norbert and Field, Kit, p14.
2 *Learning to Teach Modern Foreign Languages in the Secondary School* Pachler, Norbert and Field, Kit, p44, p55, p56.
3 *Learning to Teach Modern Foreign Languages in the Secondary School* Pachler, Norbert and Field, Kit, p53.
4 *Learning to Teach Modern Foreign Languages in the Secondary School* Pachler, Norbert and Field, Kit, p144.

CHAPTER 15

1 *Learning to Teach Modern Foreign Languages in the Secondary School* Pachler, Norbert and Field, Kit, p141.
2 *Homework: The Evidence* Hallam, Sue (2004).
3 *Reading All Over the World* Progress in International Reading Literacy Study (PIRLS).
4 *Readers and Reading* Progress in International Reading Literacy Study (PIRLS).
5 *A good read: Speech to mark World Book Day* Bell, David.

CHAPTER 16

1 Merrell, Christine and Tymms, Peter; see *Standards & Quality in English Primary Schools Over Time*, p13.

INDEX